ADVANCE PRAISE FOR

# The Nine Stages of Spiritual Apprenticeship

"Bogart calls upon his expertise as a psychotherapist and his experience as a mature spiritual seeker to discuss issues that are crucial for Western students of inner pathways. The chapter on "Separating From a Spiritual Teacher" explores the issue of the fallen guru from a particularly clear and heartfelt perspective. This is a must-read for all spiritual seekers and their teachers."

• Judith Lasater, Ph.D., P.T.
Author, *Relax and Renew: Restful Yoga for Stressful Times.*

"Greg Bogart explains how an aspirant is transformed in a teacher's enlightening presence and expands in awareness toward absolute freedom. This uniquely insightful book will become a new classic of contemporary spiritual literature."

• Master Charles, originator, Synchronicity High-Tech Meditation.
Author, *The Bliss of Freedom.*

"*Spiritual Apprenticeship* is an in-depth, well-documented and passionately written study of the guru-disciple relationship that is sensitive both to traditional views and to the unique concerns of seekers in the West today. In this time of either naive guru worship on one hand, or vengeful guru-bashing on the other, this book provides a welcome voice of balance and clarity."

• David Frawley, Author, *Ayurveda and the Mind.*

Other Books by Greg Bogart

*Finding Your Life's Calling: Spiritual Dimensions of Vocational Choice*

*Astrology and Spiritual Awakening*

*Therapeutic Astrology: Using the Birth Chart in Psychotherapy and Spiritual Counseling*

*The Nine Stages of*

# Spiritual Apprenticeship

UNDERSTANDING THE
STUDENT-TEACHER RELATIONSHIP

## Greg Bogart

***Dawn Mountain Press***

*The Nine Stages of Spiritual Apprenticeship*
by Greg Bogart

Published by
Dawn Mountain Press
P.O. Box 9563
Berkeley, CA 94709-0563
U. S. A.

Portions of this book previously appeared as
"Separating From a Spiritual Teacher"
in the *Journal of Transpersonal Psychology* (1992, Vol. 24, 1)

Proofreader: Ed Hirsch
Cover Design: Andrea DuFlon
Cover Art: Deborah Koff-Chapin
Editor: Nancy Grimley Carleton
Editorial Consultant: Linda Cogozzo, Rodmell Press

10 9 8 7 6 5 4 3 2 1

First Edition
Printed by McNaughton & Gunn, Saline, Michigan
Acid-free paper

ISBN 0-9639068-5-2
Library of Congress Catalog Card Number 97-068388
Bogart, Gregory C.
The Nine Stages of Spiritual Apprenticeship by Greg Bogart — 1st edition
1. New Age 2. Spiritual Psychology

# Acknowledgments

I would like to begin by acknowledging the important work on the topic of the student-teacher relationship that has already been done by Diana Alstad, Katy Butler, Ram Dass, Georg Feuerstein, David Frawley, Jack Kornfield, Joel Kramer, Victor Mansfield, Michael Rossman, John Welwood, Ken Wilber, and Peter Lamborn Wilson. I've learned a lot from all of them. I hope that what I've written here contributes something to the ongoing conversation.

I could not have completed this book without the encouragement, patience, and sound judgment of my editor, Nancy Carleton, and my friend and consultant Linda Cogozzo. I am deeply indebted to them both. A bow of appreciation to Andrea DuFlon, impeccable design wizard. I would like to thank Georg Feuerstein, John White, Judith Lasater, Master Charles, and David Frawley for reading the manuscript and offering their comments. I gratefully thank Deborah Koff-Chapin for granting permission to reproduce her inspiring painting on the cover.

I would like to express my gratitude to the following friends, teachers, and colleagues: Rick Amaro, Robert and Margo Bartner, Charles Billings, Michael Gliksohn, Vern Haddick, Arthur Hastings, Evaleah Howard, Ginia Laudesio, Colleen Mauro, Arlene Mazak, Don Michael, Girija Moran, Donald Moyer, Gayle Peterson, Robyn Sean Peterson, Robert Powell, Richard Rosen, Donald Rothberg, Laura Shekerjian, Swami Abhayananda, Swami Shankarananda, Barbara Somerfield, Stuart Sovatsky, Nandini Weitzman, Bryan Wittine, Janice Willis, Miles Vich, Rodney Yee, and Jeremy Zwelling. Thanks also to my mother, Agnes Bogart, whose laser-like editing untangled several passages of the text. I am deeply grateful to Diana Syverud, who keeps me grounded in daily life and makes me laugh each day. And a special thank you to Charles Mintz—advisor, elder brother, down home wise man.

I want to thank all of the individuals whom I interviewed for the book. I have changed most of their names to preserve anonymity.

For the past several years I have been fortunate to live in close proximity to two spiritual teachers, Sangye Drolma and Nur Richard Gale. I have been richly rewarded by our friendships and gratefully acknowledge all of the wisdom they shared with me while I wrote this book.

It is customary to formally give thanks to the teachers of one's lineage. I would like to offer my deepest acknowledgment of respect and gratitude to Swami Muktananda, my root teacher, powerful and dangerous as a jaguar; Andres Takra, my astrology teacher, who taught me to perceive the deeper meaning, hidden order, and cosmic humor of events; my hatha yoga guru, Allan Bateman; Judith Lasater, who taught me the meaning of balance in yoga; and Dane Rudhyar, visionary transpersonal philosopher, poet, composer, metaphysician, and painter, who guided me across a crucial threshold on the path. Each of them helped me find my own way. I would also like to acknowledge Hazrat Inayat Khan; I will always be a student of his work. And I am deeply inspired by the example of the Dalai Lama, who provides a moral compass for our world.

Finally, I offer my love and gratitude to the spiritual teachers of all ages and all lineages, whose wisdom illuminates the many paths to Truth.

# Contents

## Stage Six: Glimpses of the Goal _____ 145

## Stage Seven:
## Separating From a Spiritual Teacher _____ 167

## Stage Eight: Finding the Teacher Within _____ 211

## Stage Nine: Teaching Others _____ 237

## Epilogue: The Cycle of Apprenticeship Complete _____ 249

## About the Author _____ 151

When the cry of the disciple has reached a certain pitch, the teacher comes to answer it.

*Hazrat Inayat Khan*[1]

In order to achieve the Accomplishment, one should depend upon a Guru for the Initiation, Instruction, and Inner Teaching.

*Milarepa*[2]

An old saying is just as valid today as ever: When the pupil is ready, the Master appears. But he may appear in many disguises. What matters is not the Master, but the Mastery he "reveals." It is veiled *in* his person. It has to be contacted *through* his person, rather than *in* his person. Devotion to a guru may be the way, but sooner or later it should be transmuted into reverence: the truth within the disciple saluting in true humility the truth in the Teacher .... [This] is the essential, withal rather mysterious process of *transmission*.

*Dane Rudhyar*[3]

The spiritual pedagogy that initiates the soul into itself cannot be limited to a single form or to the Active Intelligence alone. Thus some souls learn only from human masters; others have had human and superhuman guides; others have learned everything from invisible guides, known only to themselves. This is why the ancient Sages, those who had the gnosis of direct vision, having been initiated into things that the sensible faculties do not perceive, taught that for each individual soul, or perhaps for a number of souls with the same nature and affinity, there is a being of the spiritual world who, throughout their existence, adopts a special solicitude and tenderness toward that soul or group of souls; it is he who initiates them into knowledge, protects, guides, defends, comforts them, brings them to final victory.

*Henry Corbin*[4]

1. H. I. Khan, *The Complete Sayings of Hazrat Inayat Khan* (New Lebanon, NY: Sufi Order Publications, 1991).
2. *The Hundred Thousand Songs of Milarepa*, translated by G. C. C. Chang (New York: Harper & Row, 1962), p. 45.
3. D. Rudhyar, *An Astrological Mandala* (New York: Vintage Books, 1973), p. 175.
4. H. Corbin, *Avicenna and the Visionary Recital* (Dallas, TX: Spring Publications, 1980), pp. 89–90.

*For My Father*

*Leo Bogart*

*With Love, Respect, and Gratitude*

# Introduction

In many contemplative traditions associating with an enlightened teacher is considered one of the most important and effective means of advancement on the spiritual path. In India, for example, it is common for an aspirant to seek a guru at a young age and to remain devoted to that teacher for many years. Many great illumined beings and spiritual teachers—especially those from Hindu, Sufi, Zen, and Tibetan Buddhist lineages—have maintained a lifelong connection with their own teachers and have spoken of the student-teacher relationship as essential to the alchemy of spiritual transformation. In the Jewish, Christian, and Islamic traditions it is also customary to learn from wise spiritual teachers and ecstatic mystics. Although it is common in some contemporary Western intellectual circles to ridicule gurus or spiritual teachers and to view those who associate with them as naive and immature, many people continue to pursue the age-old tradition of spiritual apprenticeship. Despite the decline of many other culturally sanctioned rites of passage, training under the guidance of a spiritual teacher can still be a powerful initiatory experience.

The great religious texts of humanity are largely the utterances of illumined men and women of the Spirit who were revered by others, many of whom instructed students. Indeed, the student-teacher relationship goes to the heart of religious and spiritual life. Some of the most momentous events in human history are an outgrowth of the influence of great spiritual teachers and religious leaders, the beacons for humanity—from Zoroaster, Patanjali, Buddha, Moses, Jesus, and Mohammed, to Martin Luther, Meister Eckhart, Rinzai, St. Theresa of

Avila, Ibn 'Arabi, Chaitanya, and the Baal Shem Tov; from Ramakrishna, Yogananda, Joseph Smith, and Crazy Horse, to Martin Luther King, Satya Sai Baba, and the Dalai Lama.

Spiritual apprenticeship is the path of training under the guidance of spiritual teachers in order to achieve inner awakening, enlightenment, or Self-realization. I use the term to denote the relationship we have to those who guide us on the path of sacred knowledge and inner wisdom, as opposed to teachers of secular subjects. In this book, I explore how association with a spiritual guide can aid a seeker on the path, and detail the challenges and difficulties that often arise in the student-teacher relationship. The book also focuses extensively on the process of separation from the teacher, which allows the student to emerge from the relationship liberated and independent.

The book examines nine stages of the student-teacher relationship:

*Stage One: Choosing a Teacher*—What impels us to search for a teacher and how we know when we have found one.

*Stage Two: Initiation*—The prerequisites, meaning, and transformative power of initiation. The link to a lineage of awakened beings.

*Stage Three: Discipleship*—Developing a person-to-person relationship with the teacher, receiving skillful instruction, and finding a spiritual practice that leads us toward inner freedom.

*Stage Four: Testing*—Examination of the student's character, motives, purity of thought and action. The exposure of imperfections.

*Stage Five: Grace and Guru Yoga*—The mysterious infusion of blessings experienced in the company of some teachers. Balancing grace with self-effort. Contemplation of the teacher's qualities and state of consciousness.

*Stage Six: Glimpses of the Goal*—Achieving the goal of spiritual apprenticeship, the experiential knowledge of the Real, the sudden realization of the Self. Moments of illumination.

*Stage Seven: Separating From a Spiritual Teacher*—Reestablishing an independent life. Resolving emotional conflicts of discipleship. Unhealthy merging. Facing a teacher's dark side. Individuation from the teacher.

*Stage Eight: Finding the Teacher Within*—Accessing inner sources of guidance, such as dreams, symbols, disembodied teachers.

*Stage Nine: Teaching Others*—Sharing what we know in appropriate ways, with appropriate intention and ethics. Tests of character for teachers. Guidelines for spiritual teachers.

Stages One, Two, and Three describe the process of entering into a relationship with a teacher. Stages Four, Five, and Six describe the ways we begin to be transformed within the relationship. And stages Seven, Eight, and Nine describe the process of integrating the relationship and internalizing the teacher. It is important to note that these are not linear stages. Not every spiritual apprentice passes through all of them or experiences them in the order discussed here. These stages intersect and blend together, and may unfold concurrently. Nevertheless, I believe that taken as a whole they describe the full cycle of the student-teacher relationship in all of its complexity.

## *Spiritual Apprenticeship in Adult Development*

Student-teacher relationships in spiritual apprenticeship have much in common with apprentice-mentor relationships more generally, while also being different in some important respects. Mentoring relationships in the general sense focus on acquiring particular kinds of skills and expertise, especially those required to learn a trade such as plumbing, carpentry, Tibetan *thanka* painting, or the practice of homeopathic medicine. The explicit purpose of the relationship is for the student to become a master of this skill or body of knowledge in his or her own right, and eventually to leave the teacher to practice this skill, art, or discipline independently.

However, in the context of apprenticeship under a spiritual teacher, matters can become somewhat more complex. The purpose of such a relationship is for the student's very consciousness and being to undergo a profound change. This may require challenging the student to overcome fears, attachments, and limiting personal beliefs. The methods may be unorthodox, even shocking, such as those used by "crazy-wisdom" teachers.[1] Thus, the relationship challenges the student on deep levels and often activates intense conflicts for the student. Further complicating matters, discipleship inherently involves a certain degree of deliberate psychic merger or union with the teacher. One may be encouraged to surrender, to give oneself over to the teacher in body, heart, mind, and speech, to meditate on the teacher, to become one with the guru. Such a practice may make the student's eventual separation from the teacher more complex to navigate than in secular forms of apprenticeship where the boundaries between student and teacher are drawn more clearly.

Despite these very real differences, both mentor-apprentice and spiritual teacher-disciple relationships have much in common. Both types of relationships involve a collaboration for the purpose of fostering the student's learning and growth. Both involve some form of instruction given by the teacher, and some form of service offered by the student, as well as effort toward task mastery on the student's part— whether this means learning to hit a target with an arrow or to focus the mind in meditation. Most relationships of both types also involve some degree of commitment of student and teacher to each other. Finally, all types of guru-disciple, teacher-apprentice, or mentor-student relationships seem to carry certain kinds of inherent tensions and difficulties, which we will examine later.

Daniel Levinson, a psychologist who wrote influential studies of human development, views a period of apprenticeship as an important stage in the personal and career development of many adults.[2] Levinson believes that mentors serve many functions: They act as teachers to enhance the novice's skills and intellectual development, as sponsors who use their influence to facilitate the apprentice's social or professional advancement, as counselors, and as exemplars the apprentice can admire and emulate. Most importantly, mentors foster the development of students by believing in them and supporting the realization of their own dreams and aspirations. All of these characteristics of mentoring relationships also apply to relationships between spiritual teachers and their students. The spiritual guide provides personal guidance, instructs the student in techniques of self-transformation, and is an exemplar of an expanded, enlightened mode of being that the aspirant can emulate. The guide sees the student's innermost spiritual potential and aids the student in achieving the goal of enlightenment or Self-realization. Thus, the spiritual guide is the mentor who guides the seeker toward awakening, holding the vision of the student as a luminous, enlightened being, and transforming the student's own vision through mysterious vibrational influence.

# Discipleship and Spiritual Apprenticeship

I have chosen the term *spiritual apprenticeship* deliberately to counterbalance what I perceive as the heaviness sometimes implicit in the term *discipleship*. The term *disciple* implies a master, a concept that often creates mistrust in Americans bred on a tradition of autonomy and freedom from bondage to masters of any kind. I do not believe the notion of masters and servants is intrinsic to the process of spiritual apprenticeship. This is only one way of framing the power relations that emerge in spiritual training. Yet it is a conception that leads to two related problems: exaggerated attempts at surrender, leading in many cases to loss of will, autonomy, and critical faculties; and the exaggerated need to angrily reject and repudiate a figure to whom we may have given too much power in the first place.

I believe we may be better served by considering spiritual tutelage as a process of apprenticeship, where we undergo deep transformation as well as acquiring knowledge of some spiritual doctrine or discipline under the tutelage of a teacher, master this knowledge to the best of our ability, and then practice what we have been taught independently. The term *spiritual apprenticeship* also more accurately reflects the varied levels of commitment that are called forth in seekers by teachers of varying levels of wisdom and spiritual realization. Some teachers who have reached the highest levels of attainment may deserve our deepest reverence, one-pointed attention, and devotion. In such cases the term *discipleship* may be properly applied. In discipleship there is an enduring commitment between student and teacher and a conscious acceptance of the teacher's guidance and authority in one's life.

However, the term *discipleship* does not accurately describe the relationship we have with other teachers who are not fully enlightened, yet can also serve as important guides for us on the Path—even though they may only be one or two steps ahead of us. We may respect such teachers and honor what they teach us, but we would not say we are their disciples. We choose to study with them to acquire specific knowledge. In such cases it is not appropriate to speak of discipleship, which implies a much more solemn commitment to a teacher. Therefore, it may be more efficacious to speak of spiritual apprenticeship, which may develop to the point of discipleship and which may also grow beyond it.

*Spiritual apprenticeship* is a term that leaves greater room for our instincts toward individuation, self-assertion, and autonomous choice to shape and steer our own lives. We approach a teacher to learn what we can, and then at a certain point we move on. That might mean a lifetime of devoted service, or a period of several weeks or months of intensive study. The term *discipleship* subtly implies that we have to surrender our lives to teachers to absorb their wisdom. Many spiritual teachers may not be worthy of such surrendering, yet we still may learn a great deal from them. The great teachers I have known merely asked that I consider their teachings, practice them to the best of my ability, and pay their basic fees for instruction—without coercion, power struggles, or a demand for absolute surrender. In some cases I believe the student may create the master-servant dynamic in the relationship as much as the teacher may insist upon it.

To illustrate why I have coined a new term for the student-teacher relationship, consider the example of David, a man of fifty-five who spent nearly a decade as a committed student of a spiritual teacher—until he began to feel uncomfortable with trends within his teacher's spiritual community. He eventually left the group, despite the fact that he loved his teacher, and honored the many teachings and gifts he had received. He now realized the teacher was fallible and made mistakes—he wasn't perfect. David then experienced a lengthy period of confusion because, as he put it:

> I've been a devoted disciple for years and now I'm on my own and I don't feel I'm living as his disciple any more. But I also don't view myself as a "former disciple." So what am I? I'm still engaged in the process of training and spiritual practice but I'm doing it on my own now. It's different. It feels like a maturing to me, more than the loss of something I once had.

Reimagining himself as a spiritual apprentice was helpful for David because it enabled him to understand his lengthy period of discipleship as a crucial, formative stage of his spiritual apprenticeship, which now had reached the stage of Finding the Teacher Within. Otherwise, he was left with the notion of a failed discipleship that had not achieved its intended purpose. Adopting this conception enabled David to recognize that the process of spiritual training may include a stage of independence and liberation from the teacher as well as a stage of dependence and surrender.

While many of the same emotional and interpersonal dynamics apply in both spiritual apprenticeship and the stage of discipleship *per se*, *spiritual apprenticeship* is a more encompassing term that allows us to discuss many types of relationships with spiritual teachers and their students. Spiritual apprenticeship is an alternative to, not a replacement of, the term *discipleship* that can broaden our understanding of how we learn from spiritual teachers. At times I will also use the term *discipleship*. Yet the term *spiritual apprenticeship* implies a greater independence of spirit. We seek out teachers to learn something that we can apply in our own lives, not to sit at their feet forever.

## Sources for This Study

As I explore the stages of the student-teacher relationship, I will periodically introduce some ideas from the history of the world's great religions. While not an exhaustive historical survey, this material will highlight the unique vocabulary each tradition has used to describe the student-teacher relationship. I hope to convey respect for every tradition. The historical material will remind us that the student-teacher relationship has been a central concern of most spiritual paths. We will see that what I refer to as *guru yoga*—in which we focus our attention on an enlightened teacher's consciousness, presence, and teachings—is one of the primary spiritual practices recommended by many traditions. In Judaism, wise rebbes, tzaddiks, and ecstatic mystics have been widely revered and are the subject of many legends. Christianity, at its heart, is centered around the faith of disciples that attunement to the presence and guidance of Christ draws them toward salvation. Similarly, those who follow the way of Islam are directed to find a mullah, sheikh, or dervish to guide them on the Path.

The student-teacher relationship and the practice of guru yoga have been described in particular depth in the Hindu, Buddhist, and Islamic traditions. The teachings of paths such as Zen Buddhism and the many Hindu yoga lineages place great emphasis on the student-teacher relationship, and present many stories of encounters and relationships between teachers and their students. I will also discuss the perspectives of Kashmir Shaivism, Sufism, and Tibetan Buddhism as representatives of the pinnacle of Middle Eastern and Asian thought on this topic.

As I researched this book I was astonished at the sheer volume of literature on this subject, including accounts by authors who have experienced either profound transformations or deep emotional trauma as a result of contact with spiritual teachers. Rather than trying to review at length the vast literature on the student-teacher relationship, I focus instead on the stories of people I have interviewed who have followed the path of spiritual apprenticeship. Their stories vividly portray the nine stages—including some of the highest peaks and the lowest valleys through which one travels on this path. I also describe my own experiences at some length. Thus, along the way the reader will learn something about me and my teachers, especially Swami Muktananda, who profoundly influenced my life. I will recount my memories of Muktananda as well as discussing as honestly as I am able some of the disturbing controversy that has surrounded him since his death.

## Problems of Discipleship and Separation

This book explores a variety of emotional and interpersonal issues that often arise for contemporary Western students of spiritual teachers.[3] This discussion is not intended to cast doubt on the validity, value, or importance of the teacher-student or guru-disciple relationship; nor will I disparage those who enter into devotional relationships with spiritual teachers. Instead, I look at factors conducive to the successful transmission of the awakened state of consciousness from teacher to student. I also explore the question of why, for many people today, a period of relationship with a spiritual teacher frequently proves to be problematic, and, in particular, why the process of separation from such a relationship can be treacherous.

I examine general features of spiritual apprenticeship as well as some of its inherent tensions and paradoxes. I am particularly interested not only in those instances where a teacher's gross misconduct precipitates a student's departure, but also in cases where the student, in a gradual, healthy, and almost inevitable process, feels a need to leave the teacher—whether this means a total severance of the relationship or simply removal from the teacher's immediate physical presence. My purpose is to deepen our understanding of the sources of disturbances and unforeseen difficulties that often arise. I celebrate the student-teacher relationship and attempt to describe it in such a way that those who travel this road will understand both its possibilities and its challenges. I draw on case material from my therapeutic work with individuals striving to clarify their relationships with spiritual teachers, pertinent historical examples, theories of adult development, and psychoanalytic and Jungian perspectives.

Thousands of Westerners have flocked to the feet of spiritual teachers since the 1960s. Some have gone to India, Burma, or Japan. Others attend weekend courses or lengthy meditation retreats. And with the more widespread public interest in spirituality and enlightenment, there have also been many casualties and cases where students left teachers feeling bitter and disappointed. While my own contacts with spiritual teachers have been exceedingly positive, I am aware that many other people have had great difficulties resolving their associations with teachers. Over the years I have met some people who have been so bruised by their experiences with spiritual teachers that it is questionable whether they will ever recover. Some of them live with a lasting legacy of regret, disillusionment, and cynicism about teachers and the spiritual path in general. So, while it can be a great blessing to have the chance to study with a genuine spiritual guide, the experience can easily go astray and end with the opposite of the desired result: confusion, bitterness, and desolation instead of clarity, joy, and illumination.

It is my hope that this book will help these individuals to better understand the complete cycle of spiritual apprenticeship, including the process of separating from a spiritual teacher and learning to rely increasingly on the inner teacher. Fully understanding the phases of this process can help turn disgruntled disciples back toward a renewed quest for enlightenment and expanded consciousness.

## Images of Spiritual Teachers in World Religions

Many contemporary images of the nature and role of spiritual teachers derive from the cultural traditions of the East. Western fascination with Eastern gurus goes back to the late nineteenth century, when religious scholars such as Max Muller and Paul Deussen began translating into

German and English the classics of Eastern spirituality such as the Vedas, the Upanishads, and the Dhammapada. The popular writings of Helen Blavatsky and Alice Bailey in the Theosophical tradition also created interest in the wisdom of Eastern sages and masters. Early in this century, great teachers such as Swami Vivekananda, Paramahansa Yogananda, and the Zen master Nyogen Sensaki[4] began arriving in the West. By the 1950s the doctrines of Hinduism, Yoga, Taoism, and Zen Buddhism were drawing serious public interest through the influence of writers and scholars such as Aldous Huxley, D. T. Suzuki, Alan Watts, Jack Kerouac, and Allen Ginsberg. In the 1960s, spiritual wisdom taught by Eastern teachers influenced the humanistic psychology movement and captured the interest of the youth subculture, and then American and European society at large. During the 1970s and 1980s, interest in spiritual teachers expanded rapidly as large numbers of Westerners embraced the teachings of Eastern spiritual leaders, and in many cases became serious and dedicated practitioners of meditative disciplines.

Many commentators have seen the arrival of Eastern spiritual teachers as a cultural innovation or novelty and assumed that apprenticeship under an enlightened teacher's guidance was alien to Western religious traditions. Yet our own Western cultures and religions also deeply respect the guidance of spiritual teachers. For example, there is a long tradition of spiritual direction and mentorship in Christianity. Two of the great Christian mystics, St. John of the Cross and St. Theresa of Avila, had a transformative teacher-student relationship. St. John was St. Theresa's confessor (even though she was his elder), and they had a profound impact on each other; they would both go into ecstatic states while discussing spiritual matters.

Thus, it is not only people in the East who revere and follow spiritual teachers, nor do the problems in such associations only arise in the case of Asian teachers and their Western students. No matter what religious tradition we follow, we recognize that there are both true and false teachers, those who are venerable and wise and those who are untrustworthy. But the basic human need to seek guidance from those who knows the mysteries of Spirit is universal.

# On Cults, Charlatans, and Spiritual Teachers

It is common for discussions about spiritual teachers to turn into discussion of dangerous and fanatical groups. Many observers see in the contemporary awakening of spirituality in the West only the coercive activity of cults. Indeed, some spiritual teachers do practice techniques of mind control and manipulate the lives of students, a point I will discuss in these pages. However, while undoubtedly corrupt spiritual leaders exist, many authentic teachers engage in transformative teaching relationships with students. A somewhat negative reaction is sometimes elicited toward *all* spiritual teachers by virtue of the fact that some teachers have a destructive influence on the lives of their students. Thus, some observers view all spiritual teachers and the groups or communities that grow around them with great mistrust. In noting this, I do not mean to denigrate the important work that cult critics and exit counselors are doing. I simply want to let the reader know from the outset that this book is written from a different perspective, one quite comfortable with the idea of the student-teacher relationship.

Of course, some deceptive charlatans do use the role of spiritual teacher to gain access to sex, power, and money. One infamous teacher was accused by a number of female ex-followers of forcing them to have sexual relations at gunpoint, in some cases after being forced to ingest LSD. The women were told that they would be possessed by the devil if they did not submit, and that this was the only way they could be protected from the forces of evil. Another teacher hired several Tibetans to dress up in monk's robes and proclaim that they had discovered through divination that she was the incarnation of Tara—one of the most powerful and beloved deities of the Tibetans.[5] The Tibetans had the last laugh, however. They demanded a large fee for perpetrating this fraud, and when the teacher borrowed the money and presented it to the Tibetans, they tore the money into pieces and flushed it down the toilet. They told her, "Sometimes even Tara has to learn a lesson."

Many exposés have been written, with juicy gossip, upsetting allegations, and, in some cases, well-documented evidence of financial or sexual impropriety. This book will not focus extensively on this issue for several reasons, not the least of which is because it has already been done so many times. The tacit discourse of such exposés is often to show that most spiritual teachers are frauds and are not to be trusted. Cynicism and suspicion of the student-teacher relationship often inform such reports. However, I believe it will better serve us to consider realistically some of the difficulties implicit in the student-teacher relationship, so that those who do choose the path of spiritual apprenticeship can be uplifted, not hurt by the experience.

In short, I am not offering a polemic against those who follow spiritual leaders, nor is it my intention to sling mud at anyone. Rather, this book is intended to be a guide for those who seek to understand the complexities of a relationship with a teacher. It is written for anyone considering studying with a spiritual teacher; anyone currently connected to a teacher and hoping to mature in this relationship; those who want to leave a spiritual teacher; or those who have already left and are dealing with the aftermath.

A major concern of this book is to show how the emotional issues of merger with, and separation from, the teacher can be resolved in a positive way. I hope this book will help even the most disillusioned former students of spiritual teachers enthusiastically renew the pursuit of the path of awakening. I am especially interested in exploring the inner sources of guidance that may begin to supplant the role of an external teacher at certain stages, and how learning to rely on the inner teacher can make possible the fruition of spiritual apprenticeship. As the aspirant experiences a sense of inner unity with the teacher, practices intensely, and achieves expanded awareness, he or she fulfills the purpose of the student-teacher relationship. Ultimately, such a person may eventually teach others in some capacity. Thus, in the final chapter I offer some guidelines for those who are called upon to share their spiritual experiences and knowledge with others. As a renewed spiritual culture emerges in the West, there is an ever-growing need for dedicated, psychologically and emotionally prepared individuals to assume the role of spiritual guides and to perform the functions of instruction and initiation for others.

This book develops the idea that we can meet the challenges of discipleship by absorbing spiritual teachings and letting them transform us, until we are ultimately liberated from the messengers who transmit them. The purpose of our association with a teacher is to awaken our own inherent freedom and clarity. As the Buddha said to his students right before he died, "Be a light unto yourself." That's what this book is about — understanding how spiritual apprenticeship can help us to become lights unto ourselves.

## *Critics of Authoritarian Power Dynamics in the Student-Teacher Relationship*

Before we begin our journey, I would like to address one further point. Recently a number of commentators have criticized the nondemocratic, authoritarian power structure that they believe is inherent in the traditional teacher-disciple relationship and the whole concept or institution of spiritual teachers. For example, Michael Rossman argued that the "pedagogy of the guru" is often bestowed in an authoritarian learning environment that contradicts, or negates altogether, the message of empowerment, enlightenment, or liberation that a teacher may espouse:

> What the student learns about learning, through engagement with the Guru and his Organization, is no new lesson at all, but a reinforcement of the metalessons taught by the usual workings of the society. . . . The student learns that to learn involves being treated as an object. . . . The student learns that to learn he or she must sacrifice autonomy — not simply by joining in something collective, but by letting another define what is of value and how to learn it. . . . The student learns not to question or to interfere with the Guru's purposes and judgments, but instead to accept the centralization of power. . . . The student learns not to question the social structure and processes of the Organization, substantively and spiritually, by reinforcing their terms by recreating them within himself or herself, . . . identifying himself or herself with the [the Organization's interests]. In all of this, the student learns . . . to accept the operation of authoritarian social forms and to integrate himself or herself in their operation. . . . This schooling is disastrous for citizens of an age of social and personal chaos and crisis; for in the absence of reliable, authoritative answers, we must depend increasingly on self-directed and genuinely cooperative skills of learning to determine our futures, or even to survive. [6]

In a similar vein, Joel Kramer and Diana Alstad's powerful book *The Guru Papers* argues that the student-teacher relationship involves implicit dynamics of control and obedience. Gurus learn to keep control over students and devotees by manipulating fear and desire, and by getting them to surrender control. They call the guru-disciple relationship, "the most extreme, clear-cut, and sophisticated example of a bond of dominance and submission not based on physical coercion."[7] They question pointedly "the great myth that external authority can be the source of inner freedom."[8] And they contend that gurus use "the absolute power of active mind control . . . to make people who are being callously manipulated believe they are freer than everyone else."[9]

Expressing similar views, Andrew Harvey has written that we no longer need spiritual teachers, because:

> most of the masters and gurus are actually the patriarchy's most brilliant way of keeping [the] always-revolutionary truths of divine identity and equality under wraps. . . . [T]he guru systems have nearly always been indirect servants of power. . . . [Gurus] have conspired with that infantilism and that incessant desire for authority that has kept the human race trapped and unempowered.[10]

While I think these commentators are making important points, the direction I will pursue here is different. I believe that we very much need the wisdom of spiritual teachers. Spiritual apprenticeship is the setting in which *gnosis* (enlightened knowing, knowledge of the sacred) is passed from one person and one generation to the next. The illumined being of today inspires and guides the illumined person of tomorrow. We have a natural need to apprentice and to be mentored, and so, too, we have an intrinsic urge to learn from men and women of wisdom and spiritual insight, to receive their blessings, and to be transformed in their company.

According to transpersonal psychologist John Welwood, there is nothing intrinsically wrong about the exercise of authority by spiritual teachers. What we must examine in each specific case is how spiritual authority is defined and exercised in the student-teacher relationship, and the source from which a teacher derives that authority:

> A given teacher has [spiritual] authority only for those who respond to his or her presence and teachings. A disciple (Latin for "learner") is one who recognizes that he or she has something

> A given teacher has [spiritual] authority only for those who respond to his or her presence and teachings. A disciple (Latin for "learner") is one who recognizes that he or she has something essential to learn from a given teacher....Just as one would turn to an acknowledged master in any field one wants to pursue in depth, so a person who feels a longing to overcome the limitations of egocentricity would feel drawn to someone who has mastered how to do that. The role of an effective teacher is to instruct, encourage, provide feedback, and inspire through the example of his or her own accomplishment. Moreover, the more effective teachers tap and nurture the inherent potential of students, rather than imposing their own style and agenda.[11]

The student-teacher relationship can indeed be complicated by issues of domination, hierarchy, and authoritarian use of power. Yet I believe that contending with power, hierarchy, obedience, and the maturation and expression of one's own inner authority are essential concerns for any person in the late twentieth century. We face these same issues in our jobs and careers, marriages and friendships, and relationships with children. We don't shy away from these relationships just because they involve complex power dynamics or imply hierarchical relations. Inevitably, these same issues are also faced in the student-teacher relationship. Spiritual apprenticeship is a path that demands our maturation—which includes both the ability to accept the authority of those whom we revere for their wisdom, *and* maturation of our capacity for authentic, reciprocal relationship. While it is always possible that we will fall prey to authoritarian power and exploitation, associating with a spiritual guide can be transformative if we are informed about the challenges implicit in the relationship. We need to develop a clear understanding of the difficulties and dangers of the path of spiritual apprenticeship so we can navigate the stages of this path wisely. That is the purpose of this book.

## Notes

1. G. Feuerstein, *Holy Madness* (New York: Paragon House, 1991).
2. D. Levinson, *The Seasons of a Man's Life* (New York: Ballantine, 1978).
3. What I am saying here refers specifically to the experience of Westerners involved with spiritual teachers. I make no claim for the cross-cultural validity or universality of my findings.

4. Nyogen Sensaki attended the famous conference on world religions in Chicago in 1895 and later stayed on in America, working as a houseboy for twenty years before he began teaching. His teacher had instructed him to wait twenty years before commencing to teach. Sensaki was the first Zen master to teach in America.

5. Sangye Drolma gave me this teaching: Tara is known as the Mother of all Buddhas. Because of her great compassion for humanity, Tara remains incarnated at all times, in twenty one forms. One account of her origins says that she sprung from the tears of Avalokitesvara, the Boddhisattva of Compassion. Another account is that in a previous lifetime she gave a large donation of food and money to a monastery. A monk said to her, "This is a great offering. Thank you. I pray that in your next life you will be born as a man so that you might attain enlightenment." She said, "You are deluded. It does not matter what the outer form is. This is all a delusion, transitory. And to prove it, I will attain enlightenment in the form of a woman."

6. M. Rossman, *New Age Blues* (New York: Dutton, 1979), pp. 54–5.

7. J. Kramer & D. Alstad, *The Guru Papers* (Berkeley, CA: Frog Ltd., 1993), p. 41.

8. Ibid., p. 99.

9. Ibid.

10. A. Harvey, "Teachers and Seekers: An Interview with Andrew Harvey," *Yoga Journal* (August, 1995).

11. J. Welwood, "On Spiritual Authority: Genuine and Counterfeit." In D. Anthony, B. Ecker, & K. Wilber (Eds.), *Spiritual Choices* (New York: Paragon House, 1987), p. 293.

# Choosing a Teacher

I know all the scriptures which are like the sea
All five branches of learning I have mastered
With grammar and epistemology
Yet without a competent Guru
The fire of my craving will not die.
If my yearning not be stilled
By the Guru's grace which is like
The nectar stream of Tantra essence
Wide as the ocean, despite my attainments
Virtues and supersensible cognitions
I have not seen Reality.
Therefore I shall rely on Hevajra
And seek firmly for the true Guru.

*The Life and Teaching of Naropa*[1]

At a certain stage on the quest for spiritual wisdom and awakening, we need a teacher to guide us on the Path. Just as we would seek a teacher to learn a foreign language or a musical instrument, if we wish to become enlightened and spiritually aware, then we need to find a person who has already achieved this condition to instruct and inspire us. As Milarepa, Tibet's most accomplished and celebrated yogi, stated, "You need a qualified and dependable Guru."[2]

Throughout human history, there have been individuals who demonstrated visible signs of spiritual realization, mystical illumination, or intimacy with God. The idea spans nearly every culture and era that certain people can, either spontaneously or through lengthy preparation, awaken higher consciousness, and become conduits for healing and spiritual truth. Whether we call them yogis, medicine men, or medicine women, prophets, illuminated beings, or ecstatic mystics, there have always been individuals who have been entrusted with the responsibility of spiritual leadership. Many premodern societies revere the figure of the shaman, who enters trance states and returns with insights from the spirit world, and who initiates apprentices.[3] In ancient China, people sought out Taoist sages such as Lao Tzu and Chuang Tzu to question them about the meaning of life and the nature of truth. In ancient Greece, philosophers such as Socrates and the Neoplatonists taught philosophies and techniques to lift students beyond ordinary consciousness into mystical experience and contemplation of higher dimensions of existence.

All spiritual traditions acknowledge the aspirant's need for a teacher. The teacher holds the highest place of respect in the mystical, esoteric branch of Islam known as Sufism, which has numerous orders of practitioners that gather for spiritual instruction by teachers known as *sheikhs*, *pirs*, or *murshids*.

> The Sheikh is the master of spiritual alchemy. . .; thus he can transform the base material of the novice's soul into pure gold. He is the sea of wisdom. The dust of his feet gives the blind eye of the beginner sight. . . . He is the ladder toward heaven, so completely purified that all the virtues of the Prophet are visible in him as in a mirror.[4]

Describing contemplative training among the Sufis, Annemarie Schimmel wrote:

> In order to enter the spiritual path, the . . . *murid*, "he who has made up his will" (to enter the Path) is in need of a guide to lead through the different stations and to point the way toward the goal. . . . The mystics . . . saw in the constant supervision of the disciple's way by the mystical guide a *conditio sine qua non* for true progress.[5]

In a similar vein, Gershom Scholem, the renowned scholar of Jewish mysticism, writes:

> A mystic requires a spiritual guide, or *guru*, as he is called in India. On the face of it the function of the *guru* is primarily psychological. He prevents the student who sets out to explore the world of mysticism from straying off into dangerous situations. For confu-

sion or even madness lurk in wait; the path of the mystic is beset by perils. It borders on abysses of consciousness and demands a sure and measured step. The Yogis, the Sufis, and the Kabbalists, no less than the manuals of Catholic mysticism, stress the need for such a spiritual guide, without whom the mystic runs the risk of losing himself in the wilderness of spiritual adventure.[6]

The teacher instructs the student in powerful methods of self-transformation such as meditation, mantra, yogic breathing, or visualization, and teaches the student to utilize these methods safely. The teacher helps the student find the most beneficial spiritual practices, prescribing techniques that are best suited to that aspirant's personality and level of maturity. And the teacher observes and supervises the student's progress in practicing these techniques, offering encouragement, advice, or actively intervening at certain stages—particularly when the student is beset by doubts or frightening experiences in meditation. The teacher also protects the student from dangers and pathologies of the spiritual path such as inflation or preoccupation with visions and psychic phenomena.[7] The teacher is a necessary guide through the mysterious terrain of the inner world.

## Spiritual Teachers in Hinduism

In the Hindu tradition, a guru is considered essential, for only one established in knowledge of the Self, the changeless Reality, can transform our perceptions  and remove the darkness of ignorance from our eyes. Innumerable realized saints in India have sung the praises of their gurus. For example, Narada, a renowned yogi, said,

> The association of the great souls is hard to acquire, hard to be had completely, but is always fruitful. For gaining even that association one requires God's blessing; for between God and His men there is no difference. So try to acquire the company of the holy soul.[8]

One of the great sacred texts of India, the Bhagavad Gita, states (IV. 34): "Those who themselves have seen the truth can be thy teachers of wisdom. Ask from them, bow unto them, be thou unto them a servant."[9] Commenting on this verse, Krishna Prem, a British-born mystic who lived in India for many years, wrote:

> The disciple must resort to the feet of a wise teacher, one who is an embodiment of that Teacher Who is already in his heart, the Eternal Wisdom. . . . [H]e needs the guidance of one who, because his whole being has become one with the Wisdom, can speak with the same voice as that Teacher in the heart and yet can do so in tones which can be heard with the outer ear. . . . But it is not by wandering . . . , by searching out the remoter corners of the earth, that the Guru can be found. The Path which leads to the feet of the Guru . . . is an interior path, and only by treading the preliminary steps by oneself can one reach the outer guide. It is only when this stage has been reached, the stage in which the disciple is ready to offer up his self in sacrifice to the Self in all, that the Guru can and does manifest himself. . . . When . . . the disciple has found his Guru, he must, by the obedience of self-effacement, and the service which consists of putting the will at the disposal of the Teacher, so unite his being with that of the latter that the Wisdom which shines in him may light up in the disciple too.[10]

The student-teacher relationship has traditionally been an integral part of the culture of India, where the first of four stages of the life cycle is that of the *brahmacharin,* the student. In this stage, a youth studies the Vedic hymns and the various branches of yoga, under a teacher's tutelage.[11] The guru gives the student initiation into *mantra* (sacred sounds and chants) and instruction in *shastra* (sacred scriptures and teachings), and may also teach meditation. In some cases, the teacher bestows *shaktipat*, a transmission of spiritual power that awakens the student's dormant kundalini energy.[12]

The Hindu tradition contains a wealth of stories about the transformative character of the guru-disciple relationship. For example, the book *Autobiography of a Yogi* describes how Paramahansa Yogananda sought a teacher, was psychically drawn to a sage named Sri Yukteswar, and became his devoted disciple. He underwent a thorough training in which Yukteswar not only initiated him but carefully guided him.

Thousands of years of Hindu meditation upon the significance of the guru are summed up in the sanskrit verse: *Om namah shivaya gurave, satchidananda murtaye*—"I bow to Lord Shiva, the Guru, Being-Consciousness-Bliss in the form of a human being" (or, "The embodied form of Being-Consciousness-Bliss"). The guru is the *murti*, the sacred form, of perfect Being, Consciousness, and Bliss. The teacher rests in a state beyond the flux of changing forms, abiding in the changeless Reality known as Atman, or the Self. The teacher is merged with limitless and all-pervasive consciousness. And the teacher is blissful, no longer being bound by the ignorance, suffering, and limitation of ordinary human life. We are drawn to such a teacher because in his or her company we begin to experience ourselves as limitless Being, consciousness, and joy. We begin to reside in the same liberated condition as the sage.

The enlightened being has come to abide in a state of pure consciousness, or communion with God or Spirit. Such an illumined one no longer identifies with the physical body, the constant turbulence of emotions and desires, or the constant flux of thoughts—but instead knows, and powerfully emanates, the light of consciousness. The enlightened sage has transcended the ignorance and contracted condition of ordinary human life, and has come to reside in a state of tranquility, full-bodied presence, and expansive awareness.

It is the presence of the teacher that communicates to us most deeply, more than the words the teacher speaks. The teacher's gaze, demeanor, and contained power open new dimensions of consciousness for us and help us go beyond our limitations into freedom. Moreover, the teacher's actions are consistently found to be compassionate responses to the needs of others, intended, above all else, to illuminate and reveal Truth.

## Illumination and Skillful Instruction

In the presence of such teachers, we find peace, have our deepest questions about life's purpose and goal clarified, or experience an interior awakening best described as mystical. Through an enlightened teacher's influence, we begin to experience inner peace and to perceive our innate perfection—also called the Self, Atman, the divinity within. The teacher's presence and guidance awaken us to the bliss and radiance of the enlightened Mind, our deepest essence.

Thus, a spiritual teacher has two main qualities: illumination or enlightenment, and skill in illuminating others. Such a person is like a Buddha, one who is awake, while others exist in the sleep of ignorance. Yet the teacher also has the capacity to wake others from their sleep. An enlightened teacher not only perceives the Self, the light of Atman or omnipresent Spirit, but he or she is able to use skillful means to convey this experience to others. One teacher may be quite illumined but may be an inept guide—irresponsible, surly, exploitative, indifferent. Another may not have complete realization but may be a very skillful teacher able to pass knowledge on to others and to lead them forward in their evolution. An effective teacher is one who combines spiritual wisdom with skill in the art of spiritual mentorship, leading to the awakening of students. As we will note again later, in identifying skill in awakening others as one mark of an effective teacher, we leave open the question of what methods are appropriate for a teacher to use, allowing room for the use of unorthodox, "crazy wisdom" methods.

## Kinds of Teachers

There are different kinds of spiritual teachers and there are teachers of different stature. One may be a teacher of physical yoga postures, while another may teach us how to train our minds through meditation. Another may be primarily a pundit able to give profound intellectual discourses on spiritual texts and doctrine. But there are some rare teachers who can awaken us and lead us into expanded consciousness by their very presence. In the words of yogic scholar David Frawley:

> Gurus are not all of one type. There are great gurus, ordinary gurus, and false gurus.... Great gurus may be sages of superhuman capacity. Ordinary gurus may be able to teach us something even though they have many ordinary human limitations. False gurus may exploit and deceive people. Some false gurus have great powers but use them wrongly. They can do great damage to their followers' minds and hearts.[13]

A fully enlightened spiritual teacher is far more than a teacher of meditation or yoga techniques. He or she is an embodiment of the highest human potentials, emanating a palpable love, compassion, or power that is often immediately evident and has a transformative effect on others. The clearest sign that we are in the company of a great teacher is that we are deeply and often inexplicably moved by this being's presence. Sometimes a teacher's stature becomes apparent by demonstrating extraordinary powers such as healing, materializing objects, knowing all details of the past, present, and future lives of devotees, or being able to appear in two different places at the same time. Indian and Tibetan cultures both acknowledge the existence of rare beings known as *siddhas,* literally "the perfected ones." Siddhas are those who possess *siddhis*, powers that transcend conventional human functioning. A siddha is a human being who has become a conduit for divine intelligence, love, and power. Siddhas have been transformed through spiritual practice and realization to such an extent that extraordinary powers manifest through them. They exhibit visible signs of having achieved advanced, "metanormal" stages of human development.[14]

According to Michael Murphy, some of the extraordinary capacities associated with metanormal functioning include the following: enhanced sensory perception of external events (extraordinary powers of seeing, hearing, etc.); self-mastery and control over autonomic bodily processes; ability to perceive internal somatic events such as awareness of cells and molecules within the body; perception of the numinous in the physical world; perception of auras or scintillae (sparks of light) around people or objects; clairvoyant perception of distant events, precognitive perceptions, and telepathic communication with others; self-existent delight; mystical illumination and ecstatic sense of oneness with God; ability to directly transmit states of illumination to others; ability to awaken the *kundalini shakti* (the "serpent power") in others; and "modification of some portion of space by mental influence, as in the apparent creation by mystics and saints of a special joy or presence in their place of contemplation."[15] In short, these are the amazing psychic powers and miraculous actions attributed to many great saints. Although these powers are no guarantee of complete enlightenment, they are visible evidence of some degree of spiritual attainment, and often elicit the faith and devotion of others.

Others may conclude that such beings are not ordinary human teachers but rather instruments of divine power and love. Those who spend time in the company of enlightened beings often experience deep meditation, awakening of inner joy, or rousing of the kundalini energy. Our evolution is notably accelerated in their company. Their presence tangibly affects our own inner state, leading to emotional catharsis, a descent of peace, visions or premonitions, or waves of tears. A teacher exhibits qualities of love, wisdom, power, or joy that we emulate, and we experience a strong desire to be in the teacher's presence as much as possible so that we can absorb the teacher's clear and radiant emanation.

Ideally, a spiritual teacher is someone of advanced attainment on the spiritual path, one who has truly achieved the state of God-realization, *moksha* (liberation), or full enlightenment. But teachers of lesser attainment can also guide us. These are what Frawley calls "ordinary teachers," but I prefer to call them "helpful guides"—emphasizing their positive contributions as well as recognizing their limitations. A person who has a commitment to a spiritual practice and has sufficient experience and preparation may serve as a teacher for others, even if he or she is not fully enlightened. While ideally all aspirants would find fully illumined teachers to guide them, such teachers are rare, and we are often led forward by persons just a few steps ahead of us on the Path. There are gradations of wisdom and there are teachers of various levels of attainment who may be helpful at different stages of the journey and can further our advancement. The spiritual apprentice learns to accept teachings that come from many sources and to respectfully acknowledge all those who assist along the way. The main concern should be to avoid becoming deeply entangled with a false teacher—who is generally much more of a conceited and manipulative rogue than the ordinary teacher or "helpful guide" who acknowledges personal limitations and imperfections.

In this book I contend that the psychological and interpersonal issues involved in forming, sustaining, and in some cases dissolving relationships with spiritual teachers of varying levels of attainment are basically the same. The more evolved teacher is only slightly less likely to fall into some of the pitfalls of the student-teacher relationship than the teacher of lesser realization. Regardless of the teacher's stature, the process of engaging in training relationships with students is always complex. Even a highly realized mystic may have many lessons to learn about human relationships and how to guide others.

The teacher is never perfect, because the teacher is human. The teacher is a stand-in for the eternal archetype of the Teacher, the Guide, the Initiator. All teachers are challenged in the course of their own development to embody this archetype as fully as possible. Some do so more adequately than others. As we will see later, a teacher has to learn how to become a teacher for others. Wise teachers always remain learners, even while others honor and respect their wisdom. Teachers also can and should learn from their students, who have much to teach them and who will eventually graduate from their tutelage.

## *Attributes of the Spiritual Guide and the Qualified Student*

In many traditions, the specific character traits of the spiritual guide and the qualified student are explicitly described. For example, according to Islamic texts, the authentic guide is supposed to possess the following attributes:

> [S]ervitude to God alone, reception of truth directly from God, privileged access to God's mercy, a heart purified of all non-divine forms of knowledge, rebirth into knowledge of the essence of God's presence, . . . correct belief, intelligence, liberality, courage, chastity, lofty aspiration, compassion, forbearance, forgiveness, sweet temper, selflessness, contentment with one's lot, dignity, tranquility, steadfastness, and a presence worthy of reverence.[16]

From this list of attributes we can see that the teacher was expected to be a person of extraordinary power, purity, clarity, and personal integrity. The student was also expected to possess certain characteristics:

> [R]epentance, renunciation, abandonment of family ties, proper belief, fear of God, patience, struggle against the lower self (the 'greater struggle' [*jihad*] as compared to struggle against external foes), courage, readiness to sacrifice, chivalrousness, sincerity, knowledge, active searching, willingness to suffer reproach without giving occasion for it, intelligence, even disposition, submission to the shaykh "as a corpse in the hands of the corpse washer," and utter abandonment to God. . . . The seeker must strive to counteract the tendency to egocentricity through the attitudes of "servanthood" or "worshipfulness," and gratitude.[17]

Qualified students are those willing to dedicate themselves to the quest for realization or enlightenment one-pointedly, renouncing competing strivings, desires, and worldly ambitions, and able to give themselves over to the teacher's guidance wholeheartedly.

Similarly, in the classical yogic traditions of India the student's readiness for the relationship with a spiritual teacher is carefully assessed. The student is expected to meet basic standards of personal competency and must be prepared to accept the rigors and challenges of training. While there are practices for less prepared students, the fully qualified practitioner, according to the Shiva-Samhita (an ancient yogic text), possesses the following attributes:

> [G]reat energy, enthusiasm, charm, heroism, scriptural knowledge, the inclination to practice, freedom from delusion, orderliness, youthfulness, moderate eating habits, control over the senses, fearlessness, purity, skillfulness, liberality, the ability to be a refuge for all people, capability, stability, thoughtfulness, the willingness to do whatever is desired by the teacher, patience, good manners, observance of the moral and spiritual law (dharma), the ability to keep his struggle to himself, kind speech, faith in the scriptures, the willingness to worship God and the guru (as the embodiment of the Divine), knowledge of the vows pertaining to his level of practice, and, lastly, the practice of all types of knowledge.[16]

Aspirants who meditate deeply on these lists of desired traits will realize that they still have far to go in character development. Thus, the student is presented with a task even before a teacher has appeared— the task of self-examination and making effort toward self-betterment. Most students do not possess many of these noble qualities when they first approach teachers. But over time spiritual apprentices will hopefully acquire at least some of these positive virtues. Indeed, the student's character and motives will be examined thoroughly and reshaped during the stages of testing that await. It is important to recognize that teachers also may fall short on many desirable traits, and, as we will see later, they too will go through many tests of character.

The main attribute of the student qualified to meet a mystic guide is longing to attain the state of awakeness and clarity, to know and experience that Being called by many names, such as Source, Spirit, Atman, all-pervading Light. Something seems to guide us on the path before we've met our living teacher face to face; and this guiding presence can appear in physically embodied or non-embodied form. As American spiritual teacher Ram Dass explains:

When you reach the stage of asking, "God, know me," or "let me be enlightened," or "I want Nirvana,". . . at that moment you call forth your spiritual guide or Guru. . . .That . . . may be any one of a number of beings, and it is not necessarily on the physical plane.[19]

# Being Guided to a Teacher

Sometimes our desire for guidance is fulfilled quickly and we are led directly to an appropriate teacher. Or, we may search for such a teacher in vain for many months or years. We may travel great distances to find a teacher, or the guide may appear right in our neighborhood, without our going anywhere. No matter where we go or what we do, the teacher will not appear until a sincere longing for truth and guidance arises within us. Once this sincerity and longing become unwavering, it will not be long before a teacher appears to help us find our way. As the traditional Indian saying goes, "When the disciple is ready, the guru appears." A woman named Pamela reported:

> One day I was in a bookstore and for some reason I picked up a magazine off a shelf that I'd never seen before. I opened it up and it had this picture of this beautiful woman saint from India. I was completely drawn to her from the moment I set eyes upon her. "Who is *that?*" I wondered. I read all about her and it gave a phone number and I called it and there was a retreat happening in our city that month. I signed up and went to see her. And the first time I was introduced to her she acted like she already knew me. I've never been drawn to a teacher before but I was drawn right to her. I had been interested in finding a teacher for a while but I had given up. Then it just happened.

While we can be moved and subtly influenced by teachers who are no longer physically alive, a living guide is generally the most potent catalyst of transformation. Many traditions contend that we will not have the chance to meet a living teacher in this lifetime unless we have exceptionally good fortune. According to Annamalai Swami (a disciple of Ramana Maharshi), "One only comes into contact with a sage when one's good *karmas* bear fruit. Only those who have accumulated good karma from many lives get the chance to meet and love a sage."[20]

We are drawn to a teacher in a variety of ways. We become fascinated by a picture that elicits an immediate interest in meeting the teacher. We read about a teacher in a book or magazine, attend a workshop, or our interest may be stirred by speaking with someone who has been noticeably transformed through contact with a teacher.

When we first meet a teacher there is often a sudden moment of recognition. Jim, a student of kundalini yoga, describes his first meeting with his spiritual teacher in 1978:

> The moment I saw him I felt an electric shock go through my body, and the whole room seemed to be illuminated. As I listened to his lecture, my heart opened and I was filled with an overflowing love. I was in ecstasy. Since then, his presence has always been with me no matter how far away I am from him physically.

We may have an immediate feeling of connection to the teacher. Or the feeling of connection may grow more slowly over time. When we first connect with a teacher it often feels like a love affair or romantic infatuation. We may become obsessed with the teacher, hanging on every word, every glance. Every photo of the teacher is a picture of our beloved. We may even share our excitement with our friends.

## My Search for a Teacher

I learned about the importance of finding a teacher from the very beginning of my journey. I first became interested in yoga when I was fourteen years old. I felt a curious excitement about the topic, and was especially intrigued by the concept of the kundalini, the serpent power. I read every book on yoga I could find and began practicing *asanas* (yoga postures), *pranayama* (breathing practices), and meditation. I read B. K. S. Iyengar's *Light on Yoga*, which hit me with the force of a thunderbolt, and I began following the courses of hatha yoga postures recommended in that book. I would begin several hours after dinner and continue until past midnight. Sometimes I fell with a thud while coming down from a headstand or handstand, and the neighbors downstairs began complaining about the disturbing noise I was making.

Several months after I started this regimen I learned why practicing yoga without proper guidance can be dangerous. One night my mother found me at two o'clock in the morning passed out on the living room floor, after I had overzealously practiced *bhastrika pranayama*, the "breath of fire." I felt a flash of light within my body, then lost consciousness. This experience frightened me. I had succeeded in rousing a powerful internal energy, yet I had no idea how to do so safely. I was not adequately prepared for such an intense practice. It was then I realized the importance of finding a teacher.

I read books about great beings such as Ramana Maharshi, Ramakrishna, and Yogananda. I read Ram Dass's stories of his life-transforming encounters with his guru, Neem Karoli Baba, also known as Maharaji. I began attending a meditation group in New York City where I received a thread of Maharaji's blanket that was distributed by some of his devotees after he left his body. The thread, which I carried attached to a *mala*, a string of prayer beads, gave forth a peaceful emanation. I began to feel the subtle presence and invisible guidance of the guru quietly assisting me.

My longing to find a spiritual teacher grew intense, and I prayed to be guided to a person of wisdom in whom I could place my trust. I visited a number of teachers, and learned important lessons from some of them about yoga, meditation, and spiritual life. But none of these teachers was right for me. One demanded a large amount of money and an immediate commitment of volunteer time to assist his organization. Another encouraged me to reject my parents and leave home when I was sixteen. Another seemed vain and totally preoccupied with himself. One observed silence and did not give lectures, which I found frustrating. I kept searching, for in my heart I knew there was another teacher.

I saw two great beings whom I loved but did not accept as my guide. I remember the expectancy in the air one summer evening at the Cathedral of St. John the Divine in New York City, where Tibetan teacher Chogyam Trungpa was scheduled to give a lecture on "The Dawn of The Age of Enlightenment." The audience was expecting a powerful confirmation of their imminent realization of the final goal. However, Trungpa was late in arriving, and the crowd began to get very restless and impatient. When Trungpa finally arrived an hour and twenty minutes late, he walked up on stage thoroughly drunk. His first words were, "To talk about enlightenment at this stage is completely ridiculous." Then

31

he burst out laughing. Obviously he didn't think that those of us present were all that close to enlightenment. The entire audience deflated at once!

Another great teacher I saw was Pir Vilayat Inayat Khan. Before his lecture one evening, he came out on stage early and sat quietly, looking around the room silently making contact with each person present. When his eyes fell on me for a moment I felt a wave of peace and inner joy. He gently smiled at me and I smiled back. Although he was not to be my teacher, I did receive a wonderful blessing from him that evening.

Mysterious karmic factors lead us to choose a particular teacher. We feel a deep inner connection that cannot be forgotten or denied, and we know intuitively that we have something important to learn from this person. The first test of spiritual apprenticeship is to exercise discernment when choosing a teacher. As Pir Vilayat once wrote, "Before you attach yourself to a master, make sure he is the master for you."[21]

I was sixteen years old when I first met Swami Muktananda, a meditation teacher and siddha guru from India. I met him the day he arrived in New York City in the fall of 1974 at the beginning of his second world tour. I had read about Muktananda in several books that described his remarkable spiritual powers, so I was excited to learn that he was staying three blocks from where I went to high school on the upper west side of Manhattan. I have often wondered whether I found him or whether he found me.

Muktananda was a short, pot-bellied, dark-skinned man who wore orange robes and a colorful maroon or red sweater. He was magnetic, moving like a restless cat, and he had a strangely fascinating and powerful emanation. His face assumed innumerable expressions, shooting quick, darting glances, momentarily irritable, then bubbling with sudden throaty laughter, then quietly blissful, appearing to move in other dimensions within himself. Dark sunglasses hid his mysterious eyes, which shone like bright suns when they were briefly uncovered.

When I first met Muktananda, I sensed that he was a man of great power and wisdom, and I also had the intuition that I was in the presence of a very ancient being whose true nature was *fire*. At first, I confess, I wasn't sure I liked him. He scared me, plus he seemed grouchy and intense, not like the serene holy man I'd anticipated finding. Yet his presence affected me in a mysterious way, and over the next few months

I began to sense that this was the teacher who could guide me. After he left New York to continue his tour I found that I was thinking about him all the time, and I yearned to meditate and began doing so diligently. Muktananda's influence in my life first became evident through an intensification of my desire to know God. I quickly shed the desires to drink alcohol and smoke marijuana and became a disciplined young yogi.

## How We Know We've Found a Teacher

Meeting a teacher may impact us so powerfully that we are seized by a desire to radically change our lives and to embrace the quest for mystical realization. When Rumi, a highly respected scholar, met his teacher Shams of Tabriz, Shams took a book Rumi was writing about philosophy and threw it into a well. Rumi became an ecstatic devotee of Shams and abandoned all else, including scholarship and family responsibilities. The most telling sign that we have found a teacher is that we begin to undergo a noticeable transformation. Our habits change and our lives become more pure. We experience inner peace, deeper meditations, or feel a blissful presence surrounding us. Our hearts open. Inner vision awakens. Our lives change. An inner fire of longing for enlightenment is kindled within us. Rumi put it like this:

> What draws Friends together
> does not conform to Laws of Nature.
> Form doesn't know about spiritual closeness. . . .
> A hand shifts our birdcages around.
> Some are brought closer. Some move apart.
> Do not try to reason it out. Be conscious
> of who draws you and who not.[22]

A common experience after meeting a teacher is for everything in our lives to fall apart. In the Koran it is said, "I am with those whose hearts are broken for My sake."[23] Old interests fall away, and we may drift away from old friendships as our interests change and turn toward matters of spirit and inner awakening. The disciples of the Indian guru Ramakrishna underwent a profound transformation as a result of their contact with their saintly master. Many were filled with a feverish devotion and burning for enlightenment. Many of them renounced worldly life soon after Ramakrishna's death and became monks in order to commit themselves completely to the pursuit of God-realization.[24]

We accept a teacher in order to attain the enlightened state, *bodhi*, the clear mind, *Atman*, the state of pure consciousness. This is the goal of spiritual apprenticeship. And the fundamental way to reach this goal is through meditation, yoga, or other transformative, consciousness-enhancing practices. Through meditation, we develop calm, contentment, and wisdom. Awareness turns inward, reflects upon itself, and becomes aware of itself *as awareness*. In Buddhist terms, meditation teaches us to recognize our *dharmakaya* nature—which is Mind, vast as space. In the Hindu tradition this is known as the realization of the Self or Atman. In yogic philosophy, Atman is one with Brahman, the Absolute, composed of the same essence as the source of all creation. No matter what terms we use to describe it, the goal is pure, unimpeded knowing, *gnosis*, the ecstatic perception of the oneness and sacredness of life.

We need a teacher not just to teach us techniques and doctrine but also to embody the enlightened state, so that we can recognize it in ourselves and achieve it. We may also choose a teacher to learn a particular method such as meditation, contemplative prayer, yoga, or shamanic journeying. Even in cases where a teacher is not a fully enlightened Buddha, sage, or siddha guru we may still grow by studying with that person for a period of time—if the teacher seems clear and balanced and we feel confident that this person can address our needs and guide us effectively through some stage of our transformation. It is enough that the teacher embodies and conveys some quality of freedom that we ourselves wish to attain.

The teacher can appear in many guises. A friend of mine once described his teacher as "a muscle-bound jock who loves to flirt with women and who also happens to be a great yogi." Some teachers may appear to be saintly, others not at all saintly. John Welwood contends that we cannot evaluate a spiritual teacher's genuineness by external behaviors alone, for we must consider the relational context in which behaviors have their meaning, and we must also avoid viewing one model of what constitutes a good teacher as ideal or exclusively valid. "Since genuine spiritual teachers come in many different shapes and forms, we will no doubt fail if we try to spell out how a good guru should behave."[25] David Frawley echoes this view, saying, "Great gurus may be saints with impeccable characters and lifestyles. However, they may also look like madmen and refuse to conform to any social norms. Society may consider them scoundrels."[26] Thus, we shouldn't accept a teacher just because everybody else says the person is an enlightened sage; nor should we immediately reject any teacher who does not conform to our expectations or conceptions of holiness. The teacher doesn't have to be famous, or an impoverished ascetic, or surrounded by important disciples. What is important is that the teacher's personal example inspires us, the teacher's words speak to us deeply, and the teacher's presence affects us intensely. The teacher helps us understand the goal of the spiritual path, and a path we can follow to reach this goal.

We can learn a great deal about how to choose and relate to a teacher if we understand some of the varied forms a spiritual guide can take, and the ways we are likely to be affected by contact with one. Thus, in this book we will consider how spiritual teachers have been described in some of the world's major religions. From the foundation of insights derived from these traditions, we will reach a number of conclusions:

1) Spiritual apprenticeship begins with a personal relationship with a teacher that tangibly affects our awareness, and that inspires us to practice a contemplative discipline in order to attain enlightenment.

2) Initiation connects the student to the influence of a spiritual lineage that transcends the individual teacher.

3) The student-teacher relationship involves the mutual meditation of the student and teacher upon one another, and the deliberate cultivation of a form of psychic merger or unity that can have a transformative effect upon the student.

4) The relationship may involve experiences of grace in which the teacher functions as a conduit for transmission of transpersonal forces.

## The Guru Principle and the Bestowal of Grace

In India the spiritual teacher has played a central role in the life of the people since time immemorial. A Sanskrit verse reads *gurubrahma gururvisnur gurudevo mahesvarah*—"The guru is Brahma and Vishnu, there is no doubt he is Shiva too." Like Brahma (the creator), the guru creates a new life within us, molds our character, initiates us, and kindles the light of consciousness in our hearts. Like Vishnu (the preserver), the guru sustains and protects us over the course of time until we reach the final goal. And like Shiva (the destroyer), the guru destroys our limitations, our identification with the body, mind, fears, and desires, so that we begin to perceive only the Absolute, the limitless freedom of Spirit.

In the Indian yogic tradition of Kashmir Shaivism the guru or enlightened teacher is more than an individual human personality but is considered the embodiment of a cosmic principle known as the *guru tattva*—literally the guru principle, or the guru function. According to Kashmir Shaivite doctrine, God or Shiva has five activities or functions: The first three are the *creation* or manifestation of forms; the *sustenance* of those forms, and their *destruction*. Within the eternal cycle of creation-sustenance-destruction, God engages in *concealment*, hiding so that we only perceive the transient show of forms and not their eternal origin and source. And the final function of Shiva is *revelation*, or ecstatic divine self-disclosure, through the *bestowal of grace*. The guru tattva, the guru principle, is identified with this power to bestow grace. Thus, the guru is one through whom the concealed power and splendor of Shiva, the Supreme Light, is revealed and unfolded within a human being. The word *guru* literally means "one who takes us from the dark to the light," thus the guru is one who transforms the night of ignorance into the dawn of inner vision and oneness. According to Paul Eduardo Muller-Ortega, a leading scholar of Kashmir Shaivism:

> The primary characteristics of the *guru* are the achieved condition of realization . . . and his capacity to transmit realization directly to his disciple. . . . The [*Siva-sutra-vimarsini*] states: "*Gurupayah*," that is, "the *guru* is the way," and he is the only method that is needed. This *sutra* can be read in two different ways. In its first interpretation, "the *guru* is the method," it means that a willing attendance upon the teacher is the sole prerequisite for the achievement of liberation. On a surface level, this means that the *guru* will then make himself responsible for the training of the disciple, and will lead him through the various disciplines and practices that will secure for the disciple the realization of liberation. On a deeper level, however, the statement that the *guru* is the method reflects the idea that the *guru* represents the embodied wholeness that is the goal of the *sadhaka*. The face-to-

face meeting of the disciple and the *guru* does not represent merely an encounter between two separate beings, one of whom happens to be enlightened and can thus aid and help the other in the search for enlightenment. Rather, by entering into a relationship of service the disciple places his finite awareness in direct confrontation with the enlightened consciousness of the *guru*, which is the same unbounded consciousness the disciple wishes to attain.[27]

We form a connection with a spiritual teacher in order to attain the teacher's same state of freedom. The Hindu tradition, and Shaivism in particular, view the guru not just as a person but as a universal principle that is embodied by certain extraordinary teachers who awaken students to the inner light of consciousness. The teacher functions as a conduit through which the concealed power of Shiva—the all-pervading Source—can reveal itself. We choose a a teacher who vibrationally entrains us to the enlightened state and draws us toward it.

## Spiritual Teachers in Buddhism

The student-teacher relationship has always been central in the Buddhist tradition. After Guatama Buddha became enlightened, he was surrounded by disciples who listened attentively to his teachings on suffering, impermanence, and the path that leads beyond clinging and attachment to freedom and enlightenment. He taught and explained how it is the nature of the human mind that gives rise to either bondage or freedom. The Buddha gave such unfathomably profound teachings as his discourses on the wheel of *samsara* (the cycle of birth, death, and rebirth), the preciousness of human birth, and the importance of striving for enlightenment in this lifetime. And he taught the noble eightfold path that leads to enlightenment. According to Lama Govinda:

The germ of Enlightenment is ever present in the world, and just as . . . Buddhas arose in past world-cycles, so Enlightened ones arise in our present world-cycle and will arise in future world cycles. . . . The historical features of Buddha Guatama, therefore, recede behind the general characteristics of Buddhahood, in which is manifested the eternal or ever-present reality of the potential Enlightenment-consciousness of the human mind. . . . The Buddha, who is worshipped, is not the historical personality of the man, Siddhartha Guatama, but the embodiment of the divine qualities, which are latent in every human being. Therefore, the Buddhas and Bodhisattvas are . . . the prototypes of those states of highest knowledge, wisdom, and harmony which have been realized in humanity and will ever have to be realized again and again.[28]

Countless beings have followed the path shown by the Buddha and found enlightenment. Some of them, known as bodhisattvas, have delayed final liberation to dedicate themselves to service and relieving suffering, and some of these, such as Avalokitesvara and Tara, are often invoked and supplicated by aspirants to enlightenment. But, in addition to meditation upon these powerful symbols of enlightenment, the relationship between a student and a living embodied spiritual teacher has always been a feature of the Buddhist way of life. In general, Buddhism tries to cultivate the attitude that Buddha nature is present in all beings, and in all the teachings life gives us. Even our enemies are identified as spiritual teachers because they teach us patience and compassion. Yet an illumined teacher's guidance is necessary to guide the aspirant through the fires of purification and transformation. The teacher inspires the student to develop *bodhicitta*, the intention to develop a clear mind and to strive for enlightenment for the benefit of all sentient beings. In traditions such as Tibetan Buddhism, the figure of the lama plays a prominent role, being the instructor in Buddhist doctrine, the officiant at ceremonies and empowerments, and the focus of devotional practice. Later, I will discuss how the teacher becomes the focal point of a transformative Tibetan Buddhist practice known as guru yoga.

In Buddhism the teacher's role is to inspire the student to undertake an arduous process of self-observation, moral training, and meditative discipline. If in Hinduism the guru is sometimes viewed as a "savior" whose grace carries the student toward liberation, the Buddhist view is generally that the teacher can only point the way that aspirants must travel through their own strenuous efforts. The teacher cannot liberate the student through the bestowal of grace. Instead, in most Buddhist traditions meditation practice is recommended as the necessary medicine for our agitated minds. Aspirants need teachers to guide them as they undertake the rigors of meditation practice and self-transformation. For those involved with intensive meditation disciplines, such as those practiced in lengthy retreats, a teacher is crucial because the student will almost inevitably go through periods of confusion, despair, physical and emotional pain, and sometimes misleading visions or states of rapture.

For example, in the book *Journey of Insight Meditation*,[29] Eric Lerner described how several Theravadin Buddhist teachers guided him through many harrowing ordeals during lengthy *vipassana* meditation retreats in India, Burma, and Ceylon. Lerner experienced stages of mental obsession and fixation, physical and emotional exhaustion, and was often overwhelmed by despair, sadness, overpowering memories, anxiety and fears of the future. At times he became so mentally and emotionally unbalanced that he feared he was verging on insanity. He described his meditative journey as an ego-wrenching experience, a "personal holocaust," a process of watching himself unravel while observing the ever-changing flow of sensations, perception, and thoughts, and while experiencing torturous inner doubts. His teachers taught him to examine, and gain insight into, the moment-to-moment experience of pain, emotional neediness, and clinging. Lerner reached a critical point in his practice when he began to experience an agonizing knot in his spinal column the size of grapefruit, which grew more and more intense over long days of sitting, causing extreme pain, tension, and discomfort. He became physically ill, and resolved to give up meditation forever. His teacher instructed him to mentally move his awareness into this energetic block instead of running away from it, and to dissolve the knot by observing its impermanent and constantly changing nature. When he worked through the physical pain, and his tendency to recoil from pain, and as he developed steady, mindful awareness of the mental states that gave rise to the sensation of the knot, the knot soon disappeared.

Later, Lerner had several glimpses of enlightenment while on retreat. He had visions and other alterations of his awareness that led him to believe he was on the verge of *nirvana*. However, when he reported these experiences to his current teacher, she reprimanded him for becoming distracted from the goal of enlightenment by the snares of blissful trance states. His teacher's assistance was crucial in keeping him on the right path at a moment when he was gripped with the illusion that he had tasted true enlightenment.

As in the Theravadin Buddhist traditions of India, Burma, and Ceylon, in Japanese Zen Buddhism a relationship with a spiritual teacher, known as a *roshi*, is considered one of the foundations of the path.

> In the person of a genuine roshi, able to expound the Buddha's Dharma with a conviction born of his own profound experience of truth, is to be found the embodiment of Zen's wisdom and authority. Such a roshi is a guide and teacher whose spirit-heart-mind is identical with that of all Buddhas and patriarchs, separated though they may be by centuries in time.... Zen, as a transmission from mind to mind, cherishes pulsating, living truth.... Like sound imprisoned in a record or tape, needing electrical energy and certain devices to reproduce it, so the Heart-mind of the Buddha, entombed in the sutras, needs a living force in the person of an enlightened roshi to re-create it. [30]

In the course of Zen practice, students meet regularly with a roshi to report their experiences in meditation and progress in solving perplexing, paradoxical questions known as *koans*. Over time, zazen meditation, grappling with the koan, and encounters with the teacher jar loose the practitioner's familiar thoughts, perceptions, and concepts, leading to an enlightenment experience known as *kensho*, or *satori*. Innumerable Zen stories describe the process by which a roshi leads the student to enlightenment by supervising the rigors of disciplined meditation practice, *koan* contemplation, and through periodic teaching encounters known as *dokusan*—in which the student and teacher discuss the student's progress in meditation and understanding of the Dharma. According to Roshi Philip Kapleau:

> Dokusan (individual instruction) ... is the time allotted for bringing all problems pertaining to practice before the roshi in private. This tradition of individual teaching started with the honored Shakyamuni himself and has continued unbroken until today.... This "eyeball to eyeball" encounter with the roshi within the privacy of his inner chambers can be anything from an inspiring and wonderfully enriching experience, giving impetus and direction to his practice, to a fearful ordeal of mounting frustrations.... An accomplished roshi will not scruple to employ every device and strategem, not excluding jabs with his ubiquitous baton (*kotsu*), when he believes it will jar and rouse the student's mind from a state of dormant unawareness to the sudden realization of its true

nature. . . . The teacher may repeatedly frustrate the student by summarily dismissing him, rebuking him for not solving a koan, or cracking the student with the baton while he is prostrating. . . . This strategy of placing the student in a desperate situation where he is relentlessly driven from the rear and vigorously repulsed in front often builds up pressures within him that lead to that inner explosion without which true awakening seldom occurs.[31]

The tradition of private meetings between the roshi and the student provides an important model for the relationship of teacher and student. In contrast, many popular contemporary spiritual teachers are remote figures constantly surrounded by large mobs of students and devotees. It is often difficult for students to have regular personal contact with such teachers and to have their questions answered. This is not to say that one cannot have a transformative relationship with such teachers. Indeed, a lot of personal contact is not always necessary, and the teacher's charismatic presence or lucid public discourses are sometimes sufficient to answer students' questions and resolve doubts. Students also learn to find answers to their questions through meditation.

Nevertheless, regular interaction with a teacher, and a personal relationship, rather than an impersonal one, can be very helpful to the aspirant. Even if the teacher has hundreds or thousands of devotees and disciples, there is ideally some setting in which the student can communicate directly with the teacher. The basis of spiritual apprenticeship is contact with the enlightened consciousness of the guide—contact that will inspire us to practice meditation, uproot our fears and illusions, and help us break through to deeper clarity. A living teacher can be a more potent catalyst of awakening than one who is no longer alive because we have more opportunity for contact with the teacher's awakened mind, for in-depth instruction, and for thorough testing and purification. Most importantly, with a living teacher we are able to receive close supervision, instead of going out on the turbulent waters of transformation alone, without guidance. The teacher observes us as we proceed on the path. Later, as we mature in spiritual practice, the teacher will encourage us to become independent. But at this stage reliance upon the teacher serves our transformation.

The Buddhist traditions of spiritual instruction teach us two main lessons: First, we choose a teacher because we receive a clear and convincing articulation of the truth. The teacher elucidates the doctrine that enables us to understand the importance of enlightenment and the means to attain it. Second, a teacher wins our trust as he or she demonstrates skill and compassion in guiding us through the ordeals of metamorphosis that we face when we become practitioners of a spiritual discipline. In short, we choose a teacher who demonstrates the ability to guide our inner journey.

## Examining a Teacher

Choosing a teacher is not something to jump into quickly, and it is best to proceed cautiously. It is essential that we closely examine the character and behavior of a person we are considering accepting as our guide, as well as noting what changes we feel in ourselves as a result of contact with this being. If there is a powerful inner shift of our consciousness after meeting a teacher, we may feel instrinctively drawn to seek further contact and instruction.

The first test of spiritual apprenticeship is discrimination in the choice of a teacher. While we can never know for certain whether or not a teacher is enlightened and will truly serve our growth, we have to utilize our hearts and our intuition to try to answer this question. Of course, there is no guarantee that our intuition won't mislead us. We could be preyed upon by a magnetic, persuasive, and misguided person who exploits us or hurts us. We could always get burned. This is a risk implicit in spiritual apprenticeship—but this is a risk that we accept because we sense the transformative power of associating with a spiritual guide. Every mystical tradition tells us of the importance of finding a teacher, and our own experience confirms this. Yet this is no moment for haste. We proceed with cautious receptivity to the teacher's transmission or instruction. We are neither rigidly skeptical nor overly starryeyed. We size up the teacher and listen within ourselves to sense if we feel an inner connection. Now is the time for us to listen to the voice of our own heart, which is always our most reliable source of guidance.

Later we will discuss how the teacher tests and examines the student's character. But the student also needs to examine and test the teacher before proceeding further. It is not necessary at this stage to commit one's life to the teacher, to surrender fully. Self-giving, devotion, and abiding trust in the teacher will emerge with time, as the teacher proves worthy, and as the student's doubts are addressed.

Observe the teacher's character. What are the teacher's human qualities, and do you find these appealing? Is this a person you want to become like? What idiosyncrasies of character do you note? Does this teacher emanate a palpable spiritual energy that affects you inwardly? How does the teacher treat other people? What changes in your awareness have you noticed since meeting this being? Is the teacher willing to listen to your questions and to address these directly, humanely, and satisfactorily? Is this person able to responsibly lead a community of students? Is the teacher a sufficiently convincing embodiment of purity, serenity, and truth to serve as your vehicle to freedom?

As we approach a teacher, it is important to assess whether we are being subjected to any cultish dynamics and pressures. Will we be expected to go out on the streets to sell flowers or newspapers to raise money for the teacher? Does the teacher demand that we sever all other ties with family and friends? Traditionally, willingness to renounce ties to the world and attachment to personal relationships was considered a necessary attribute of a sincere aspirant. Yet in our era a more integral spirituality is emerging that can be pursued in the midst of (not despite) a complex life of relationships with others and engagement with the challenges of the world. Renunciation may emerge spontaneously but should not be forced or demanded at this stage.

Closely examine the teacher's other students. Do they look healthy and radiant, or are they haggard and undernourished? Do they seem balanced, or do they try too hard to look happy and blissful? If you are unimpressed with the teacher's long-time students, you will probably not be happy with the outcome of your own association with this teacher. We may feel a vague discomfort in the presence of some teachers and the community of students surrounding them. These feelings may be a keen intuition that something is amiss and that this may not be a place where our growth will be furthered. Daniel Goleman has described these "Early Warning Signs for the Detection of Spiritual Blight":

> Taboo topics: Questions that can't be asked, doubts that can't be shared, misgivings that can't be voiced. For example, "Where does all the money go?" or "Does Yogi sleep with his secretary?" Spiritual Clones: In its minor form, stereotypic behavior, such as people

who walk, talk, smoke, eat and dress just like their leader; in its more sinister form, psychological stereotyping, such as an entire group of people who manifest only a narrow range of feeling in any and all situations; always happy, or pious. . . . Groupthink: A party line that over-rides how people actually feel. "You've fallen, and Christ is the answer"; or "You're lost in samsara, and Buddha is the answer"; or "You're impure, and Shiva is the answer." The Elect: A shared delusion of grandeur that there is no Way but this one. The corollary: You're lost if you leave the group. No Graduates: Members are never weaned from the group. Assembly Lines: Everyone is treated identically, no matter what their differences. Loyalty Tests: Members are asked to prove loyalty to the group by doing something that violates their personal ethics; for example, setting up an organization that has a hidden agenda of recruiting others into the group, but publicly represents itself as a public service outfit. Duplicity: The group's public face misrepresents its true nature. Unifocal Understanding: A single world-view is used to explain anything and everything; alternate explanations are verboten. Humorlessness: No irreverence allowed.[32]

It is also important to examine a prospective teacher's lineage. Who were this teacher's teachers? Does the teacher have a background in an identifiable lineage of spiritual practice, realization, and instruction? Or is the teacher self-taught and self-proclaimed? This in itself is not always the sign of a charlatan, for there are many examples of well-qualified teachers with the full authorization of great lineages who abuse their position as teachers. But be especially careful with any teacher who say that your evolution is solely dependent on them, or that there is no other path to realization than to become their student. I am personally mistrustful of any teacher who claims to have a mission or role of unique importance in the course of history. Nevertheless, many teachers and their followers do make such claims—a fact that has its roots deep in our history. In forming an association with a spiritual guide, we should be keenly aware of the tendency to place messianic hopes on teachers. To explore these issues further, I will briefly examine the role of spiritual teachers in Judaism and compare two colorful examples.

## *Spiritual Teachers in Judaism*

In the Jewish tradition, *rebbes* have always been greatly respected and revered figures, guiding others on the path of moral action, righteousness, and commitment to Biblical teachings and commandments. In contrast to Hinduism, where it is often said that an enlightened teacher merges with God and becomes divine, in Judaism it is believed that while a mystic may have a vision of God or angelic realms, it is not possible for a human being to ever attain union with God. Even the most enlightened teacher is always seen in human terms. We will see later that perceiving the essential humanity of the teacher is crucial if we are to assess realistically a teacher's character. Nevertheless, a teacher may be viewed as close to God and able to lead others toward God through his example and moral influence.

In medieval Hasidic Judaism, a figure emerged known as the *tzaddik* ("the righteous one"), to whom great powers and healing abilities were often attributed. The tzaddik was a charismatic figure said to be in constant communion with God, a visionary possessing extraordinary powers who provided spiritual and prophetic leadership to his community.[33] Like the *siddha guru* in India, the Jewish tzaddik was viewed as an instrument for an influx of divine energy and vitality, which streamed through him from God down to his contemporaries. Tzaddiks were holy men little concerned about formal religious services and scriptural study, and more interested in the living spirit of prayer, devotion, song, and community.

In Judaism the perception that a spiritual leader can play a redemptive role in the world has frequently been filtered through two lenses that still color our perceptions of teachers in our own era: messianism and apocalypticism. *Messianism* is the hope for the advent of a religious and political leader who will be the savior and liberator of the exiled Jewish people. For example, the great spiritual leaders of ancient Israel were patriarchs and prophets who provided leadership in times of crisis and made prophecies regarding the future destiny of Israel—the hopes for reestablishment of the House of David, the future glory of an Israel returned to God, the beginning of an era of everlasting peace, and the turning of all nations toward the One God. Thus, the role of spiritual teachers in the Jewish tradition was intricately connected to collective hopes for changes in historical, social conditions. Messianism was concerned with the collective historical destiny of the Jewish nation, not with the attainment by individuals of special mystical knowledge achieved through states of inwardness.[35]

Messianism often appears in connection with *apocalypticism*, the belief in the imminent end of the world. According to Scholem, messianism is both "a content of religious faith... and also living, acute anticipation."[36] This apocalyptic expectancy is heightened during moments of communal suffering and desperation, where people begin to believe that the end of the world is imminent. It seems to be an intrinsic part of human psychology to look for an external savior who will liberate us. Every religion has the myth of the expected return of a universal teacher. Hinduism has Kalki, the next avatar of Vishnu. Buddhism has Maitreya, the Buddha to come. Christians await the return of Jesus. Shiite Muslims expect the return of Mahdi, the twelfth son from Ali, nephew of Mohammed. This expectancy of return is closely connected to the recurrent mythic theme of hope in the return of paradise on earth, the restoration of a once sacred world.[37]

Even today, many of us view teachers through the lens of messianic expectation, placing on them the burden of redeeming the entire world. We look to spiritual teachers not only to instruct us in contemplative techniques but also to provide leadership for a community or social movement and to liberate us from the sufferings of history. This desire for leadership and salvation is often filled with the same "living, acute anticipation" that Scholem noted. Indeed, some spiritual apprentices fervently believe that their teacher has a uniquely important historical mission, and is indeed the long-awaited savior of humanity. Some teachers also believe this about themselves.

A case in point from the history of Judaism is the figure of Sabbatai Sevi, the "mystical messiah." Sevi was a complex figure, an ecstatic mystic with an illuminated gaze who also fell periodically into states of deep depression—a classic bipolar personality. Born in August 1626, he began to live ascetically and study Kabbalah from youth, practicing frequent ritual baths, fasts, and mortifications. Often called a fool, lunatic, and madman, he exhibited recurring cycles of anguish and depression, followed by manic euphoria, ecstasies, and illumination. In these latter phases his face would turn red and was said to "burn like fire" while he was in prayer or song.[38] In 1648 agitation swept the Jewish community due to mass murders of Jews in Poland. This crisis coalesced with one of Sevi's phases of inner euphoria, during which he heard a voice proclaiming him the Savior of Israel. He began to act as if, and to proclaim that, he was beyond the authority of rabbinic Judaism and subject to a higher law. Nobody paid any attention to him; people thought he was crazy. He had himself wedded to the Torah in a public ceremony. Rabbis flogged him and drove him out of town.

Then a man named Nathan had a vision and began announcing publicly that Sevi was the messiah. Sevi denied it. Nathan spent weeks trying to convince Sevi of his messianic mission. In May, 1665, Sevi went into a manic rapture and proclaimed himself "the anointed one," giving rise to an acute public frenzy and a flock of followers. He was later excommunicated from Jerusalem and fled to the city of Aleppo, but his movement spread due to the feverish activity of Nathan, Sevi's prophet. His life reached a climax when he was captured by the Muslims and converted to Islam, essentially renouncing Judaism. His followers were left desolate and disillusioned. Many tried to interpret the secret logic of his bizarre actions through the doctrine of "the holiness of sin." Such a doctrine posed a grave threat to the rabbinic orthodoxy, who spared no effort to suppress the movement. The Sabbatian movement thus ended in catastrophe for thousands of his followers, who desperately tried to explain his actions. The story of Sabbatai Sevi is a classic example of how a teacher's psychological imbalance and delusions of grandeur, coupled with the messianic hopes of followers, can lead to catastrophic outcomes for disciples. Later I will cite an example of a contemporary false teacher who caused great harm to others.

The history of Judaism also informs us about spiritual teachers who work selflessly for the benefit of others, and who exercise a positive and uplifting influence. Consider the life of the Baal Shem Tov, an ecstatic wise man who taught a celebratory spirituality and whose movement revitalized the Jewish communities of Eastern Europe. The Baal Shem Tov was the original tzaddik. Whereas the Jewish tradition tends to be strongly intellectual, the Baal Shem Tov brought spirituality into the body, encouraging others to express the love of God and the spirit of joy through ecstatic songs, dancing, and renewal of the living spirit of religious community.[39] Elie Wiesel, in his book *Souls on Fire*, writes:

> Historically speaking, the character barely emerges, his outlines
> blurred by contradictions. Nothing about him can be said with
> certainty. Those who claim to have known him, to have come close
> to him or loved him, seem incapable of referring to him in terms
> other than poetic. . . . [He was] a man who almost single-handedly
> opened the soul of his people to a new creativity, a creativity here-
> tofore unexplored, of man come to grips with what crushes or
> lifts him toward infinity. The man who left his mark on so many
> survivors of so many massacres in Central and Eastern Europe...
> The master who gave song to despairing communities, managed
> to disappear without leaving . . . even a fragment of valid autobio-
> graphical material. Obsessed by infinity, he neglected history and
> let himself be carried by legend.[40]

Born either in 1698 or 1700, the Baal Shem lived his early life in
obscurity as an impoverished innkeeper in the country. One day a "mad-
woman" told him, "I know who you are. . . . I know that you possess
certain powers. I also know that you may not use them before the age
of thirty six."[41] At age thirty six, observers witnessed the Baal Shem
flooded with light, thus launching his public work. He was said to be
able to see into a person's soul and to respond to the unspoken thoughts
of others. He exhibited an unusual, prolonged trembling, as if he was
continuously aware of some fear- and awe-inducing presence.[42] He traveled constantly, appearing here and there, accosting strangers, making
followers of them all. Generous and kind, he showed interest in the details of every person's life. Every human being deserved his attention.

> A man of contagious intensity, he changed all who approached
> him. The most mediocre of men vibrated at his contact; an en-
> counter with him was the event of a lifetime. To have his gaze rest
> on you meant feeling his fire run through you. . . . He wished to
> remain accessible to all who came to him to share their worries,
> their anguish. . . . What he wanted was to end all waiting, per-
> sonify all hope. If one believed his legend, he succeeded. He be-
> longed to all.[43]

The Baal Shem loved peasants, ruffians, sinners, drunkards, and
brought hope to those who had no hope. The movement he spawned
sustained communities through the devastation of exile, pogroms, and
the Holocaust—despite the fact that he himself possessed no notable

ancestors, no exalted social status, no official titles or influential friends, no material possessions, or even talmudic learning.

> He explained . . . that abstract erudition is not the sole vessel of truth or the sole path leading to saintliness. And that saintliness is not the only link between man and the eternity he carries inside him. Song is more precious than words, intention more important than formulas. . . . [W]hy despair? Why give up the fight? One tear, one prayer can change the course of events; one fragment of melody can contain all the joy in the world, and by letting it go free, influence fate. . . . When he died in 1760 . . . there remained in Central and Eastern Europe not a single Jewish town that was left unaffected. He had been the spark without which thousands of families would have succumbed to gloom and hopelessness—and the spark had fanned itself into a huge flame that tore into the darkness.[44]

The life of a teacher such as this confirms our belief that there are rare beings who can inspire and liberate the hearts of others, lifting them beyond suffering into joy. While there are false teachers who bring about their own downfall and bring disaster upon their followers, there are also true teachers who serve humanity and leave an indelible mark on all they touch. When we meet a being aflame with the light of truth, we feel it in our bodies. In their presence, our own souls are set on fire.

Spiritual apprenticeship begins with the recognition that one has found a guide who illuminates a path to freedom, making that freedom available not in the distant future, but in this very moment. The kindness, peacefulness, and powerful intensity apparent in the teacher inspire the student to seek deeper stillness and refinement of being through a life of contemplation and spiritual practice. Thus, the guide is both the catalyst and harbinger of the student's own inner awakening.

The presence of great teachers awakens in us a recognition of our own potentials and inspires us to seek the same enlightened, expanded way of being. Inspired by the teacher's example, we embark upon the journey of spiritual apprenticeship. The teacher becomes our model of greatness and the focus of our reverent attention. Led forward by a courage that will be tested and strengthened over time, we take a breath and step forward.

# *Notes*

1. *The Life and Teaching of Naropa*, translated by H. Guenther (New York: Oxford Univ. Press, 1963), p. 28.
2. *The Hundred Thousand Songs of Milarepa*, translated by G. C. C. Chang (New York: Harper & Row, 1962), p. 51.
3. J. Halifax, *Shamanic Voices* (New York: Dutton, 1979).
4. A. Schimmel, *Mystical Dimensions of Islam* (Chapel Hill, NC: Univ. of North Carolina Press, 1975), p. 237.
5. Ibid., pp. 100–101.
6. G. Scholem, *On the Kabbalah and Its Symbolism* (New York: Schocken, 1969), p. 18.
7. K. Wilber, "Pathologies of the Spiritual Path." In K. Wilber, J. Engler, & D. Brown (Eds.), *Transformations of Consciousness* (Boston: Shambhala, 1986).
8. W. T. De Bary (Ed.), *Sources of Indian Tradition, Volume 1* (New York: Columbia Univ. Press, 1958), p. 329.
9. *Bhagavad Gita*, translated by J. Mascaro (Middlesex, England: Penguin Books, 1962), p. 64.
10. K. Prem, *The Yoga of the Bhagavat Gita* (Baltimore: Penguin Books, 1958), pp. 34–36.
11. W. T. De Bary (Ed.), *Sources of Indian Tradition, Volume 1* (New York: Columbia Univ. Press, 1958), p. 16.
12. G. Krishna, *Kundalini: The Evolutionary Power in Man* (Boston: Shambhala, 1970); A. Avalon, *The Serpent Power: The Secrets of Tantric and Shaktic Yoga* (New York: Dover, 1974).
13. D. Frawley, "All Gurus Great and Small," *Yoga Journal* (March/April, 1997), p. 28.
14. M. Murphy, *The Future of the Body* (Los Angeles: Jeremy Tarcher, 1992).
15. Ibid., p. 47.
16. J. Renard, "Islamic Tradition of Spiritual Guidance," *The Way*, 28, 1, 1988, p. 62.
17. Ibid., pp. 62, 64.
18. Cited in G. Feuerstein, *Yoga: The Technology of Ecstasy* (Los Angeles, Jeremy Tarcher, 1989), p. 25.
19. R. Dass, *Grist for the Mill* (Santa Cruz, CA: Unity Press, 1977), p. 81.
20. D. Godman, *Living by the Words of Bhagavan* (Tiruvannamalai, India: Sri Annamalai Swami Ashram Trust, 1995), p. 278.
21. V. I. Khan, "What Is Initiation?" In *Initiation* (New Lebanon, NY: Sufi Order, 1980), p. 10.
22. Rumi, *This Longing*, translated by Coleman Barks and John Moyne (Putney, VT: Threshold Books, 1988), p. 18.
23. Islamic saying, cited in A. Schimmel, *Mystical Dimensions of Islam* (Chapel Hill, NC: Univ. of North Carolina Press, 1975), p. 190.

24. *The Gospel of Sri Ramakrishna,* translated by S. Nikhilananda (New York: Ramakrishna Vedanta Center, 1974).

25. J. Welwood, "On Spiritual Authority: Genuine and Counterfeit." In D. Anthony, B. Ecker, & K. Wilber (Eds.), *Spiritual Choices* (New York: Paragon House, 1987), p. 292–93.

26. D. Frawley, "All Gurus Great and Small," *Yoga Journal* (March–April, 1997), p. 28.

27. *The Triadic Heart of Siva: Kaula Tantricism of Abhinavagupta in the Non-Dual Shaivism of Kashmir* (Albany, NY: State Univ. of New York Press), pp. 164–66.

28. L. Govinda, *Foundations of Tibetan Mysticism* (New York: Samuel Weiser, 1969). p. 90.

29. E. Lerner, *Journey of Insight Meditation* (New York: Schocken, 1977). Unfortunately, this excellent book is long out of print and difficult to find.

30. P. Kapleau, *The Three Pillars of Zen* (Garden City, NY: Anchor Books, 1980), p. 96.

31. Ibid., pp. 54, 93, 94.

32. D. Goleman, "Early Warning Signs for the Detection of Spiritual Blight," *CoEvolution Quarterly,* Winter, 1983, pp. 127–28.

33. G. Scholem, *On the Mystical Shape of the Godhead: Basic Concepts of the Kabbalah* (New York: Schocken, 1991), p. 127.

34. G. Scholem, *The Messianic Idea in Judaism* (New York: Shocken, 1971).

35. Indeed, the concept of "enlightenment," as it is known in Eastern religions, is never discussed in Jewish mysticism, where the focus instead is on the community's redemptive hopes and aspirations.

36. G. Scholem, *The Messianic Idea in Judaism* (New York: Shocken, 1971), p. 4.

37. I am indebted here to the insights of Richard Gale.

38. G. Scholem, *Sabbatai Sevi: The Mystical Messiah,* translated by R. Werblowski (Princeton, NJ: Princeton Univ. Press, 1973).

39. I am indebted here to the insights of my friend Michael Gelbart, a contemporary Jewish wise man.

40. E. Wiesel, *Souls on Fire: Portraits and Legends of Hasidic Masters* (New York: Simon & Schuster, 1982), p. 13.

41. Ibid., pp. 7–8.

42. M. Buber, *Tales of the Hasidim* (New York: Schocken, 1947).

43. E. Wiesel, *Souls on Fire: Portraits and Legends of Hasidic Masters* (New York: Simon & Schuster, 1982), pp. 19–20.

44. Ibid., pp. 26–27.

# ══════════ STAGE TWO ══════════

# *Initiation*

There is a trust between the murshid (master) and the mureed (disciple) which establishes a link between them.... The initiation is the outward sign of that link, a link which can only be maintained by the faith that a mureed has and by the confidence which the murshid returns in answer to that faith. Initiation by a spiritual teacher means both a trust given by the teacher to the pupil and a trust given by the pupil to the teacher.

*Hazrat Inayat Khan, The Sacred Link.*[1]

In most traditions, the student approaches a teacher to receive initiation, which is a specific introduction to a transformational technique, an investiture of grace, or an acknowledgment by the teacher that the student has been accepted for instruction. It may involve either a formal ceremony or a quiet, private exchange between teacher and student. It may involve instruction in meditation or prayer, a vow to serve the teacher, or a ceremonial initiation into a contemplative order.

Before the student is allowed to take initiation there is often a preliminary period of preparation and purification, which may range from a few days or weeks to several years. It is by fulfilling these conditions without complaint that the student demonstrates genuine readiness. Teachers often put students through various trials to test their courage, resolute intention, and ability to make a commitment to practice the teachings that will be given. Through these preliminary tests, the teacher examines the student to determine whether he or she is a suitable candidate for initiation. The student may be asked to refrain from consuming intoxicants, to avoid certain foods, or to observe celibacy for a certain period. One may also be asked to offer service to the teacher for some time prior to receiving initiation. Traditionally, for example, the aspirant might spend several years tending the teacher's fields or working in a barn shoveling cow manure prior to receiving initiation. The student may be asked to pay a fee or make a financial contribution to support the teacher's work. In Native American cultures, those seeking instruction from a medicine man or woman offered tobacco and blankets as payment. In these varying ways, the student proves genuine worth, sincerity, and persistence.

A practitioner of Transcendental Meditation gave this account:

> I clearly remember my initiation into TM twenty five years ago. I listened to the preliminary lectures closely and absorbed their meaning. I paid my fee. I was asked to avoid using alcohol or drugs for two weeks prior to the event. The day of my initiation I received the mantra and chanted prayers of thanks to the teachers of the TM tradition. My first meditation was peaceful and deep. It felt so peaceful I didn't want to come out of meditation. All through the day afterward I felt a soft glow throughout my body.

In some cases initiation may be a relatively simple matter. The student may have a private meeting with the teacher in which instructions are given. In some traditions, the teacher places his or her hands upon the novice's head to bestow a blessing. Or it may involve a more elaborate rite of passage. One woman gave this account of her initiation:

> We were told to spend the two days before initiation observing silence, reflecting on what we were about to undertake. We were to be absorbed inward, to fix our minds on God, and to eat lightly. Then on the morning of the ceremony, we were each given a special robe to wear and we were asked to take off our own clothes and leave them by the banks of the river to signify our leaving behind of our old lives and former selves. We put on these beautiful sky blue robes, which were called Robes of Glory, representing our renewal and purity of spirit. We put on the robes and walked in a procession from the river into a lush forest, accompanied by drumbeats. Finally we were called one by one to come before the teacher. She wore a special velvet robe we had never seen before, and a silver necklace shaped like a coiled serpent; she looked very powerful. Quietly she spoke to each one of us, explaining about our lineage and the importance of the practice she was now teaching us. She instructed me in meditation and

prayers I was to offer every day. I was asked to not tell anyone about the specifics of these practices.

The initiate is often sworn to secrecy to preserve the sanctity of the experience and the customs surrounding it. Secrecy is a way of honoring the specialness of this experience, which is a sacred event, not a profane or everyday occurrence. It preserves the power of the initiation. To speak about one's initiation experiences may dissipate their power. It may also expose us to the doubts and cynicism that others might display toward our experiences. This can cause us either to devalue the experience, or to experience anger toward others—which is not the purpose of receiving initiation. In other words, speaking too soon or too openly about such experiences, and divulging secret instructions creates a variety of mental and interpersonal distractions. It is better to keep silent and allow the initiation to work inside of us.

## Initiation Among the Sufis

To explore this theme further I will describe the meaning of initiation among the Sufi mystics of Islam. In the Mevlevi order of Sufis, the novice first learns to perform various kitchen functions, learns to recite and interpret Rumi's *Mathnawi,* and learns the technique of the whirling dance—fulfilling a preparatory period of 1001 days prior to formal initiation.

> After the [novice] had performed the three years of service he might be considered worthy of receiving the *khirqa*, the patched frock, "the badge of the aspirants of Sufism." The relation of the novice to the master is threefold: by the *khirqa*, by being instructed in the formula of *dhikr* (recollection), and by company, service, and education. In investing the murid with the patched frock, Sufism has preserved the old symbolism of garment: by donning a garment that has been worn, or even touched, by the blessed hands of a master, the disciple acquires some of the mystico-magical power of the sheikh.
>
> During the initiation ceremony—a festive day in the dervish community—the adept had to pronounce the *bay'a*, the oath of allegiance, and was invested with the *khirqa*, the Sufi frock. An essential part of the ceremony consists of the novice's putting his hand into the sheikh's hand so that the *baraka* is properly trans-

mitted. Another important act is the bestowing of the *taj*, the dervish cap.[2]

Initiation is often a joyous event, a celebration of connection to a lineage of awakened beings, an expression of gratitude for the blessings and instruction being offered, and an expression of hope in our ability to travel the spiritual path toward its goal. Now that we have made our offerings of gifts or service to the teacher, we are ready to receive the gifts offered by the teacher, as a symbol of our initiation. The teacher may give a special blanket, a piece of clothing, a pair of sandals, or a cap—objects invested with the teacher's spiritual power that become a continuing reminder of the teacher's blessings and inner psychic influence. Receiving a gift from the teacher as a mark of acceptance of the student is found in many traditions. The objects are empowered by the teacher's *shakti* or *baraka*. The one object I received from my teacher's hand was a shawl he gave me in 1978. I have worn that shawl while meditating for many years. To me, it is more than a piece of cotton cloth; it is a special object that reminds me of the teacher's presence.

The real garment of initiation is a subtle but tangible blessing the disciple receives that he or she feels as a tingling or bliss in the crown of the head, an inner stillness, a descent of peace, exhiliration, or a feeling of love and connection with everything. This is the real event of initiation. An electricity within us is kindled, a sense of connection to Spirit, the Absolute. Something new is alive within our being. It dwells within us and begins to grow—especially as we intensify our efforts and thereby activate a miraculous inner awakening that will propel us into a new life. This is the interior event of which external initiation is the occasion and the symbol.

Sufi sage Pir Vilayat Inayat Khan has explained the deeper significance of initiation as follows:

> What is the meaning of initiation given at the hands of a human being? The initiator is like a catalyst who sets in motion the forces that have been building up in that process of incubation. We find the same principle in alchemy: there is a process of transformation taking place, and it takes just that spark to trigger it off. . . . You cannot say the guru does it for you, but you can say that if you are in a state of readiness, that action upon you can really trigger off something that is on its way very intensely.[3]

# *Experiencing the Spiritual Power of Lineage*

The teacher is the catalyst we need to grow. Our intense desire for illumination makes us ready to catch a single spark of the awakened Mind that sets the process of self-transformation on fire. This spark that awakens us is a gift, a blessing not just from the teacher but from an unending lineage of awakened beings. In Sufism it is said that the student-initiate is linked, through the teacher, to the *silsila*, the chain of initiation and spiritual guidance. Thus, the aspirant who becomes connected to a teacher also becomes connected to the teacher's teacher, Mohammed and all the other great prophets, and ultimately to God.

> The fact is that if an initiator is a genuine initiator, he is never alone. According to the tradition of the Sufis, the initiator who is always present behind any initiator is Khidr, the same being as Elijah. . . . The initiation links you up with the masters of that particular line through the whole hierarchy, . . . and in so doing it links you with all the masters of all the other religions. . . . A karmic connection is established, which means that from the moment Murshid gives you *bayat* (initiation) he feels responsible for you.
>
> One looks for a guide who is suffiently in harmony with the hierarchy of masters to act as a go-between or even lift the consciousness of the pupil to the point where he is able to reach some measure of guidance directly. If such a master is authentic, he will refer to the one hierarchically above him (whether incarnated or not) for his briefing. This is the chain of transmission which reaches to the source of all initiation, the One beyond, of whom naught can be said. . . . Initiation is the reiteration of the covenant which was made at the birth of one's soul, the vow to proclaim the divine sovereignty. . . . According to the Zoroastrian Gathas, when we were still in the angelic state we vowed to incarnate upon earth in order that we might become channels for the transfiguration of the world, to insure the victory of light over darkness. Our struggle on earth is the enactment of this pledge. The *bayat* (initiation) is the renewal of the pledge we made in eternity. . . . One is linked . . . to the whole hierarchy of masters, saints, and prophets, who form the spiritual hierarchy of the government of the world, the embodiment of the master, the spirit of guidance.[4]

Hindu and Buddhist traditions also emphasize the importance of lineage, contending that the spiritual power and awakened consciousness of lineages of enlightened beings—many of them no longer physically alive—support and guide sincere seekers of Truth. Thus, as we receive initiation, we may also be asked to acknowledge and celebrate our connection to those who have proceeded us on the path to enlightenment, the instructions they have left behind, and the blessings and mysterious assistance that flow to us from the lineage of instruction.

Ideally, our teacher is the descendant and inheritor of a lineage of spiritual instruction and illuminated consciousness. It is the spiritual power of the lineage that comes through great guides and empowers their teaching. As Pir Vilayat noted, the transmission of truth does not just come from one person but from an unending chain of illumined souls. In ancient Indian yoga there was said to be a lineage descended from Shiva down to sages such as Matsyendranath, Goraknath, Patanjali, Narada, Shankara, Guadapada, and Ramanuja, and continuing through the chain of instruction to contemporary practitioners. In Tibetan Buddhism, there is a vast lineage of Buddhas and Bodhisattvas from Shakyamuni Buddha to Lokeshvara, Tara, and Manjushri, to Padmasambhava, Atisha, Tsonkhapa, to the great yogis Tilopa, Naropa, Marpa, Milarepa, and Gampopa, and to the Dalai Lamas and other reincarnating *tulkus*.

Often in the course of initiation we are asked to learn about the great practitioners of our lineage. Later we may come to realize the power of lineage through experiences of guidance from our "grandfather gurus," that is, our teachers' teachers, or other teachers of our lineage. One man reported:

> After I had open heart surgery I felt the presence of Bhagwan Nityananda, my guru's guru at my bedside. He left his body in 1961, but there he was with me. He rubbed my forehead and told me to meditate upon the sound of Om. I felt completely peaceful. The apparition lasted several minutes and left me in a state of ecstasy that continued unabated throughout my period of recuperation. Now I feel a deeper reverence for my teacher but also for his entire lineage, because I could so clearly feel the greatness of *his* teacher.

A woman who had been initiated into techniques of meditation had a vision of a famous teacher of her lineage:

Several months after my initiation I was grappling with my desires for sex and beer and pot and I didn't feel like meditating anymore. I resisted it for weeks. One day I sat in front of my altar, on which sit the pictures of the gurus of my lineage. I prayed to them for assistance and guidance. I felt R (my teacher's teacher) was there with me. He repeated my meditation instructions to me very slowly and softly. My third eye began to throb and I saw a brief flash of light. Then my mind became silent and I glided into a long, peaceful meditation. I feel that R's spirit blessed me and helped me meditate. This experience definitely increased my desire to meditate more regularly.

This last example illustrates the fact that in some cases an aspirant receives initiation from a teacher who is not in a physical body. Many Christians have reported visions and visitations of Christ. Hindus may have visions of saints such as Shirdi Sai Baba or Ramakrishna. In Islam, there is a long tradition of initiation by the Prophet Mohammed or other saints and masters who had died long ago:

A final possibility of initiation from a source other than a human master was through Khidr. Khidr, identified with the mysterious companion of Moses mentioned in Sura 18 [of the Koran], is the patron saint of travelers, the immortal who drank from the water of life. Sometimes the mystics would meet him on their journeys; he would inspire them, answer their questions, rescue them from danger, and, in special cases, invest them with the *khirqa*, which was accepted as valid in the tradition of Sufi initiation. Thus, they were connected immediately with the highest source of mystical inspiration.[5]

## Progressive Initiations

In some traditions, the student takes not one but a series of initiations, which mark different stages of the student's understanding and commitment to the teachings. In Buddhism, the first, most basic basic initiation, "Taking Refuge"—in which one takes refuge in the Buddha, the Dharma (the teachings), and the Sangha (the community of practitioners)—is followed by subsequent empowerments or initiations, such as the Bodhisattva vows or the Tibetan Vajrayana foundation practices (*ngondro*, pronounded "noondro"). Later on, further initiations will be given, depending on the student's character and needs. Each initiation conveys a particular piece of the vast teachings of the Buddhist tradition, and also introduces the student to a new mantra, prayer, visualization, or meditation practice. Initiation is not just a single event but also a process of gradual transmission to the student. Periodic initiations revitalize the student's commitment to practice and awaken increasing determination and resolute intention to attain enlightenment. A student may also periodically reaffirm vows or commitments made during the original initiation.

Initiation marks a transition into a new condition or way of being. As in all effective rites of passage, its goal is to transform the initiate so that he or she will be deeply and permanently changed by the experience. It is meant to be a moment of metamorphosis. Nowhere is this transformative quality of initiation clearer than in the tradition of *shaktipat diksha* in India.

## *Shaktipat Initiation*

In the Indian yogic traditions, initiation is known as *diksha*, which Georg Feuerstein describes as "a form of spiritual transmission by which the disciple's bodily, mental, and spiritual condition is changed through the adept's transference of spiritual energy."

> By means of initiation, which may occur informally or in a more ritual setting, the spiritual process is either awakened or magnified in the practitioner. It is always a direct empowerment, in which the teacher effects in his disciple a change of consciousness, a turnabout, or metanoia. It is a moment of conversion from ordinary worldliness to a hallowed life, which alters the initiate's state of being.[6]

In the Indian Tantric tradition, the process of spiritual transmission is known as *shaktipat,* which literally means "descent of the power."

> Shakti-pata is the event and the experience of the descent of a powerful energy current into the body. . . . Shakti-pata can be inaugurated by the adept through a verbal command, his touch, his glance, or . . . even his mere presence.[7]

Through shaktipat, the teacher transmits spiritual energy and awakens the aspirant's dormant kundalini energy, which then begins to unfold and expand, purifying the student's body, mind, and heart, leading the individual toward enlightenment or realization. This may occur rapidly in the case of a highly prepared aspirant, or more gradually in the case of a less mature student. Shaktipat can be bestowed through the teacher's touch, gaze, or thought; or in other cases it may occur spontaneously in a vision or a dream, or simply by being in the teacher's presence. Through the teacher, an enlightened awareness and spiritual power begins to awaken and gradually transform the aspirant.

The effects of shaktipat can be quite varied and are often dramatic. According to Swami Vishnu Tirth, the symptoms of an awakened kundalini include involuntary bodily movements, trembling, shaking, laughing, weeping, states of intoxication and bliss, involuntary retention of the breath (*kumbhaka*); spontaneous *bhastrika pranayama* (deep, rapid inhalation and exhalation, a cleansing and stimulating form of *pranayama*); speaking in strange, unknown languages; frightening or blissful visions; smelling inexplicable aromas; currents of energy rising up the spine; spontaneously assuming yogic postures, or making animal sounds; vibrations in the chakras (energy centers); and experiences in which the mind stops and plunges into an ocean of bliss.[8] One woman reported the following shaktipat experience:

> I was sitting there listening to his lecture when his eyes fell on me. They were dark and intense and open wide. The next thing I knew I felt this pain at the base of my spine. Then I felt something explode inside me, and all this energy started rushing up my spine. My body began to move violently. Soon my head started rotating very fast. Later my eyeballs began to spin and to look upward into the crown of my head. I felt like I was moving up into higher centers of my brain. Then I started hyperventilating and then I don't know what happened but I just disappeared. I sat there meditating for over two hours. There was no me, just formless, blissful light everywhere. Later I learned that yogis call this state *nirvikalpa samadhi*, which means meditative absorption without form.

In many yogic schools shaktipat is considered to be the key to spiritual liberation. Yogis often toil fruitlessly for decades without genuine attainment, but upon receiving shaktipat, they may proceed much more rapidly toward awakening. Indeed, shaktipat often gives the student an immediate experience of the goal of the spiritual path, a taste of enlightenment. This increases the student's enthusiasm for the inner quest, and it increases the student's faith in the teacher who serves as a conduit for this transmission. The power of shaktipat does not appear to be dependent on the recipient's efforts or conscious intention, and the transmission can occur quite unexpectedly by being in the presence of an enlightened teacher, or even by seeing a picture of such a teacher.

Shaktipat initiation may also precede our choosing a teacher. Indeed, we might not be ready to accept a teacher until after experiencing this powerful transmission, which provides convincing evidence of the teacher's capacity to guide us toward a transformed condition.

Receiving shaktipat can be problematic for some individuals who are not psychologically balanced. Awakening powerful internal energies can stimulate underlying emotional problems and mental disorders, making these rise rapidly to the surface. This is one reason why anyone with an active kundalini should remain under skillful guidance throughout the process of awakening. This is also a reason why some people believe that shaktipat is not advisable. Take, for example this brief discussion with H. W. L. Poonja:

> *I have had shaktipat from a Guru and it made me feel very quiet and stoned, as if I just smoked three chillums.*
> So why go to a guru when you can have some hash for one rupee behind the Gandhi ashram in Hazrat Ganj? This high will stay for three hours and then you can have more. In this same way shaktipat of power without knowledge of Truth will turn the guru-disciple relationship into dealer-addict dependence. Don't cultivate a habit which is dependent on anything. You have nothing to do and you will not get anything. Here there is no transmission or shaktipat but all that happens is within you. I don't transmit anything. I don't give shaktipat. All that I do is remove your dependence on anything else. . . . Just remove your dependence on God and on methods and everyone else and It will shine and reveal itself without any method. Don't depend on gurus.[9]

These provisos aside, shaktipat can be a powerful catalyst of inner transformation for the spiritual apprentice. In shaktipat initiation the awakened consciousness of the teacher is felt to enter the student, often giving the latter a glimpse of the goal of the spiritual journey, the enlightened state. Of course, the initial ecstasy or expansive bliss usually doesn't last permanently; the aspirant has to make continuous efforts at self-purification to become a worthy receptacle of this bestowal of power. After this initial glimpse of the goal of the path we strive to deepen our experience and to become stabilized in an expanded state through our own efforts. This is the work of the stage of discipleship. But having received shaktipat initiation, the awakening kundalini energy subtly leads the aspirant forward from within. Shaktipat is like the planting of a seed within the student. If properly watered through devotion, meditation, and remembrance, this seed can sprout and flower into the tree of spiritual attainment.

## *My Initiation*

The occasion of initiation is a moment to remember with love and gratitude. After my teacher left New York, I felt drawn to learn from him further, and thus I resolved to visit him again soon to receive initiation. In the summer of 1975, when I was seventeen, Muktananda was going to conduct a retreat in Arcata, California. To be able to attend I needed to pay the fee and buy a plane ticket. I bused dishes in a restaurant for several months to earn the money. Right before I left to fly to California I learned that Baba had been very ill, and to my chagrin, he actually missed the first several weeks of the retreat. For all of us present, it was a test of faith to remain there despite his not being physically present. Many times I thought of asking for a refund and leaving. Indeed, he did not arrive until two days before I was scheduled to depart to return to the East Coast for my first year of college. I had come to California despite the strong displeasure of my parents, who could only look with horror as their son pursued this Indian swami—whom they assumed was probably a dangerous cult leader like so many others. My friends also thought my choice of summer vacation was rather strange. During the weeks of waiting for Muktananda's arrival at the retreat, I became quite distressed, thinking that perhaps I had made a terrible mistake spending so much money and traveling so far. I worried that I would not receive the uplifting transmission of awakened consciousness that had motivated my journey. I was desperately afraid that I would return home without receiving shaktipat.

The afternoon before I was scheduled to depart, I was called before Muktananda's throne by his secretary, Arjuna.[10] Muktananda pulled my hair to draw me close to him. Then he tapped on my glasses, indicating that I should remove them. He grabbed me by the nose, right between the eyes. With the palm of his hand he slapped my forehead, then pounded me hard on the top of my head several times. He ran his hand up and down my spine. He pulled me next to him, practically into his lap, looked into my eyes, and repeated "Guru Om Guru Om Guru Om Guru Om Guru Om Guru Om." His eyes were bright and powerful. I repeated the mantra back to him. Then he told me to sit next to him with my eyes closed. While I sat beside him I felt as if I were sitting next to a furnace; he emanated intense heat. After about ten minutes he told me to return to my seat. I did so, walking through the crowd of devotees giddy and wobbly-legged and dazed.

I was expecting something really intense to happen. Some people, upon receiving shaktipat, begin to sway, tremble, or burst into tears; or they have visions of saints or distant places. Instead, nothing much happened to me at first. There were no thunder bolts. What I felt at first was a soft glow in the top of my head and a warm electrical current running through my spinal column. Soon enough, I would begin to feel more dynamic effects of this initiation.

The next day I returned home to my family. My father, whom I love dearly, was grouchy when I got into the car at the airport. He didn't want to hear anything about the retreat; he only wanted to know that I was okay and ready for school. In time my father would reveal to me how upset he had been that I had turned myself over to this man from India. He felt I had rejected him, and it hurt him very deeply. Perhaps some of my father's pain would have been alleviated if only I had been able to explain to him that it was an ageless tradition in India for a young man or woman to seek out the guidance of a guru and to go to him for instruction. At any rate, I had received my initiation. Now I needed to become a disciple, to practice my teacher's teachings.

## Stages of Initiation and Discipleship

At this point, it will be helpful to gain an overview of the unfoldment that occurs as a result of initiation. Sufi master Hazrat Inayat Khan, in his book *The Path of Initiation*,[11] details the proces that begins when the student finds a guide on the path. The student's faith is central, and even if the teacher proves to be false or not fully enlightened, the student's sincerity of purpose will itself be sufficient to lead to spiritual advancement. The student must then go through various tests, which are often confusing. The teacher tests the student's faith by doing things that appear strange, bizarre, cold-hearted, meaningless, or unjust to test the student's faith, sincerity, and patience. (We will return to the topic of testing shortly.) Inayat Khan contends that only students who endure the stage of testing will reach the next stage, in which they receive knowledge attentively, meditate upon it patiently, and assimilate it fully.

According to Inayat Khan, the external teacher's primary role influence occurs relatively early in the process of spiritual unfoldment, and will soon end. The seeker still has a long road to walk.

> Several initiations may be given to the pupil whom the teacher has taken in hand, but his progress depends upon the pupil himself. . . . There is another kind of initiation which comes afterward, and this initiation is also an unfoldment of the Soul. It comes as an after-effect of the initiation that one had from the teacher. It comes as a kind of expansion of consciousness."[12]

In the next stage of discipleship, the seeker is initiated by his or her own ideal, the ideal of his imagination and highest aspirations. But Inayat Khan emphasizes that the student must strive to become the embodiment of this ideal. As Inayat Khan puts it, "The savior will not save him." The student who has reached this stage begins "to radiate his initiator who is within him as his ideal."[13] Discipleship becomes an interior process of dedication to spiritual practice and the refinement of one's own consciousness and one's character, rather than focusing primarily on devotion to the teacher.

The student begins to discover the teacher as a living entity within himself or herself, present at all times, especially in times of trouble and difficulty. The subtle link between teacher and apprentice grows stronger and is discovered in a variety of life situations.

Finally, Inayat Khan says, the disciple undergoes the initiation in God. The student "rises above the ideal he has made, to that perfect ideal which is beyond the human personality, which is the perfect Being. . . . One sees no other than God."[14] The student now communicates with God, who becomes to the initiate a living presence. Discipleship or spiritual life is not just a matter of belief in God, or service to a human teacher. It is a process through which we actually are transformed, assimilating that knowledge and power that we feel in the presence of the guide, until we are one day raised to the same joyous state of exaltation and Self-arising freedom.

> No one can give spiritual knowledge to another, for this is something which is within every heart. What the teacher can do is to kindle the light which is hidden in the heart of the disciple. . . . The work of the teacher is most subtle. It is like that of a jeweller who has to melt the gold first in order to make an ornament out of it.... When the pupil has received the initiations that the teacher has to give, then the teacher's task is over, and he sends him on. The teacher does not hold the pupil indefinitely; he has his part to perform during the journey on the path, but then comes the inner initiation. This comes to the disciple who has become meditative.[15]

External initiation received from the teacher activates an internal process of awakening. The aspirant's priorities and lifestyle change, becoming focused on attainment of Self-knowledge—the knowledge of the heart as a temple in which a living Spirit dwells and unfolds. Initiation is like the sounding of a gong that resonates for weeks, months, years, even decades, until the student's whole life has been transformed.

## Notes

1. H. I. Khan, "The Sacred Link." In *Initiation* (New Lebanon, NY: Sufi Order, 1980), pp. 13, 20.
2. A. Schimmel, *Mystical Dimensions of Islam* (Chapel Hill, NC: Univ. of North Carolina Press, 1975), pp. 102, 234.
3. V. I. Khan, "What is Initiation?" In *Initiation* (New Lebanon, NY: Sufi Order, 1980), p. 7.
4. V. I. Khan, "The Link with the Spiritual Hierarchy." In *Initiation* (New Lebanon, NY: Sufi Order, 1980), pp. 8–9, 23–25.·

5. A. Schimmel, *Mystical Dimensions of Islam* (Chapel Hill, NC: Univ. of North Carolina Press, 1975), pp. 105–6.

6. G. Feuerstein, *Yoga: The Technology of Ecstasy* (Los Angeles, Jeremy Tarcher, 1989), pp. 25, 27.

7. Ibid., pp. 28–29.

8. V. Tirth, "Signs of an Awakened Kundalini." In J. White (Ed.), *Kundalini, Evolution, and Enlightenment* (Garden City, NY: Anchor Books, 1979), pp. 94–97. For more on the symptoms of awakened kundalini, see L. Sannella, *The Kundalini Experience* (Lower Lake, CA: Integral Publishing, 1987).

9. H. W. L. Poonja, *Truth Is* (Huntington Beach, CA: Yudhishtara, 1995), p. 75.

10. Arjuna is now known as Master Charles.

11. H. I. Khan, *The Path of Initiation* (Katwik, Holland: Servire, 1979), pp. 62 ff.

12. Ibid., p. 74.

13. Ibid., p. 67.

14. Ibid., p. 68.

15. Ibid., pp. 77, 97.

# Discipleship

Look with unswerving faith and love
At the Jewel of a Guru:
Drink the pure water of instruction.
*The Life and Teaching of Naropa*[1]

The relationship between spiritual teacher and aspirant is founded on the recognition of a need to associate with a person who has fully traversed the process of inner transformation, who has achieved some degree of illumination (if not complete enlightenment), and who has the skill and interest to guide students on the path. The student has made the effort to approach a teacher and has received initiation. Now the student's task is to assimilate the teacher's message and transformative influence. The spiritual apprentice begins to build a life around the teacher, a life that constantly refers to, and acknowledges, the teacher's influence. This is the beginning of the phase known as discipleship.

In some cases recorded historically (for example, the Indian poet-saint, Kabir[2]), a single encounter with an enlightened being has led to awakening of the student. In other cases (for example, the Tibetan yogi, Milarepa[3]), the student engages in an extended period of study and service to the teacher. In some instances we become devoted students of teachers who are no longer physically alive. Regardless of the form it takes, the relationship is consciously chosen by the student as an outgrowth of a deepening desire to grow spiritually, to know the truth of existence, to come closer to God, to awaken Buddha mind, to wake up from the sleep of spiritual ignorance. This goal may become so compelling and so central to the aspirant that other concerns, such as the pursuit of wealth, romantic love, fame, or worldly power may pale into insignificance. The commitment of discipleship is usually an outgrowth of encounters with a teacher that demonstrate the teacher's greatness and wisdom, and move the student to respond with respect, gratitude, devotion, and a desire to receive instruction. In this stage, the spiritual apprentice becomes a disciple, a follower of the teacher's way, one who accepts the teacher's authority and looks for ways to invite and allow the teacher's deeper influence in his or her life.

According to Georg Feuerstein, the aspirant to enlightenment who approaches a teacher begins as a student inspired by the teacher's presence and discourses but not yet seriously engaged in spiritual practice, wavering still in commitment, and often pulled by worldly desires and interests.[4] Gradually, however, the student advances to the stage of the disciple, more aware of the subtle, nonphysical, psychospiritual link to the teacher and willing to honor and cultivate this link. Finally, the aspirant reaches the stage of the devotee, in which the teacher is experienced as a spiritual reality rather than as a human personality, giving rise to a devotional attitude toward the teacher.

For some, discipleship means performing direct service to the teacher or living in a spiritual community, such as an ashram or monastery. For others it means practicing meditative, yogic, or contemplative techniques, following vows or precepts, or carrying the spirit of the guru's teachings into daily life. Some students accept a teacher whom they have never met on the physical plane and assume the stance of discipleship simply by meditating on the teacher's words or pictures, or through frequent inner remembrance of the teacher. Discipleship may be a total commitment, or it may take its place next to other pursuits such as family life, professional responsibilities, and artistic activities. In either case, the student willingly embraces a reverent or devotional relationship with a spiritual teacher who is acknowledged as a primary guiding influence. For the purposes of this discussion, I am going to assume that the major emotional and interpersonal issues involved in student-teacher relationships will be virtually the same for various forms of discipleship—although a student in direct service to a teacher may be more likely to have intense personal interactions with the teacher than one who lives at a distance and sees the teacher less frequently.

As the relationship unfolds and accelerates the disciple's spiritual progress, an abiding devotion, faith, and love between teacher and student begins to grow. The teacher's personal example and direct transmission of spiritual energy can have such a profound impact that the student feels a natural and enduring gratitude, and thus willingly submits to the teacher's discipline and authority. Clare, a student of a Zen teacher for over twelve years, reports:

> His sanity and clarity of mind are a beacon for me. He teaches me how to live with dignity, simplicity, and humor. I will always honor him for that.

And Beth, a student of a teacher with a worldwide following, says,

> My guru has shown me my own divine essence. He has led me to God. For me, the guru is the final destination. He is my Krishna, my deity, my Beloved. There is nothing else for me to accomplish beyond this relationship. I have left my personal concerns at his feet because I feel most fulfilled just being his devotee.

Statements such as these demonstrate that some seekers organize their lives to a large extent around discipleship. In some cases, the relationship with a teacher who provides the guidance needed to reach the goal of spiritual illumination becomes all-important, the fulcrum around which the student's entire life is balanced. One woman reported:

> It just got to be the daily pattern of our lives that when we got up in the morning we raised prayers to Guruji, meditated in front of his pictures, and remembered him through chanting. In the evening we waved lights to his picture just as if he were present with us in the room and the whole atmosphere became charged with an atmosphere of love and devotion. Every day our sense of closeness with our beloved guru and with God grew deeper. Our lives were completely those of devotees.

A young man named Ted reported:

> I was so grateful to receive such lucid instruction in Buddhist doctrines and I was so inspired by the lama's presence that there was no way I wasn't going to practice a lot. I wanted to follow his example, to wake up and become an enlightened Buddha like him.

Finding an illumined teacher may elicit feelings of ecstasy, bliss, relief, and a feeling of inner openness to the teacher from a space beyond the rational mind. For some students, recognizing the cord of love that connects them to a teacher is the beginning of a lifelong commitment. Such individuals may follow the spiritual mentor's teachings toward the final goal of enlightenment without ever experiencing a significant disturbance in the relationship. For such students, the teacher is a trusted friend, companion, and guide on the spiritual path.

In this chapter I describe the stages of spiritual apprenticeship in which we develop an ongoing relationship with a teacher, listen to instruction, receive individualized guidance, establish a spiritual practice, and have regular opportunities to meet the teacher's enlightened mind (known in India as having the teacher's *darshan*). Regular visits to the teacher are very helpful at this stage. This in itself requires effort and sacrifices. By putting aside other interests to spend time in the teacher's company we signify the growing priority of the spiritual quest in our lives. A desire for enlightenment begins to burn within our hearts; we long to experience a deeper awareness of Spirit.

## *The Phase of Instruction*

Part of the teacher's role is to explain things to us, introducing us to some form of doctrine or spiritual teaching. Each aspirant needs clarification of some details of meditation practice, spiritual doctrine, or understanding of the dynamics of the mind. Providing these explanations may or may not be the teacher's forte. Some teachers hardly speak at all. Others chat with students or answer simple questions but never give formal discourses. Others lecture with great skill. In any event, at this stage of spiritual apprenticeship the student begins to attend darshan or study groups on a regular basis, or reads written materials in order to absorb the teacher's discourse of instruction.

Through our regular contact with the teacher, we have our questions answered directly. The teacher's words gradually remove our doubts and help us understand how to proceed in working with ourselves so that we can evolve spiritually. The teacher's skill in removing our doubts helps deepen our confidence in his or her guidance and in following the path. We feel that we are washing our minds and hearts clean with the truth the teacher conveys. We begin to experience the delight of living disciplined lives and purifying our minds and hearts.

We start to feel the transformative effects of practicing a spiritual discipline, which increases our enthusiasm and interest in hearing what the teacher has to say.

## *Establishing a Spiritual Practice*

Seeing the teacher's state of freedom and joy and receiving instruction inspires us to practice disciplines such as meditation, prayer, asanas and pranayama, mantras, or visualizations. We learn methods of attunement to the inner light, methods for developing peace and equanimity. Now it is time for the spiritual apprentice to practice these methods, which shift awareness away from ordinary thinking, perception, and mental chatter, toward the activity and presence of consciousness itself. Such practices transform us and reveal the intrinsically clear and peaceful mind that is our true nature. By practicing methods of meditation or Self-inquiry we gradually begin to become like the teacher.

At first we learn a set of practices within one particular tradition. Later, we may develop a spiritual practice of our own that blends elements of several disciplines or traditions. My own practice, for example, combines my training in meditation, hatha yoga, depth psychology and dreamwork, astrology, and music. Gradually we find a practice that is in alignment with our personalities and inclinations. I am not partial to devotional practices, but I am quite drawn to the physical rigors of hatha yoga. We must find our own way.

The spiritual apprentice also learns what conditions are conducive to practice. For example, I like to practice hatha yoga before sunrise and meditation near sunset. I also like to practice yoga while listening to music and to meditate while soaking in hot springs. Thus, we identify what factors or environments are helpful to us in intensifying our inner work. We also identify what hinders us or creates obstruction to cultivating mindfulness and a quiet mind. I find the sounds and images of television advertising very disturbing to my peace of mind. Music, on the other hand, draws me naturally toward meditation.

Wash the mind clean through the purity of spiritual discipline. Be serene. Rest with God. Melt your mind into the mantra of your choosing. Face all that arises with dispassion, yet focus your intention always on serving the highest outcome for all beings. Make yourself a worthy vessel for whatever destiny places in your hands. Make yourself stainless and you will know freedom. Refine your mind, body, heart, speech, and actions. Abide as the Self and perceive the divine light in others, treating all with respect.

Find the yoga or discipline that works for you and then practice it so that it tunes your consciousness, so that you become fully aligned with your inherent radiance, intelligence, and joy. Maybe your practice is sitting zazen, or contemplative prayer, or martial arts, or ecstatic dancing, or Sufi *zhikr* (remembrance of God). Hazrat Inayat Khan said, "The path you choose is the path for you."[5] When you find the right practice or combination of practices, you will know. It will feel good. Doing this practice feels like a place you want to return to again and again. There is no doubt in my mind whatsoever that I have found the right spiritual practices. For me, the disciplines of yoga (such as asana, pranayama, mantra repetition, and meditation) are reliable ways of coming into balance, refining my awareness, accessing expanded consciousness, and attaining inner peace. So is the discipline of dreamwork, of which I will have more to say later.

## Obstacles and Pitfalls

Many obstacles arise as we attempt to establish a spiritual discipline. Our busy lifestyles often make if difficult to find time to practice. Innumerable distractions appear, many of which seem entertaining, pleasurable, and stimulating when compared to the hard work of self-examination and inner purification. When we *do* practice we may inwardly resist and rebel. Old habits and desires rear their heads and divert us from practice. It may seem like more fun to go to the movies than to sit on a meditation cushion and observe the restless chatter of the mind. Also, our environment may not be conducive to quiet contemplation. This is the stage where we must rouse the will to overcome all obstacles so that we can pursue our practices. In Buddhism, this is known as the generation of *bodhicitta*, the resolute intention to eliminate defilements of consciousness and impurities of thought, word, or action in order to attain enlightenment.

One potential pitfall at this stage of establishing a spiritual discipline and lifestyle is a feeling of superiority to others. We may even become fanatical or try to convert others to our path. We have different life goals than others; we have an excitement about a spiritual practice or lineage that our family, friends, and neighbors may not share. This can give rise to feelings of being radically separate and isolated from others.

Another pitfall is imbalance, such as that which manifests when we get too intense about our practices—a bit overzealous. A man named Roger gave this account:

> My teacher had spoken a lot about the importance of physical purification, and I became totally obsessive about fasting and detoxing. I'd go on week-long fasts on water and do all kinds of bizarre enemas, like prune juice, and drinking all this psyllium seed. I was also meditating for hours every day and hardly sleeping. At one point I went to see my parents for a month and I found a place where I could go get colonics. So for that month I was working as a grill cook in a greasy Italian restaurant cooking veal cattiotore while I was fasting and doing a month-long program of daily colonics while visiting my parents. It was totally out of hand. My parents were so glad when I left! Finally, when I went back home and saw my teacher, he said, "You're taking all of this a little too far, aren't you?" I saw that I had gotten way out of balance with all the practices I was doing. It just wasn't appropriate to my environment.

## Learning One Thing Well

In the stage of discipleship our task is to master specific instructions or techniques that the teacher imparts. Part of the teacher's role is to teach us a few basic practices that we can do consistently. In 1979, my hatha yoga teacher, Allan Bateman, taught me a series of sixteen yoga postures, three breathing exercises, and relaxation. As I explored other systems of yoga over the years I noticed that many of them were more complex and exhaustive than Allan's method. I was always curious to learn new exercises, so I once asked Allan to teach me new poses and yogic techniques. To my surprise, he declined, asking in response, "Have you mastered everything I have shown you?" I had to admit that I had not, and that I could still learn to do the basic poses with greater effortlessness and precision. Thus, over the years I keep going back to the basics, rather than worrying about whether I have achieved the most advanced and difficult poses. The basic practices have always been abundantly nourishing. I have been doing this same sequence of poses since 1979. Periodically I branch out and learn other methods and new postures, but I always come back to the basic sequence I learned from Allan. This discipline has been deeply transformative for me.

I believe it is better to find one method and to work deeply with it, whatever it is, rather than learning many different methods and techniques that we will never practice on a regular basis. Such learning is useless window shopping. Many spiritual teachers convey methods that are too complicated, too demanding, and too time-consuming for the average person to utilize as a regular practice. A wise teacher passes on a manageable, useable set of practices that the student can take home and practice consistently.

As we change our habits and evolve our own daily practice, we may soon notice remarkable changes in ourselves. For example, we begin to wake up earlier, to rouse ourselves from slumber to stretch, to breathe, to chant or repeat a mantra, to rouse the fires of the inner life, to greet the day with joy and devotion and dedication to our upcoming day's labors. We may sit to feel the setting of the sun, quieting down into a state of deep absorption that reflects the evening's beautiful dark blue radiance. We remember our teachers with love. Most importantly, we begin to feel more peaceful, mindful, and loving in our daily lives. This is often a time of wonder and amazement as we see the initial results of our new spiritual practices and experience unexpected expansions of our consciousness.

## My Early Experiences of Discipleship and Spiritual Practice

For me, the initial stages of discipleship took the form of spending summers with my teacher and then practicing his teachings while living in the world, working, and going to school. It meant returning home and practicing the teachings I had received. The fundamental teaching was that God is within me, that the highest aim of life is realize my innate divinity, and that the means to do this is to turn my mind within to contemplate its own root and origin, the field of pure consciousness that

witnesses and encompasses all phenomena. The path is also one of respecting the divinity of others, recognizing the Self, the one consciousness, in everyone, even the lowliest person or creature. I was taught to
see God everywhere, alive in everything that exists and every event
that occurs.

After my initiation at the Arcata retreat, I went off to college at
Wesleyan University in Connecticut. I installed myself into my dormitory room and unpacked my yoga books, my meditation blanket, and
pictures of my teacher, which I placed on top of a suitcase in a make-
shift altar inside the small closet that would serve as my yogi's cave. It
was here that my meditative journey was to be launched. I spent hours
meditating in this space, especially in the early morning hours of 4:00
to 5:30 before anyone was awake, even the birds. Sometimes I also visited a small chapel, which was the quietest place I could find on the
campus. I was determined to pursue the path of yoga and meditation,
despite the fact that this placed me somewhat at odds with others in my
environment.

When I arrived at college I was entering a period of abstinence
from most ordinary forms of recreation and enjoyment, which contributed to some degree of isolation. Over time I did make wonderful friends
at Wesleyan, but at first it was a bit awkward for me. I was trying to
meditate while everyone else in the dorm was getting loaded, playing
their stereos and losing their virginity at top volume, and generally enjoying a healthy, post-adolescent freedom to go completely wild now
that we were all finally away from our parents for the first extended
time. The problem was that I had already done my share of partying in
high school. I went to my first Grateful Dead concert at age eleven with
my sister, Michele. I'd been to the Fillmore East several times—even
once personally ejected from the premises by Bill Graham himself.[6] I'd
seen Jimi Hendrix and the Rolling Stones at Madison Square Garden,
and heard the Who play their rock opera *Tommy*. My neighbors in the
dorm at Wesleyan were all too intent on keeping the rock and roll spirit
alive, ever so noisily. Yet this was a moment when more than anything
else I longed to know God, the universal consciousness, the all-pervasive Spirit. I was more interested in Ramakrishna and Meister Eckhart
than in Bruce Springsteen and the *Rocky Horror Picture Show*. I was
more interested in books on yoga philosophy than guzzling beer at par-

ties. I was generally viewed by others as a total bore. But I didn't feel naive, prudish, or judgmental. I didn't mind that other people wanted to do drugs and party, but it simply wasn't what I wanted to do at that point. I was focused in my intention to follow the spiritual path. The lack of support and the difficulties I faced trying to meditate in that environment only made my resolve and commitment grow stronger.

One of the challenges of discipleship is to persevere in following a spiritual teaching or way of life when no one else around you is doing so. Our faith and one-pointedness is thoroughly tested in such circumstances. We face many internal and interpersonal crises, sometimes causing us to feel ostracized by others, or to doubt our own path. We may be ridiculed or shunned, as I was on several occasions, for pursuing a contemplative life; consequently we may withdraw and limit our social contact with those who do not support or encourage our spiritual quest.

A spiritual apprentice learns the importance of keeping the right company, spending time with other seekers as much as possible—or else staying alone and quieting the mind, keeping the company of God, the vast inner silence. Later on, we will learn to sustain our inner peace amidst any company and under all conditions. But there are stages where it is indeed desirable to establish a protected place of peace. This is one reason why many aspirants enter monasteries, ashrams, and spiritual communities where they can dedicate themselves to spiritual practice in a quiet and supportive environment.

I became filled with the urge to meditate, and I began to do so intensely, three times a day. I awoke and went to sleep early. I practiced hatha yoga postures and breathing exercises every day. I stayed in my room, focused my mind inward, and read books on yoga, mysticism, Jungian psychology, anthropology, mythology, and the history of religions. I was absorbed in my private world of studies and stayed to myself much of the time.

Occasionally I formally honored the guru, waving candles and incense sticks as I gazed at pictures of Muktanandaa, Nityananda, Ramana Maharshi, Shirdi Sai Baba, and other great teachers. I would sing various chants and prayers. I was a little uncomfortable about this as I had been raised in a family that avoided all religious beliefs and observances, and I felt a little skeptical about my own tentative forms of worship.

Nevertheless, my meditations were always noticeably deeper when I did this, a fact that increased my sense of subtle protection by a lineage of enlightened beings who supported me in my efforts to awaken.

Each day I sat to meditate before dawn, before dinner, and before sleep. With each successive session of meditation I plunged deeper within. I locked my legs into lotus posture and in moments my breath became very soft, very light, very shallow. Often I stopped breathing altogether. As the ripples of breath and thought subsided, my mind became completely still. I began to rest in a place between the in-breath and the out-breath. At first I could only sustain this experience for a moment. Gradually I was able to sustain my concentration and remain in a state of breathless awe for longer periods—suspended outside time. At such times, my sense of solid physical boundaries dissolved into pure consciousness. I *was* that consciousness. In this state I felt an extraordinary peace and exhilaration, and a sensation of contained power.

I melted my mind into the sound of the mantra, Guuuuurrrrrrrrrrroooooo Oooooooooooommmmmmmmmm. This mantra felt totally alive with shakti. All other thoughts dispersed as the mantra imprinted its vibrations into my awareness. Sometimes it felt as if the sounds and I were merging into infinity. The boundaries of my ordinary awareness dissolved. On some occasions my awareness floated up above my body, and from this elevated vantage point I looked down upon myself. Every cell of my body vibrated and tingled with consciousness. I perceived strange liquid forms around me, and saw myserious shapes, lights, and images with my eyelids closed. Once I had a vision of a mountain scene that I intuitively knew was located in the Himalayas. Another time I perceived an image of an event that actually occurred a day later.

The mind, when calmed and purified, when its customary agitation subsides, becomes as calm and clear as a lake high up in the mountains of Tibet. In this tranquil condition, the individual mind becomes entrained to the mind of the universe, the infinite consciousness that pervades everything. The calm mind can travel to all realms, opening to dimensions beyond ordinary reality. And so I began to travel in the inner world.

Sometimes I felt that my body had become as small as a grain of sand. Other times I expanded so that I was as vast as the entire universe. I was all-pervasive consciousness. I perceived that I am not just this physical body, this personality, these desires, thoughts, plans, and emotions. I am the Self, all-pervasive Being. My initiation had propelled me directly into some of the states of consciousness described in classical yogic texts. These meditations were profoundly moving, and after I ended my sessions and had finished massaging my feet (which often fell asleep during long periods in lotus posture) I was often filled with peace and a perception of the sacredness of everything, the beauty of all life. The *shakti* (spiritual power) and the initiation of my guru had propelled me into a period of accelerated spiritual growth, and had even given me a glimpse of the mystic vision, the awareness of the all-pervasive Spirit.[7]

## *Personal Contact with the Teacher*

Once we begin to sincerely and intensively practice yoga, meditation, or contemplation of the Self, we have even greater need for the teacher's company to deepen our understanding and to guard us from pitfalls such as laziness or inflation. One sign that our spiritual apprenticeship is being properly guided is that we feel our teacher's willingness to engage in open communication. No matter how great a teacher may be, if he or she won't relate to you as a person then you may decide that this person in not your teacher, even if he or she is widely considered to be an awakened sage. What good is a teacher who is never available to talk to you or answer your questions? A teacher should not act like you're asking for a big favor because you request to speak to him or her about a matter of personal importance.

A man I counseled named Doug was a close student of a Tibetan Buddhist teacher whom I will call Lama Z. Doug's girlfriend became pregnant and he decided to marry her. His new responsibilities, in turn, began to cut into the long hours he had been dedicating to working for a business owned and operated by the Lama's spiritual community. After he had heard the news, Lama Z's only comment to Doug was, "Too bad about the girl." Doug was hurt by this statement, which seemed to imply strong disapproval of this turn of events. The implication was that Doug would no longer be able to do his spiritual practices because he would be tied down by his family responsibilities. Another student, his supervisor at the business, said, "You're compromising your position with Lama Z." Doug felt misunderstood and perplexed by their statements and their negative attitude toward his marriage.

I asked Doug if he felt there was anything nonspiritual about marriage and child rearing. Could not these activities and commitments, like any other endeavors, be fields or vehicles for the practice of the Dharma, the path to enlightenment? Maybe the lama and his other student were falling into the dualistic trap of making a distinction between Dharma practice and worldly life. Doug agreed. His next impulse was to leave the teacher immediately. I asked Doug whether it had ever occurred to him to simply talk to his teacher about his concerns, and to ask him directly if there was some reason why his teacher should disapprove of his becoming a householder. I told him, "If your teacher is unwilling to speak with you about your concerns and questions, and to address them in a personal way, then perhaps he is not really your teacher. If he makes you feel bad about your choices, if he makes you doubt the positive value of your human commitments and responsibilities, then you should question whether you have found the right teacher for you."

Doug gathered up his courage to speak to Lama Z, who, when he better understood how his words had affected Doug, graciously apologized and gave Doug his blessing to marry. Doug has continued to have a long and fruitful spiritual apprenticeship under Lama Z's guidance, and this episode was a critical turning point in their relationship. Both Doug and Lama Z learned important lessons, illustrating how both student and teacher can learn from one another in the process of spiritual apprenticeship. This story illustrates how students have the responsibility to speak their minds to teachers and to not submit unquestioningly. It is also an example of how teachers have the responsibility to listen to students and to not be inflexible or claim to be infallible. I will return to these themes in later chapters.

Through face-to-face contact, we establish a personal relationship with the teacher. One day I left the ashram's morning chanting program early to go to work. I was kneeling down to tie my shoes when suddenly Muktananda appeared and started walking toward me. He stopped and stood right in front of me so that I could touch his feet. He placed his hand on my head. As I looked up into his eyes for a moment I saw infinite space and the stars and a man drunk with inner ecstasy. For an instant I disappeared into formless vastness with him. I glimpsed his state of consciousness. As he walked away I started spontaneously re-peating to myself the words of an ancient Buddhist chant: *Gate Gate Paragate Parasamgate Bodhi Swaha* (Gone! Gone! Gone Beyond! Gone Totally Beyond! Hail the Pure Enlightened Mind!) While I couldn't fully perceive Baba's state of consciousness, I could feel that in some sense he had gone beyond the ordinary human condition. After this experience I felt more connected to my teacher, more reverent toward him, more respectful of his greatness.

A man named Stuart gave this account of his transformative per-sonal contact with a great spiritual practitioner:

> In 1983 I got introduced to Swami Kripalu's sole remaining renunciate disciple living in America, Swami Vinit-Muni, who lived in Canada. He was taking on no new students. He had only two students living with him in a secluded place. I wrote a letter, hop-ing he would let me come visit. He had turned several of my friends away. To my surprise he told me I could come and visit him. Vinit did ten hours of sadhana a day from four or five a.m. until noon and then again in the afternoon. That was all he ever did for the last thirty years. He lived in a tiny shack. Very simple. Humble. Cooked for me. Wouldn't take any money from me. Put me up for two or three weeks at a time. Taught me on a one-to-one basis for six to eight hours at a time, reading the *Hatha Yoga Pradipika*, translating it and going over it line by line. It was like a father-son relationship in addition to the teaching. Then during that first re-treat, either he gave me an experience, or I had it through the intensity of the practice: I did the *simhasana* (the lion pose) with my tongue sticking out for two or three minutes. And when my tongue came back in my mouth it was exactly like peaking on LSD. I had a sense of infinity, and that any thought I had was amplified greatly. If I had a thought that was self-deprecating I felt like I was in hell. If I had the thought of recognizing the vast-ness of everything it was utterly inspiring and silencing with awe. That went on all night. Anything I worried about would be very exaggerated. Anything I was happy about would be just wonder-ful. The next day I saw Vinit. I had been doing sadhana in this little building separate from where he lived and I was in there with the windows completely blocked off with blankets. Vinit said, "Last night you had an experience. But then some thoughts from your life came in and the experience ended." I then learned that he had some kind of psychic ability.

## *Life Guidance*

The teacher not only initiates the process of spiritual unfoldment, but also guides it toward completion. This can include both supervision of the aspirant's spiritual practice and guidance of the student's worldly life and personal development. It is the teacher's responsibility to see to it that an initial transmission is well integrated. For example, if shaktipat has been given, the teacher can advise the student if the awakening of kundalini is intense and frightening.[8] Some students receive individualized instruction regarding their spiritual practice:

> My teacher told me I was meditating too much and that I needed to stop and eat more and work outdoors and use my body. Once I was more grounded he suggested I start meditating more intensely again. The timing seemed much better and my meditations had better results. I had better concentration, less strain, and I felt more clarity and peace and happiness, rather than feeling spacy and disconnected and burned out like I did before.

Another of the teacher's functions is to serve as a source of practical guidance through some of our most important life transitions and decisions. Part of how we ascertain the stature of a teacher is by examining how effectively he or she guides students' lives. The teacher's guidance either leads students to change themselves and their lives in positive ways, or it does not. One way we deepen our trust in the wisdom of teachers is through seeing the concrete results of following their recommendations. One woman was very grateful to her teacher for advising her to go to medical school—even though he taught a very intensive form of meditation practice and often advised students to minimize their worldly ambitions and pursuits. She said:

> Many of his students were having a hard time making it in the world. A lot of them didn't have any money and people were more into hanging out and meditating than going out and getting a job. It was pretty striking when I started doing this intense school thing. Years later, when I was a practicing physician, he said to me, "Lots of people can sit and meditate a lot, but not many can live an enlightened life while remaining active in the world. The measure of your spiritual advancement is your ability to do this work with a cheerful dedication to service always in your heart." He taught me that my work in the world is my spiritual practice.

Once I wrote Muktananda a letter saying I wanted to quit college so I could go to India and dedicate myself to meditation. I thought that becoming a yogi meant deemphasizing the intellect and transcending the thinking mind. He replied that I *must* finish college and that I was not under any circumstances to quit school. He said, "Nurture your interests in your studies like a small, fragile flame, until it grows into a blaze." There was no room for hesitation. I trusted his guidance, and I feel to this day that he instructed me responsibly. He correctly perceived that for my personal evolution continuing education and intellectual development were quite necessary. He guided me based on what was best for my character and long-term personal development.

Of course, sometimes the best teachers are the ones who don't tell people what to do at all. Ultimately, the student will have to develop discernment and the ability to make his or her own decisions. But at this stage, the student may rely heavily upon the teacher's guidance. It is indeed a remarkable stage of the spiritual journey to find ourselves guided by someone who seems to know our character and our needs so deeply that we come to implictly, and sometimes unquestioningly, trust the teacher's judgment and instructions.

## Great Answers to Deep Questions

Great teachers address our deepest questions in unexpected and brilliant ways, jolting us out of rigidified perceptions to open up our vision of reality. Once I asked the Zen master Joshu Sazaki Roshi a question. He had been sitting completely still for two hours and had not moved at all except to take a few sips of tea. My question, asked with some degree of urgency and over-seriousness, was "Roshi, what Zen discipline do you recommend for Western students?" His reply: "The highest discipline of Zen is to manifest silence when you meet others." He certainly lived what he taught. This was a great response because it undercut my urgent question about formal practices and showed that Zen was a way of being, not a set of techniques one applies to oneself.

Someone once asked Lama Tarthang Tulku his views about sexual morality and conduct. He said, "The best sexual morality is complete relaxation."[9] Similarly, someone once asked Kalu Rinpoche, the venerable Tibetan Buddhist yogi, a question about sex and how it could be utilized as a vehicle of inner transformation. Some members of the audience were appalled that such a question was posed of the elderly monk, who presumably had little experience of sexuality in his own life, which had been dedicated to intensive spiritual practice. To everyone's surprise, Kalu Rinpoche responded: "When you reach the moment of truth, tell yourself, 'Now I have finally arrived!'"

A teacher may also uproot all of our questions. I experienced this once in the presence the French Vedanta teacher, Jean Klein. He seated himself in front of his audience and sat for half an hour without uttering a word. He silently conveyed Self-knowledge, Self-realization. After that half hour sitting I had no questions at all. He quietly conveyed the peace, presence, and awareness that is in itself the highest teaching and transmission, the answer to all questions. It is contentless, and has no beginning or end. No technique is needed to realize it. We only need dissolve our consciousness back into its source.

## Silent Transmission

Some great teachers are able to communicate the enlightened state not by lecturing, but through a wordless transmission of Being. The illumined teacher communicates the enlightened state simply by *being* it, by abiding in that state of consciousness. We have seen that sometimes teachers instruct us in techniques such as meditation, prayer, or visualization. Sometimes they explain complex philosophical doctrines, the teachings of the masters of the lineage, or the meaning of mystical texts. A teacher may prescribe a set of practices for the student, such as a certain number of mantra repetitions or breaths to count, or a course of yoga postures. But the most profound instruction may occur when teachers convey peace and expanded awareness through their silent presence.

One teacher famous for the power of his silent transmission was the Indian sage Bhagavan Ramana Maharshi. Annamalai Swami, a contemporary teacher in the lineage of Ramana Maharshi, has stated:

> If you enter a dark place with a lamp, light falls on everyone who is near you. You don't have to tell people, "I have a light" because they will all be aware of its presence. In the presence of a *jnani*

like Bhagavan the spiritual darkness of devotees is put to flight by the radiant light of *jnana*. In Bhagavan's case this light cleaned and calmed the minds of all who were near him. When mature devotees basked in this light they sometimes had an experience of the Self. The radiation of this spiritual power was Bhagavan's *mauna diksha* [initiation through silence]. He radiated this power quite effortlessly. It was not done by an act of volition, it was a natural consequence of his realization. Bhagavan didn't need to speak about the Self. He *was* the Self and he radiated its power all the time. Those who were receptive to this power needed no verbal explanations from Bhagavan. The spoken teachings were only for those who were not able to tune into his silent radiation.[10]

Ramana Maharshi himself explained:

> The highest form of Grace is silence (*mouna*). Guru's silence is the loudest *upadesa* (spiritual instruction). It is also Grace in its highest form. All other initiations are derived from *mouna* (silence). They are therefore secondary. *Mouna* is the primary form. If the Guru is silent the seeker's mind gets purified by itself.[11]
>
> The books say that there are so many kinds of *diksha* (initiations). They also say that the Guru makes some rites with fire, water, *japa, mantras*, etc., and call such fantastic performances *dikshas*, as if the disciple (*sishya*) becomes ripe only after such processes are gone through by the Guru. . . . Such is the Guru. Such is Dakshinamurti [a legendary yogi of antiquity]. What did he do? He was silent; the disciples appeared before him. He maintained silence, the doubts of the disciples were dispelled, which means that they lost their individual identities. That is *jnana* and not all the verbiage usually associated with it. Silence is the most potent form of work. However vast and emphatic the *sastras* may be they fail in their effect. The Guru is quiet and peace prevails in all. His silence is more vast and more emphatic than all the *sastras* put together.[12]

# Darshan

One of the joyous and transformative aspects of the student-teacher relationship is having the opportunity to see illumined teachers in person, to have their *darshan*. Darshan literally means a gaze or a look. Thus, it means having a look at the teacher. It is also the the time when the teacher has a look at us and when we may receive the teacher's glance—which can be a conduit for direct transmission of the teacher's love, power, and awakened consciousness.[13]

With ordinary teachers ("helpful guides") we attend classes or meetings, or have interviews with the teacher, but we do not speak of having darshan *per se*. However, in the case of great teachers, we often find that simply being in their awakened presence and having a look at them profoundly inspires and intensifies our own striving for Self-realization. These precious times with the teacher activate our own ability to rest in a state of pure, unconditioned awareness. They also confront us with everything in ourselves that creates limitation. Finally, darshan can be a transformative, life-altering experience, as meeting the gaze of the teacher can feel like looking directly into the eyes of God. A man named Robyn recounted this powerful darshan experience:

> Years ago I went on a pilgrimage to India with my teacher at the time, Pir Vilayat Inayat Khan. We had the opportunity to have the darshan of a very powerful and very elderly saint in Delhi, named Baba Sita Ramdas Onkarnath. My teacher told those of us present, "If you go in there and look this being in the eye and ask for something, then afterward you have to be willing to not carry grudges, to not tell lies, to live in truth." There was a tremendous commotion at the back of the tent as the saint's followers arrived and they all began to go nuts with devotion toward this guy. Finally the sadhu comes into the tent, held up on one side by Pir Vilayat and by a man named General Uban Singh on the other side. The old Baba was nothing but skin draped over bones. He could barely sit up, he was so old. We were told that he could barely hear because there was so much cosmic sound in his ears, and that he could barely see because the divine light was so pervasive in his awareness. We were told that darshan would now begin and immediately there was a stampede of Indian devotees. Big mobs started rushing up to the front. General Uban told everybody to calm down and that they were going to separate men and women on different sides of the room. Things began to quiet down a bit as soon as they divided the sexes. So all the women go up first for darshan and this takes a long time, and I'm sitting there raking myself over the coals. Everyone was taking from this guy, mentally asking him for this or that, and I don't know if I can do what Pir Vilayat said—if I can be truthful and let go of all my grudges. So I don't know if I can ask him for anything. Finally the men start going up and eventually I'm about third from the front of the line.

Then suddenly, all of these people rush up in front of me and I am pushed way to the back by a swelling wave of lunatic Indian devotees. This gives me more time to think about what I would like to ask this guy for. All of this took a really long time so I ended up being one of the last few people to go up for darshan.

When I finally get up there I kneel down. All this time, Baba has not spoken to anyone. General Uban is in a trance now and Baba is speaking through General Uban. People come up and ask the guy for different things like enlightenment or healing for themselves or some family member. Baba responds to these people through General Uban. My turn comes and I go up and kneel down at his feet. I am really afraid. I can't bring myself to look up into his eyes at all. I was in a place of really low self-esteem because I was in India with people who were all having all these high mystical experiences and I wasn't having any. I reached over and touched his feet with a garland of flowers each of us had been given. And inside, at the deepest level of myself where no one could hear, silently I said, "Look, I don't know what to ask you for. I see everyone taking from you. So if you can see anything in me that is worthy as a gift to you, please take it." Right then I looked up at him and he started to open his eyes. And I was so scared I looked away. And then General Uban spoke and said, "He wants you to know that he accepts your gift." I just shattered. I started to weep uncontrollably. In this place where no one else could hear or know, he was able to know what was in my heart.

Darshan can be quite informal or highly formal. It is an occasion to offer flowers, pieces of fruit, or other gifts to the teacher as an expression of our gratitude or as a sign of our sincere interest in receiving transmission. Students may bow before the teacher or greet the teacher in some other way. The teacher may sit quietly or may openly greet students and inquire about their well-being.

It is often only in the setting of formal darshan that students of renowned teachers with many followers are able to establish a personal relationship with the teacher. It can be in this setting that students' questions are addressed, their inner needs are met with a loving response by the teacher, and their faith is awakened and renewed. As we sit and look at an enlightened teacher a variety of responses can be elicited. We feel deep peace or become very emotional for no apparent reason. Tears come to our eyes, or an inexplicable ecstasy arises within us. We feel heat in our bodies, or pressure in the head, or energy moving through one or more chakras. We experience *kriyas*, spontaneous physical movements initiated by the awakening kundalini; or we go into meditation effortlessly. We may even experience rays of light emanating from the teacher's eyes into ours. Or a feeling of love envelops us. We also find our deepest fears and insecurities stirred and brought out into the open by our contact with the teacher. We are often amazed to witness our own neurosis becoming highly activated in the teacher's presence.

I used to find that complex feelings came up for me during daily darshans, where anyone who wished to could approach Muktananda. He greeted each person with a quick brush or tap with a large wand of peacock feathers that he wielded like a royal sceptre. My experience was that he always reflected my own inner state. When I was angry or not doing my practices, he would ignore me. When I was in a serene, loving, and centered state of consciousness, he would greet me with love and respect. When I was very emotional and uncertain, he responded with compassion, concern, and a reassuring gaze. When I made sincere efforts to meditate, I felt that he knew it.

As an example of just a few of the internal dramas elicited by darshan, I would like to offer some brief selections from my journal recording several months of nightly darshans I had with Muktananda in 1976:

> 3/28/76: Had his darshan, gave him bananas. One hit with peacock feathers.
> 4/1/76: Baba stormed around the ashram furiously turning off lights and thermostats. Everyone knows he's been angry all day. At evening darshan he came in and said, "You're all fools! Why should I talk to you?" Everyone cowered! Then he said, "Don't you remember what day it is? April Fools!" Everyone was in hysterics laughing at this little prank!
> 4/3/76: This morning I prayed for him to give me something special and powerful so my faith in him will grow. During afternoon meditation Baba walked over and touched my lower back with his big toe. I felt a spark of electricity that jolted my body forward.
> 4/6/76: The inner shakti is working subtly in my head for the past few days. Body heating up during meditation.
> 4/15/76: I inwardly offered Baba my self-pity when I bowed to

him during darshan. Two bops with the peacock feathers.

4/20/76: I went up for darshan angry with Baba. He completely ignored me. No bops.

4/23/76: I feel senselessly content and happy. I feel like Baba is the sailor of the ship over the sea of life. There's nowhere else I'd like to be.

4/24/76: I hate all this fucking chanting and bowing. I gotta get out of this place.

4/26/76: I've been having big problems with mom and dad. They were pretty upset when I told them I wanted to drop out of school and go to India. Tonight Baba said, "You shouldn't get fed up with this world. You will never find God if you run away from your affairs."

4/27/76: As I approached Baba for darshan I inwardly surrendered myself to him, to the divine will, and to universal consciousness, of which he is the embodiment. I let go and surrendered to whatever will happen. He bopped me twice very hard with the feathers. I looked up at him and he looked at me, then he bopped me again.

5/6/76: Many subtle kriyas, energy in my 3rd chakra. My body is burning with intense heat.

5/29/76: Very calm meditation, hardly breathing, prana steady.

6/11/76: I told Baba on darshan line that I am still doubting the connection between us and whether he is really guiding me. He assured me there is a strong connection between us, that I will understand it more over the course of time. When I returned to my seat I began to feel an intense throbbing and twitching of kundalini energy at the base of my spine. Baba, in mid-sentence, raised up his sunglasses, looked at me grinning, and pointed right at me.

At first we offer gifts to the teacher: flowers, fruit, pictures we have painted. All of these are offerings of love, gestures of respect, and expressions of gratitude. But gradually, we begin to offer something more subtle. It is ourselves that we offer. We come to meet the teacher from the place of our own growing mindfulness or realization of the Self. We offer the joy that is rising inside us as we continue to meditate daily, as we learn to walk the path of peace.

# *Tapasya*

During the phase of discipleship we listen to the teacher's instructions, begin to practice the techniques recommended to us, have the opportunity to see the teacher and ask questions, and are inspired by the teacher's presence. We also learn that to achieve a transformed condition we must burn and consume our inner limitations. In yoga philosophy this is the principle known as *tapas*, which means heat or burning. Thus, we begin to perform *tapasya*—austerities that eliminate impurities of body and mind, hone our concentration, and prepare us to hold the intense energies of deeper meditation. The aspirant gradually becomes on fire with the desire for enlightenment, for union with God, for absorption in the One. Ramakrishna is perhaps the best example of a teacher who demonstrated this burning desire for God in his own life.[14] The fire of practice is what drives us into constancy of awareness, so that we begin to dwell unceasingly as ever-expanding, sourceful consciousness.

In most schools of mysticism, it is taught that, before experiencing illumination, the aspirant must engage in a lengthy process of purgation through penances and austerities. In the words of F. C. Happold:

> The Mystic Way is usually ... divided into three stages: the Way of Purgation, the Way of Illumination, or the Illuminative Life ... , and the Way of Union, or the unitive life.... The Indian philosopher Radhakrishnan uses a somewhat different scheme to describe this path to perfection. The three stages of the way of perfection he calls Purification, Concentration, and Identification.... He who would tread the Mystic Way is bidden not only painfully to learn to annihilate the selfhood but also to turn his attention more and more from the multiplicity of the phenomenal world, with its classifying and image-making, its logical reasoning and discursive thinking, so as to attain that "simple seeing" of which the mystics speak; for not until the eye has become single can the whole body be filled with light.[15]

During this phase of purgation or purification, the teacher may inspire the student to undertake intensive practice that the student might not have undertaken otherwise, for example, doing a Buddhist vipassana retreat or a Zen *sesshin*, during which one meditates for hours each day. Sufi practitioners may do a forty-day retreat. All Jesuits go through the strenuous Exercises of St. Ignatius. Or we can create our own rigorous program for self-transformation.

## The Dark Night

One effect of intensely embracing a spiritual discipline is that we may experience a dark night of the soul—described by the Catholic mystic St. John of the Cross as a time of inner desolation, a desert of the heart, an extended period of dryness, depression, and inner emptiness.[16] Old interests and sensual pleasures no longer bring joy, and there is a heightened awareness of their ultimately unsatisfying nature. Only enlightenment will quench our thirst for peace and inner freedom. Our old desires and worldly interests have dried up, yet the blissful experience of enlightened awareness or the presence of God has either not revealed itself or has withdrawn from our awareness. This is considered a time of testing for the spiritual aspirant, who must continue to purify the mind, body, and heart through this difficult period in preparation for a deeper experience of inner peace and communion with God.

In the book, *Pilgrims of the Stars*, mystic and singer Dilip Kumar Roy describes the torments he experienced after coming into contact with Sri Aurobindo, the great mystic, sage, and guru.[17] Roy's career as a musical performer began to feel totally empty, yet it took a long time before he could let go of the fame, adulation, and aesthetic pleasure his career brought him so that he could dedicate himself completely to the interior journey at his teacher's ashram in Pondicherry. Only as old interests, ambitions, and desires fall away are we able to focus one-pointedly on the goal of spiritual apprenticeship—enlightenment or Self-realization. During such a phase, we may feel profound doubt in the path we have chosen, for we do not yet feel the transformative effects of our practices, or the presence of the Beloved, yet no human gratification or sensual pleasure quenches our thirst for inner peace and enlightening knowledge.

His ways are strange, bewildering!
   To fathom Him I fail.
How He fulfills our hearts with His love
   O Friend, I cannot tell.

I learned to laugh through tears and staked
   My all to glimpse his Face:
I won him by becoming His,
   Lost all and gained His Grace.

Relentlessly He weaned me from
   My lesser loves, my kin,
Till even the mate I once had hailed
   Loomed far and alien.

Now dead I am grown to fear and shame
   In my lone quest for Thee:
Strange, none befriends when thou becom'st
   One's friend, O Mystery![18]

I consciously experienced a dark night: As I began meditating intensely I lost interest in music, which had been my strongest interest, as well as in sports, movies, novels, and other pastimes. My attention turned inward, and I spent most of my time meditating, reading, and repeating my mantra quietly to myself. I often spent time with Charles Gonzalez, a gentle Jesuit priest who taught at Wesleyan, discussing issues that arise for mystics, such as conflicts about desire and renunciation, and the loneliness of the path. Father Gonzalez was a radiant man who exuded love, purity, and a spirit of service. I was fortunate to have such a spiritual friend during that desolate period.

There is both sadness and joy in the spiritual apprentice's eyes. There is sadness because the aspirant inevitably suffers while passing through stages of purgation. Old attachments are released, often through painful ordeals, and one may repeatedly see the futility of trying to achieve lasting happiness by seeking fulfillment of ordinary desires and ambitions. As Inayat Khan once said, "The bringers of joy have always been the children of sorrow."[19] Yet, the aspirant also finds joy and resonant peace in a life dedicated to contemplation and service. This joy and deep sadness gradually merge into compassion, which becomes increasingly apparent in the directness and sincerity of the spiritual apprentice's gaze.

## Finding a Community of Practitioners

At times the transformational process demands that we leave the past and all former companions behind. Yet as we become more solidly rooted in our spiritual practice we may find ourselves drawn to a new set of friends who share our interests and commitments. We may meet regularly with other people for study, meditation, chanting, or discussion of our experiences and difficulties on the path. Sometimes this becomes a more formal involvement with a spiritual group or community, which can be very joyous. I remember with gratitude times I spent with friends and fellow seekers at ashrams and meditation retreats. There is a power and joy in chanting, meditating, or practicing yoga or other disciplines with other people in a group. We are supported by spiritual company to intensify our own efforts to know Truth, to be awake. Pursuing the spiritual path in community with others can have its memorable moments. A man named Tim reported:

> I was the head cook at the Maharishi University during the first "7000 Course," when seven thousand people meditated together twice a day for three weeks. I was the guy who got to cook breakfast and lunch for all those people. For one meal I cooked one ton of broccoli! The first day of the course a storm blew through town with the darkest clouds. It felt incredibly ominous, as if the evil gods were out to destroy us. The water line to the kitchen broke. I had to organize a big water brigade to ferry water into the kitchen. This huge obstacle came up, but we got through it. I had this great crew of people. After that, for the next three weeks it was blissful. We'd met the initial resistance. Everything flowed. Everything worked. It was a marvelous experience of living and working in community.

## Dangers of Involvement

Our involvement with a group or spiritual growth movement could be life-transforming and a source of enduring benefit. But involvement in a spiritual community can also pose dangers for the spiritual apprentice. We could fall under the influence of a psychologically imbalanced individual or become involved in a movement that ends in disaster. These days there are so many stories about spiritual teachers leading their communities of followers into group suicide or confrontations with civil or military authorities that all students should carefully consider the implications of involvement with a group. It is important that we look closely not just at the bliss and infinity we think we see in the teacher's eyes but also at the environment that is growing around the teacher. Is there a prevalent atmosphere of paranoia within the group? Are visitors greeted with warmth and welcomed without being subjected to an aggressive sales pitch? We should be especially cautious whenever attendance at a meeting, a retreat, a seminar is coerced or if we feel that recruiters are too actively courting our participation.

We should feel free to come or go from a group at any time. Many years ago, a friend of mine was involved with the Hare Krishna movement. For some time he enjoyed the austere life and the daily *kirtan* (chanting of divine names) on city street corners. Then he became an attendant to one of the head swamis of the movement, who used to beat him frequently. This same swami was later convicted of murder. He was clearly a violent and abusive individual not worthy of the rank of a spiritual leader. Once my friend figured out that he no longer loved or trusted his teacher and announced that he was considering leaving, he was given the "silent treatment" by members of his community. For weeks he was constantly followed around so that he was never left alone. And he was not permitted to use the telephone or to speak with anyone outside the group. Eventually, he escaped from the group by punching his kirtan group leader in the nose and making a run for it.

## Another False Messiah

Lest anyone minimize how destructive it can be to participate in a group led by a deluded, false teacher, consider the example of Shoko Asahara, leader of the Japanese cult AUM Shinrikyo (The True Teaching of Aum), the group responsible for poisoning thousands of people in a nerve gas attack on the Japanese subway system in March, 1995. Asahara claimed to have achieved enlightenment during his travels in India and became a proponent of yoga and meditation. Most of his followers only saw Asahara on TV or video. Those who tried to leave AUM were told they would burn in a Buddhist hell. Members were subjected to severe privations, torture, and near starvation. Some were kidnapped or murdered. Members were encouraged to seek ordination, taking vows of chastity, cutting all ties with the world, renouncing their families, and signing over all worldly possessions and property to Asahara. The group also coerced members into turning over assets of other family members. In 1995, the group's assets were estimated at more than a billion dollars.

Asahara believed that the whole world would acclaim him as the new Buddha and the savior of humanity. He began preaching Judaeo-Christian themes of the approaching Armageddon, and that World War III was imminent. To survive, he believed AUM needed to be armed for self-defense, and thus AUM began buying weapons of mass destruction to wage war against Japan, the United States and rest of humanity. This war, he said, would end in victory for AUM. He predicted earthquakes, volcanoes, and chemical and nuclear war. Driven by these paranoid delusions, AUM began developing chemical and biological weapons, including strains of the deadly Ebola virus collected in Zaire by AUM scientists. Asahara was in short, a megalomaniac predicting war, with limitless funds to buy weapons and deadly chemicals. When Asahara was finally tracked down by police after the sarin attack in the subway system, he was found in a crawl space less than three feet tall holding the equivalent of $100,000 in cash.[20]

## Signs of Mind Control

The sobering reality is that there are many charismatic teachers who prove to be charlatans, and many religious and spiritual groups that turn out to be destructive and dangerous cults.[21] It can be a nightmare to discover that the community with which we are affiliated is actually utilizing elaborate strategies to keep us bound to the group and serving its interests, which are not always in our own best interest. In this century, complex and effective means of controlling thought and behavior have been developed to dominate individuals and groups, and many of these methods are routinely employed within some groups ostensibly dedicated to spiritual awakening.[22] Thus, any seeker considering involvement with a community should be thoroughly familiar with the signs of manipulation or coercion. It is best to be informed about the shadow side of discipleship.

In his book, *Combatting Cult Mind Control*, Steven Hassan described the components of mind control, "a system of influences that disrupt an individual's identity. . . and replaces it with a new identity."[23] Mind control is a social process,

> achieved by immersing a person in a social environment where, in order to function, he must shed his old identity and adhere to the new identity desired by the group. . . . The person usually shows a radical personality change and a drastic interruption of his life course. [Mind control refers to] those systems that seek to undermine an individual's integrity in making his own decisions. The essence of mind control is that it encourages dependency and conformity, and discourages autonomy and individuality.[24]

According to Hassan, there are four main components of mind control often seen in cult groups: Control of behavior, control of thoughts, control of emotions, and control of information. *Behavior control* is control of the group members' environment, where they live, what they wear, what they eat, the amount of sleep they get, and the jobs they have. Rigid schedules are often maintained, with free time greatly restricted. People work, eat, and live together, and any form of individualism is discouraged. All are subjected to an authoritarian chain of command. *Thought control* refers to:

> Indoctrinating members so thoroughly that they internalize the group doctrine, incorporate a new language system, and use thought-stopping techniques to keep their mind 'centered.' In order to be a good member, a person must learn to manipulate his own thought processes. . . . [Cult] ideology is internalized as "the Truth," the only map of reality.[25]

The group doctrine filters all incoming information and determines how information can be thought about. Thinking becomes black versus white, "us versus them." Good is equated with the leader and the group; and bad, with everything outside the group. It is claimed that the group's doctrine is scientifically proven and provides answers to all problems. Students learn to block out criticism of the group, and to defend their new identity as group members against their former identities. Denial, rationalization, justification, and wishful thinking prevail.

> If information transmitted to a cult member is perceived as an attack on either the leader, the doctrine, or the group, a hostile

wall goes up. Members are trained to disbelieve any criticism. . . . Paradoxically, criticism of the group confirms that the cult's view of the world is correct. The information presented does not register properly.[26]

Group members are taught to use thought-stopping practices to counteract "bad" thoughts, to drown out the negativity. Thought-stopping short-circuits a person's ability to test reality, so the individual can think only positive thoughts about involvement with the group.

*Emotional control* manipulates and narrows the range of a person's feelings. Guilt and fear are used to keep members under control, often by creating an outside enemy believed to be persecuting the group (Satan, FBI, psychiatrists, family, rival sects, deprogrammers). Within such a group, loyalty and devotion are the most valued emotions. Members are not allowed to express any negative feelings, except toward outsiders. Members are taught never to complain or to criticize a group leader, only themselves.[27] Interpersonal relationships are strictly controlled and members constrained as to whom they can marry, go to bed with, or spend time with. Members are kept off balance, receiving praise one minute, castigation the next. Feelings of dependency and helplessness are fostered through forced confession of past sins. These confessions are often used against members later on to keep them in line. Participants are also subjected to *phobia indoctrination* so that they have panic reactions (sweating, rapid heartbeat, feeling lost and defenseless) at the thought of leaving the group. They are told that if they leave they will die, burn in hell, go insane, or commit suicide. Members are made to feel that security is possible only within the group.[28]

*Information control* is the process of denying people information they need to make sound judgments so they become incapable of doing so. Members of such groups have no access to newspapers, TV, radio, magazines, or books. They have no free time and read only material disseminated by the groups. They are not allowed to discuss anything critical of the leader, doctrine, or organization.

Members spy on each other and report improper activities or comments to leaders. New converts are not permitted to talk to each other without an older member present to chaperone them. Most importantly, people are told to avoid contact with ex-members or critics.[29]

Group leaders screen members' letters and phone calls, while members know nothing about scandals, lawsuits, or internal disputes occurring within the group.

Those who have been subjected to mind control often experience considerable conflict and difficulties in trying to sever their connection with such a group. Often they need assistance in the form of exit counseling to free themselves from a coercive group and its insidious mental, emotional, and behavioral programing. I refer the reader to Steven Hassan's book for further information on this process.

Some degree of behavioral control is to be expected in any spiritual community—including healthy groups. Regular scheduling of work, study, and other activities can free the mind so that we can focus on intensive spiritual practice. In traditional Buddhist monasteries no food is taken after noon for precisely this reason, and during meditation retreats silence is often observed. When we detect behavioral control within a group, we can ask ourselves several questions: Have we consciously chosen austere living conditions (such as practicing meditation in silence for long periods of time, limiting food intake, or accepting a period of celibacy) because these disciplines support us in one-pointed pursuit of enlightenment? Having lived within these behavioral strictures for some time, do they still serve our spiritual growth? Or do they weaken us physically and emotionally? And is the group flexible enough to allow us to find our own discipline and daily rhythm of activities— including both a reasonable amount of work and enough quiet time for sleep, meditation, and personal care? Or are we pushed to the point of exhaustion by a dehumanizing schedule of grueling labor? Is every moment's activity rigidly prescribed? Is there room for us to be ourselves, or do we have to suppress our true feelings, thoughts, or personalities—or else face group censure? Our answers can help us decide for ourselves whether or not we are involved with a healthy community. A life of hard work and intensive pursuit of expanded consciousness through contemplative discipline is one thing. To have every aspect of our existence dictated by others so that we have no free will is another matter entirely. Such an atmosphere stifles all creativity and prevents students from growing. It is a wholly unsuitable atmosphere for higher evolution.

Regarding thought control, it is normal for a spiritual group to teach its doctrine to members and for members to be enthusiastic about these teachings. The question is, are other views considered and discussed? Are questioning and open inquiry welcomed and accepted, or does an oppressive atmosphere prevail? Are members punished for holding a different opinion or viewpoint? Does a hostile and defensive atmosphere prevail, rather than a joyous and accepting one? These are important questions, as we will note again in Stage Seven when we discuss the need for open and honest discussion within spiritual communities.

Where emotional manipulation is present, a dangerous atmosphere may exist within a group. The practices of phobia indoctrination are especially destructive and "crazy-making." A woman I once knew had just left a community and was panic-stricken because the group had indoctrinated her that those who left the group would be cursed in all undertakings. Whenever she faced any difficulties, she attributed it to "the guru's curse." In contrast, a healthy community uses no coercion to establish commitment. Moreover, a healthy spiritual community provides some support for an individual's emotional response, in contrast to groups where all individuality is submerged to the group will. Looking, acting, and thinking like a clone is not conducive to spiritual growth, notwithstanding the ways this might help us "transcend ego."

While not all spiritual groups exhibit these forms of mind control, we should be cautious about deeper involvement if we become aware that they are being employed. Equipped with knowledge of some of the danger signals we can proceed into deeper involvement with a teacher or community. Another thing to keep in mind is that groups change over time. A community that started out innocent, joyous, and free and can grow quite rigid, controlling, and oppressive. We need to continue to monitor our feelings about the teacher and the group throughout our time of involvement.

If we are students of an ordinary teacher or helpful guide, Stage Three may be as far as we proceed on this path. We may receive instruction in a technique and then go our own way. We may experiment with participation in a spiritual group but decide at some point that it does not suit us. Or we may proceed into deeper transformation under a teacher's guidance, by undergoing a process of testing that allows us to receive the teacher's most transformative influence.

# *Notes*

1.  H. Guenther, *The Life and Teaching of Naropa* (New York: Oxford Univ. Press, 1963), p. 40.
2.  D. Lorenzen, *Kabir Legends* (Albany, NY: State Univ. of New York Press, 1991).
3.  L. Llalungpa, *The Life of Milarepa* (Boston: Shambhala, 1978).
4.  G. Feuerstein, *Yoga: The Technology of Ecstasy* (Los Angeles, Jeremy Tarcher, 1989), p. 26.
5.  H. I. Khan, *The Complete Sayings of Hazrat Inayat Khan* (New Lebanon, NY: Sufi Order Publications, 1991).
6.  When I was 13 years old a family friend, Ruth McGhee, took me to the Fillmore East to meet B. B. King, an old friend of hers. We were on the guest list and went backstage, but Mr. Graham was unimpressed by our backstage passes and showed us to the door. Rudely.
7.  It is important to note that the kinds of yogic phenomena I experienced are not the same things as enlightenment. Nevertheless, such experiences are fascinating and deepen our faith in the teacher and enthusiasm for meditation practice.
8.  Some people have criticized Muktananda for giving shaktipat too freely, in some cases bringing about a powerful kundalini awakening for which the student was not prepared—in some cases leading to imbalance. Traditionally shaktipat was a secret initiation given only to the most seasoned and qualified spiritual aspirants. Muktananda gave shaktipat to anyone who approached him in a halfway respectful and receptive manner. Some were able to take that powerful transmission of shakti and use it to do sadhana and undergo deep transformation. Others experienced physical and psychological difficulties as a consequence of shaktipat. Not all were properly prepared and some casualties have been reported. In any great adventure there are some who do not make it to the goal. Not all climbers of Mt. Everest reach the summit.
9.  J. Needleman, *On the Road to Self Knowledge* (New York: Alfred Knopf, 1976), p. 109.
10. D. Godman, *Living by the Words of Bhagavan* (Tiruvannamalai, India: Sri Annamalai Swami Ashram Trust, 1995), p. 335.
11. *Talks with Sri Ramana Maharshi* (Tiruvannamalai, India: Sri Ramanasramam, 1984), p. 501.
12. Ibid., p. 370.
13. It is said that one can receive the grace of great beings through even a moment's contact. In 1996 while traveling on a tour through Southern India with my father, we arrived one day at Srinageri, site of an ancient Shaivite temple, and home of one of the four Shankaracaryas, among the most powerful and widely respected Hindu spiritual leaders. A yogi only rises to the rank of a Shankaracarya after a lifetime of sadhana and demonstrated spiritual attainments. We were informed by other visitors that we had just missed darshan but that the Shankaracarya would soon pass by where we were standing. My father had never seen a *sadhu* of this stature before but he instinctively assumed a respectful stance with his hands placed in the gesture of *namaste*. The Shankaracarya stepped outside and started walking past us. He looked at us for only a moment, but I felt the power of his glance. He had tremendous shakti.

He was observing a day of silence so no words were spoken, but everyone was much moved, as I was, by his presence. He had a wild, fierce expression, as well as a look of supreme detachment. It was a marvelous darshan, a glimpse of an awakened being.

14. L. Hixon, *Great Swan: Meetings with Ramakrishna* (Boston: Shambhala, 1992).

15. F. C. Happold, *Mysticism: A Study and an Anthology* (Middlesex, England: Penguin Books, 1963), pp. 56–57, 59.

16. The dark night of the soul is an important stage in spiritual unfoldment not dealt with in other traditions such as Hinduism, Buddhism, or Sufism. No one has described this phase of the spiritual journey as clearly as St. John of the Cross. *The Dark Night of the Soul,* translated by E. A. Peers (Garden City, NY: Image Books, 1959).

17. D. K. Roy & I. Devi, *Pilgrim of the Stars* (New York: Dell Publishing, 1973).

18. Ibid., p. 253.

19. H. I. Khan, *The Complete Sayings of Hazrat Inayat Khan* (New Lebanon, NY: Sufi Order Publications, 1991).

20. M. Sayle, "Nerve Gas and The Four Noble Truths," The New Yorker, April, 1996.

21. M. Singer, *Cults in our Midst* (San Francisco: Jossey-Bass, 1995).

22. See R. J. Lifton, *Thought Reform and the Psychology of Totalism* (New York: Norton, 1961); and R. J. Lifton, "Cults: Religious Totalism and Civil Liberties." In *The Future of Immortality and Other Essays for a Nuclear Age* (New York: Basic Books, 1987).

23. S. Hassan, *Combatting Cult Mind Control* (Rochester, VT: Park Street Press, 1990), p. 7.

24. Ibid., pp. 54–5.

25. Ibid., p. 61.

26. Ibid., p. 62.

27. Ibid., p. 64.

28. Ibid., p. 65.

29. Ibid.

# *Testing*

> The master who had to teach the method and the exercises had first
> to test the [student] to determine whether he was willing and able to
> undergo the hardships that awaited him on the Path. The newcomer
> was sometimes made to wait for days at the Sheikh's door, and some-
> times as a first test was treated very rudely. Usually three years of
> service were required before the [student] could be formally ac-
> cepted in a master's group.
>
> A. Schimmel, Mystical Dimensions of Islam[1]

Once the student makes the commitments of discipleship and has begun in earnest to pursue a spiritual practice, a more or less protracted
period of testing ensues. There are two main types of tests: tests of the
student's faith in the teacher and commitment to the spiritual path; and
tests of the student's character, often through the exposure of imperfections and distorted perceptions.

## *The Sheikh and The Lamb's Bladder*

My friend and teacher Sangye Drolma recounted the following story: A
man went to a sheikh for teaching. The sheikh was very simple and
austere, sitting by himself in a mosque. He had no other students. After
visiting the sheikh for several months the student thought, "How great
it would be if my teacher had more disciples to receive his teachings."
The following day, the teacher was surrounded by a huge entourage of
followers. Each day thereafter large crowds came to the mosque for his
blessings and guidance. Now the student could barely see the teacher,
much less have personal conversations with him. He thought to himself, "How I long for the close personal contact I used to have with the
sheikh. I wish all these people would go away."

The next day when the man went to the mosque he noticed a strange thing. Every time the sheikh moved in any way people began holding their noses and complaining that the sheikh exuded nauseating odors. The crowd started yelling and cursing at the sheikh and calling him a fake. Some threw vegetables at the sheikh. The student sat watching in amazement. The mosque soon cleared out completely and the student was left alone with his teacher once again.

When they were alone together, the teacher pulled up his robe and revealed that he was holding a lamb's bladder under his arm, next to his body. When the sheikh rubbed it or moved his body, the bladder made the farting sound. It stank abominably. The sheikh said, "I heard your request and granted your wish. Everyone else thought I was disgusting and began to doubt and denounce me. But you sat here and never wavered. You didn't lose faith in me despite my strange actions. This is how I know you are worthy to be my student."

## Tests of Faith in the Teacher

As this story demonstrates, the teacher will often behave in quite a strange manner to instill doubt in the student's mind about the teacher's sanity, purity, or good intentions. Indeed, many teachers contend that their most seemingly strange or inexplicable behaviors are actually means of testing their disciples. One man reported that he was working at his job as a house painter in a town nearby his teacher's ashram (spiritual community):

> I was painting away and I looked up and there was Swamiji. He looked so happy. He smiled and asked me to join him for a walk. I said of course. After we had walked for a few minutes Swamiji pulled a cigarette out of his pocket. He lit it and began to puff on it. Immediately all my judgments came up about smoking—it's not healthy, it's not spiritual, a yogi would never do it. He smoked that whole cigarette and kept looking me straight in the eye. After that, for the next few days I became filled with doubt. Could it be that Swami X was a fraud, that I had been deceived, that he was not enlightened? I felt that he was a hypocrite, telling us to live these pure lives, but here he was polluting his body. I started to think about leaving Swami X. But then I realized that Swami X's strange behavior did not change how I felt about him. The

core of his presence was unchanging. He was serene, loving, and filled with inner dignity and power. These were the qualities of the man that I loved and admired. I didn't care if he smoked.

Sometimes the scalpel of the guru's surgery on the student's ego is very painful. For example, the teacher may make some outrageous demand, ask us for a large sum of money, yell at us, or even strike us physically. Consider this example from the story of the Tibetan Buddhist guru Naropa and his teacher, Tilopa :

> When Naropa made his mandala and venerated him with folded hands, Tilopa glanced once at him. Naropa prayed and asked for instruction. "If you want instruction, give me your girl." When Naropa did so, the girl turned her back to Tilopa, looked at Naropa, smiled and cast sidelong glances at him. Tilopa beat her and said: "You do not care for me, you only care for Naropa." Naropa did not lose faith in the propriety of his Guru's actions, and when he sat there happily without the girl, Tilopa asked him: "Are you happy, Naropa?" And Naropa answered: "Bliss is to offer the mudra as fee to the Guru who is Buddha himself, unhesitatingly."[2]

One contemporary teacher tested the faith of two of his close, long-time students very fiercely. He stabbed one of them, his personal attendant, with a fork. The disciple received the blow without complaint. He never spoke of it to anyone, and his devotion to his teacher remained constant. The other student got burned more profoundly in the fires of testing. The teacher began making sexual advances toward the student's teenage daughter. Outraged, the disciple left the teacher immediately.

Through such tests, we are confronted with our deepest fears and attachments, and we are asked to make an offering of our doubts and fears. Doubt in the teacher is deliberately instilled to determine our level of trust. Many traditions teach that it is only when the student trusts the teacher unquestioningly and submits to whatever demands or outrageous behavior the teacher exhibits that the student becomes ready to receive the deepest transmission the teacher is capable of bestowing.

Another test of the student's faith occurs when the teacher completely ignores the student for a long period of time, until the student becomes convinced of having been completely rejected by the teacher. At this juncture, the student who is uncommitted or incapable of trusting the teacher is likely to flee, while the student who has understood the teacher's instructions will be undeterred and will steadfastly practice meditation and Self-inquiry. Such a student demonstrates an unshakable commitment not only to the teacher but also to the discipline and inner mastery that discipleship entails. Indeed, this is often a moment when students can deepen their attunement to the Self and begin to dwell more deeply in a state of tranquility and mindful awareness.

## Crazy Wisdom or Abusive Conduct?

From the perspective of some spiritual teachings, any effort to resist the teacher or depart from the teacher's company is viewed as a defense or protection of the ego, a sign of an inability to bear the intensity of spiritual discipline and of the teacher's exposure of our masks, fears, and limitations. In many yogic traditions, for example, one is exhorted to hold on to the guru's feet (figuratively speaking) and submit to the guru's testing, no matter how difficult this may be.

Many adepts are forceful slayers of the ego, impersonal and sometimes cruel. Association with such a teacher can set a fire under us that can burn to cinders every vestige of ego that stands in its path. Whether this proves to be a purifying fire or a destructive one depends to a large extent on the integrity of the teacher and the courage of the student to consciously live through this shattering of ego. The awakened teacher's job is to liberate us, and to accomplish this goal, spiritual shock therapy is sometimes necessary.

There is a long-standing tradition of "crazy wisdom" spiritual teachers who make outrageous demands of students or who engage in actions that seem outrageous or inexplicable. Georg Feuerstein has described crazy wisdom as:

> the world-wide tradition of spiritual adepts whose behavior and teaching prove shocking to ordinary moral sensibilities and challenge widely held norms of thought and conduct. These are the crazy adepts of Tibetan Buddhism, the eccentric teachers of Ch'an (Zen), the holy fools of Christianity and Islam, the *avadhutas* and *bauls* of Hinduism, and the tricksters and religious clowns of tribal traditions. In order to teach spiritual truths, these masters often adopt quite unconventional means—certainly means that are not

ordinarily associated with holy folk. They resort to alcohol and other drugs, and they use sexuality for instructional purposes. . . . Their generally outrageous behavior does not at all conform to our cherished ideas of religiosity, morality, and sanctity. . . . Their seemingly crazy deeds have the express purpose of topsy-turvying consensus reality in order to lead to spiritual breakthroughs. . . . The crazy-wise teachers are eccentrics who use their eccentricity to communicate an alternative vision to that which governs ordinary life. They are masters of inversion, proficient breakers of taboos, and lovers of surprise, contradiction, and ambiguity. . . . That which tricksters, clowns, mad lamas, Zen masters, holy fools, rascal gurus, and crazy-wise adepts have in common is *active* rejection of consensual reality. They behave in ways that outwardly manifest the reversal of values and attitudes intrinsic to all genuine spirituality.[3]

It is often difficult to discern whether a teacher's outrageous behavior and difficult demands are actually tests and true expressions of crazy wisdom, or whether they are, in reality, abusive conduct. In evaluating a teacher's conduct, it may be helpful to consider these comments by Richard Gale, a scholar of comparative religions:

In the Eastern Christian (Greek and Russian Orthodox, Syrian, and Coptic) traditions, they have always emphasized the doctrine of humility. The disciple is always cautioned against "vainglory" in a teacher, which means deceit, or pride in oneself and one's image that raises oneself above others. This is the most dangerous sign in a teacher. Humility is always said to be the antidote to vainglory. And the way to discern if a teacher is lost in vainglory is to observe his or her state of humility.[4]

Often a teacher's abusive behaviors are rationalized as tests of the student. For example, suppose a teacher keeps demanding more and more money from us and then claims that this is for our own good, to free us of our attachment and clinging. Is this exploitation, or a crazy wisdom teaching? Or what if a teacher asks us to dance naked in front of others at a party? The answer can only be found in the context of instruction. Has the teacher been shining a spotlight on particular attachments so that this test makes sense to us, difficult as it may be? Is the teacher honest about controversial actions and their rationale? Does the teacher make reference to this as a teaching situation so that we are able to recognize and integrate the lesson? If so, then it might be considered a valid teaching gesture. My own guideline is that if a teacher tests us in a way that challenges our deepest fears and arouses our defenses and suspicions, then the teacher has a responsibility to help us understand it as a test and to give us some reasonable understanding of its meaning or purpose. Then we may feel grateful that the teacher is revealing our attachments, fears, rigidities, self-righteousness, and lack of humor. After all, we may have "signed on" as disciples with the clear understanding that our egos are to be uprooted in the process, by any means necessary.

## Fierce Teachers

In some cases students feel profoundly liberated by a teacher's purifying fire of testing. There are teachers who deliberately and effectively use their intensity as a means of transforming and liberating students. However, to be an effective means of instructing us, the teacher's fierceness must be compassionate. We can receive and benefit from fierce instruction if we feel that, behind the drama of our ego crisis, we are truly loved by our teacher. When we lose the sense of our teacher's compassion, our trust is shattered, and inwardly we begin to revolt. At this juncture some students proceed directly to the stage of Separating From a Spiritual Teacher.

In other instances, we recognize that the teacher has been quite compassionate in bringing us face-to-face with our deepest fears and exposing our weaknesses—our lack of courage, our wounded pride, our intolerable arrogance, our desire to be rescued by others—shedding light on these areas so that we can become stronger. If we are fearless and trust the teacher, we can be purified by these fiery teachings, instead of getting burned. One man gave this account of a lesson from a hatha yoga master:

> I went to Hawaii for a week-long retreat with a very intense yogi. He annihilated me completely. He kept us moving all the time and my body started to get burning hot. I felt weak and uneasy and he kept pressing me to my limits in every exercise. After the

first day I was exhausted. By the second and third day I was mentally and emotionally drained and defeated. He was so strong and powerful and demanded so much of us that I became terrified that something terrible was going to happen to me. A few times he yelled at me for being so afraid. I kept saying, "I can't do it." And he looked me firmly in the eye and he kept saying "You can. Come on. Do it." We did so many handstands and so many back bends. After a while I just let go to it and my body stretched to its limits, which were far beyond what I thought my limits were. That was amazing to me. By the fourth and fifth days I had faced a lot of my fear and gone beyond it.His fiery teaching liberated me by forcing me to go beyond my limits. I felt more powerful and confident than I ever had before.

## Tests of the Student's Character

The human heart must first be melted, like metal,
before it can be molded into a desirable character.
*Hazrat Inayat Khan, Complete Sayings*[5]

Discipleship is usually understood to be a difficult process in which the teacher tests the student's character, obedience, intelligence, and level of spiritual insight and realization. Discipleship is sometimes characterized as a fire of purification, difficult to endure, to which the disciple is asked to surrender. In making the commitment to enlightenment through spiritual apprenticeship we implicitly give the teacher permission to expose personal limitations and imperfections of character that keep us in bondage and ignorance. Part of a teacher's job is to challenge us to confront our deepest fears and to transcend habituated perceptions—thereby making it possible for us to see with new eyes and to assimilate new knowledge. Inevitably the process can be intensely uncomfortable for the student.

The mystic Gurdjieff once recounted a story about an esoteric school he had visited during his travels. This school practiced an exercise in which students were instructed to freeze in the exact physical position in which they found themselves at the moment of a designated "Stop" signal. Usually students were taken by surprise and did not have time to compose themselves before freezing. The stop exercise was to apply to thoughts and emotions in addition to the position of the physical body. One day a student of the school faithfully obeyed his teacher's instruction to freeze while he was standing in the rising waters of an irrigation canal. The water nearly drowned the man as he courageously obeyed his instructions and stood there immobile, and he barely escaped with his life. Nevertheless, the man was transformed by consciously witnessing his own confrontation with death.[6] This story illustrates in a rather dramatic way the depth of commitment asked of us at this stage of our training. We are pressed to go "all the way"—to unconditionally trust and let go, beyond ego, beyond fear.

Testing may involve specific instructions that are difficult for the student to carry out. The teacher may ask the student to give up sex, drugs, a career, or a relationship, or to embrace a particular job, diet, marriage, or spiritual practice. A student who loves to meditate but is not very grounded or practical may be asked to work long hours at a job so there is no time for meditation.

One man, who had been exceptionally promiscuous in his young adulthood and who confessed to having sexually exploited innumerable women, was commanded by his teacher to marry a woman whom at first he found exceptionally homely. After struggling with this instruction, he decided to marry the woman, and later reported that this marriage enabled him to make major breakthroughs on the spiritual path. He began to perceive the Goddess in his wife's face and he dedicated himself to her service. In this way, a difficult instruction led to a profound transformation of his capacity to love another human being. His character was tested and transformed. His heart changed, and from a sex-obsessed man filled with lust and strategies of seduction, he was transformed into an ecstatic devotee of the divine feminine.

In some instances, a test will reveal the maturity and personal integrity that the student already possesses. One teacher arranged to have someone offer a bribe to a disciple who was a policeman. The disciple refused the bribe, and his good character was demonstrated. Another teacher spread rumors about a student to see if he would get angry. The disciple remained silent while other people gossiped about him. He remained steady and continued meditating without being distracted by other people's opinions and criticisms.

Some tests challenge the student to exceed old limitations, and to express his or her greatest strengths and talents. The test may help refine the student's character and visibly transform the student into a more evolved person. A woman named Jessica reported:

> My teacher sent me to way to start a human service project where we set up kitchen facilities and shelters for indigent children and adults in northern India. We clothed and fed indigent people and made sure they got some kind of medical care. At first, I was put off by this assignment. I thought when I finally found a teacher I would do intense meditation practices in a retreat somewhere. Instead, I got thrown right into the thick of life in an enormous overcrowded city with many social problems. I learned so much from that experience. I grew as a human being. I discovered what compassion means. Above all, I learned courage, especially as I watched these people coping with so many adversities. And I learned to instill courage in others, to strengthen them to carry on. I am so grateful for the test that my teacher set for me.

## The Exposure of the Student's Ego

One of the primary tasks of the teacher is to expose and uproot the student's impurities, limitations, and imperfections. This may involve painful tests and some humbling of the student's egotism or pride. To awaken true spiritual vision, we need to relinquish our misperception that our real identity consists of our bodies, our desires, our thoughts, our social status or position. The Yoga Sutras call this *asmita*, the false identification of consciousness with the vehicles through which it is expressed—physical, mental, or astral.[7] We misidentify with the instruments of consciousness—body, mind, emotions—but not with consciousness itself, our deepest essence. The teacher's tests challenge us to relinquish attachments to transitory forms and rigid concepts, so that we can perceive our true identity as the Self, Atman, the ocean of timeless Being. These tests show us where our consciousness is fixated— whether it be on past or future, pleasure or pain, or on personal identity, desire, and ambition. As we let go of these points of clinging and attune to the unchanging presence that is within and around us, then, very naturally, we begin to perceive the Truth: that our true nature and identity is the transcendental light that shines forever in all things, tranquil and boundlessly aware. The tests we undergo are simply means to remove obstacles to that awareness. When the false is removed all that remains is the Real. This is knowledge. The great Advaita Vedanta philosopher Shankara wrote:

> O prudent one, lose all sense of separation and enter into silence. Realize that you are one with the self-luminous Brahman, the ground of all existence.... The Atman is the reality. It is your true, primal self. It is pure consciousness, the one without a second, absolute bliss. It is beyond form and action. Realize your identity with it. Stop identifying yourself with the coverings of ignorance, which are like the masks assumed by an actor.[8]

To liberate us, teachers test us in ways that expose our false identification with the ego and root out impurities such as a sense of self-importance and superiority (or inferiority). These tests present us with the choice to either cling to our illusions, or to relinquish these to perceive reality more clearly. We are given opportunities to let go of our lesser identities so that we might awaken to our greater Identity.

An image that captures the nature of this phase of spiritual apprenticeship is seen in an eighteenth-century Indian painting called "Mahavidya Cinnamasta," which means "the seduction and destruction of illusion."[9] The image depicts illusion as a man's body seated on a lotus with a slithering, black, octopus-like creature coming out of his throat and holding in one hand his own head on a platter. The teacher's job is to hand us our egos on a platter. If you don't want to get burned, then don't stand near the fire. If you don't want to get chopped, then stay away from the guillotine.

A skillful teacher teaches us lessons that help us become free of impurities such as bigotry, fear, disdainful attitudes, negative thinking, excessive pride, and arrogance. Most students who approach teachers do not possess all of the refined qualities of character listed earlier; thus, in the course of our training we need to refine our character and to have our egotism exposed. When the student is a very difficult, arrogant, or hard-headed person with personality flaws that are evident to everyone but himself, the teacher may be quite forceful in exposing these qualities. I once saw Muktananda give a thorough tongue-lashing to a man who had been observed many times breaking ashram rules, and had even stolen money. Afterward, the man was much humbled and very remorseful, and gradually his character appeared to change. Let us note that this humbling of the student's ego is not the same as abject *humiliation* of the student, where the student is seriously traumatized and emotionally damaged by the experience. Of course, in some cases the line between humbling and humiliation may be very blurry indeed. (See Distortions of Discipleship below.)

Muktananda began the process of exposing my ego from the very beginning. The first time I ever spoke to Baba directly in 1974, I asked him a question about spiritual pride. Ah, what a foolish lad I was! I had been reading Chogyam Trungpa's book, *Cutting Through Spiritual Materialism*, which was relevant to me because at the time I was feeling slightly superior to some of my high school classmates who hadn't yet discovered the wonders of the spiritual path. In response, he said, "There was once a young boy who was a great yogi. He was such a great yogi that he developed *siddhis*, powers. One of his siddhis was that he could say a mantra over a bowl of oatmeal and make it expand so much that it covered the entire surface of the earth. Do you have any such powers?" When I nodded no, he said, "Well, wait until something happens. Then you can get conceited about it." I had never in my life been so thoroughly put in my place. His response deftly deflated my sense of superiority. I felt extremely stupid, but afterward I had a good laugh at myself.

My weaknesses were also exposed through some difficult lessons in the area of work. For a long time I was condescending and egotistical about my assigned jobs in the ashram. My ego used to get steamed up over being asked to clean toilets, vacuum hallways, and mop floors. I did my jobs quietly and without complaint, but inwardly I was huffy and disdainful. I often wondered why I couldn't be assigned to work in the library, or to do editing work for ashram publications, anything more interesting than these other menial tasks. I particularly disliked jobs that felt like they were made up just to keep us ashram residents occupied.

Once I spent over a month engaged in an absurd work project: I was part of a crew that was charged with the task of using buckets to transport an enormous pile of rocks from a parking lot to the basement of a building, which had a very low ceiling. I kept dropping the rocks, the heavy buckets were throwing my spine out of alignment, and I kept bumping my head on the low ceiling. I began to get really tired. And bored. Then I became intensely angry about all the time I was wasting on this task. Then I began to plan how I would make my escape from this ashram gulag.

This job made me think frequently about a story that epitomizes the phase of testing in spiritual apprenticeship. This was the story of Milarepa, the Tibetan yogi whose teacher, Marpa, made him spend twelve years building numerous stone houses, tearing them down, and then rebuilding them. Years of back-breaking labor brought Milarepa many times to the brink of absolute despair, extreme physical exhaustion and pain, and the loss of all hope that he would attain enlightenment in this lifetime. Later, Milarepa came to understand why he had been tested so severely. It turns out that, prior to seeking instruction from Marpa, Milarepa had been involved in black magic. He had learned to cast spells to seek revenge against an evil uncle who had stolen Milarepa's father's property and deprived the rest of the family of its rightful inheritance. Milarepa was informed that it was because of the negative karma he had accrued through his violent, destructive magical acts that Marpa had needed to test him so ruthlessly—to purify him fully. Only then was he fit for instruction and initiation.[10]

Reflecting on this story, I became absorbed in the fantasy that I was being tested like Milarepa and purified, through my arduous labors, of all my past karma. However, after a while, I began to realize that perhaps this was no great spiritual test. And I returned to the ordinariness of the task, the naked sensation of the weight of the rocks, their density and smoothness, the sensations of my tired, aching muscles carrying the buckets.

For a while I made quite a show of how hard I was working. When people passed by, I would let out grunts and moans so everyone would see how difficult my job was, and how hard I was working. I also made a point of appearing strong and energetic and showing off how muscular I was. I was lost in the drama of it all, the sheer heroism of my being out here in the sweltering heat working like a prisoner on a chain gang. Then I realized that nobody gave a damn what I was doing. I was just a skinny, long-haired teenager puffing out his scrawny chest doing some stupid job. This realization was for me a total ego defeat, the final blow to my sense of specialness.

I had been doing this job for so long, yet the task was nowhere near completed. The pile of stones was enormous. There was no clear reason why we were being asked to do this. Yet there was nothing else to do. And so I began to surrender to it. This was my assigned task. And so I tried to do it better. I began to grow more mindful, ducking carefully to avoid beheading myself. I began to feel invisible and to disappear into the activity of doing the job. I was not invested in the outcome. I became the work, practicing meditation in motion. The job was doing itself; I was just the instrument. I felt a sensation of emptiness and im-personality, but also a deep peacefulness in doing the work in this man-ner. Soon thereafter I was assigned to a new job.

I learned a tremendous amount from this experience. I burned out a lot of my egotism, my feeling of being "above" doing ordinary labor. I came to respect the value of every task and occupation and learned to do daily labor with love. I came to feel joy in doing simple jobs thor-oughly and well. One day I was sent off to sweep a remote pathway in a corner of the ashram grounds. I did the sweeping very carefully and mindfully, and as I did so I felt that I was sweeping the leaves from my mind, as well as from the footpath. I was very peaceful as I did this. As I swept leaves that afternoon I told myself that I would sweep the path so well that Baba himself would be pleased to walk upon it. To my amazement, just as I was about to finish my day's work, Baba showed up and walked down the path, followed by a trail of people. He stopped and looked at me, and whispered "*bahut accha* (very good)."

## *Self-Surrender*

Austerity, self-study and resignation to Isvara constitute preliminary yoga.
*Patanjali, Yoga Sutras*[11]

Some of the most significant tests of spiritual apprenticeship are those that challenge us to conquer the inner demons of doubt and lack of faith. We cannot experience contentment and serene inner wisdom as long as we continue to kick, scream, and complain inwardly, saying, "Why aren't I rich and famous yet" Or, Why haven't I had any visions?" Or, "Why haven't I met my soul mate yet?" Or, "Why isn't my kundalini awakening faster?" An important lesson of discipleship is to learn to trust whatever the universe has in store for us and to accept the present moment as it is. As we pass through the stages of testing, we begin to lay our egos and our lives increasingly at the feet of the divine.

One day in Ganeshpuri I went up to Baba's seat and laid my head at his feet. Inwardly I felt myself let go completely. In that moment I surrendered to the divine will, to whatever was going to happen in my life. I let go of the desire to attain enlightenment. I let go of the desire for amazing meditation experiences. I let go of the desire for fame and recognition, or for special favor in the eyes of my teacher. I let go. When I looked up at him, he was very loving and compassionate. And while I have not always sustained this state, I have continued to try to remember this moment of self-offering, because when I surrender I am at peace. I feel blessed even in the midst of suffering because I trust that even this is a lesson intended for me. As Hazrat Inayat Khan said, "No one will experience in life what is not intended for him. . . . There is nothing that is accidental; all situations in life work toward some definite end."[12]

We only become true disciples when we surrender. Then our lives are in the hands of a greater intelligence, and enfolded by its design. We trust the forces of guidance to lead us to our destination. It is only when we surrender that we experience serenity. In surrender, our hearts reach out to meet our source and origin, saying: "All that I am, all that I do is for you, Spirit. I leave the results in your hands, for I do not know what is best for me and for the good of all beings. I leave all that for you to decide. I strive to be an instrument of healing, integration, learning, social evolution, the betterment of life, through whatever work I do. Lead me, for I do not know what to do. And when I do see and understand what my next task is, give me the strength to do it purely and thoroughly, with all my heart, to serve all, awaken all, heal all, feed all. Act through me so that your intention may be fulfilled. I am your servant. Use me as you deem most fit. Let me see and know what you want for me, even if it is not always what I want for myself."

Meister Eckhart, the great Catholic mystic, said:

> In general it is the will of God that we surrender our wills. . . .
> Apart from complete surrender of the will, there is no traffic with God. . . . Yield completely to God and then be satisfied, whatever he does with his own. The only true and perfect will is the one that has been merged with the will of God, so that the man has no will of his own. . . . Relax and let God operate you and do what he will with you. The deed is his; the word is his; this birth is his;

and all you are is his, for you have surrendered self to him, with all your soul's agents and their function and even your personal nature. Then at once, God comes into your being and faculties. . . . For this birth in the soul God will and must have a pure, free, and unencumbered soul, in which there is nothing but him alone, a soul that waits for nothing and nobody but him. . . . When he finds you ready he must act, and pour into you, just as when the air is clear and pure the sun must pour into it, and may not hold back.... You need not look either here or there. He is no farther away than the door of the heart. He stands there, lingering, waiting for us to be ready and open the door and let him in. You need not call to him as if he were far away, for he waits more urgently than you for the door to be opened. You are a thousand times more necessary to him than he is to you. The opening of the door and his entry are simultaneous.[13]

## Surrender, Not Submission

Some people mistrust the idea of self-surrender, seeing it as a naive response that invites exploitation by those who would gladly exercise power over us. But surrender to the divine will doesn't necessarily mean to submit to whatever the teacher asks us to do. We have every right to ask the teacher why a particular test or acceding to a difficult request will serve our growth and wellbeing. Testing by a skillful teacher has only one goal: to free the student of ignorance, fear, unhealthy attachment, areas where the student is resistant to change. Where we sense that the teacher has other motivations, driven more by his or her own desires, then we may feel quite justified in resisting the test. Brenda, a longtime student of a teacher from India, gave the following account:

> Once I felt a very strong sexual energy emanating from my teacher toward me. It was intense. He didn't say anything, but intuitively I knew that he wanted to have sex with me, and he was checking out whether I was interested or not. I totally ignored it. I wasn't interested at all. I was a yogini, a meditator, not one of his gopis, worshipping him. That wasn't my path at all. He never bothered me again after that.

In some situations we may have to refuse to comply with a teacher's request or command, or to reject unwanted advances. And all youngsters need to be taught to say no to any older person who fondles them or asks them to take their pants down, even if it is in Swami's room. One outspoken mother told her teacher very directly, "If you ever molest my daughter, I'll come into this ashram and cut your dick off." She figured that ought to keep the Swami in line. And she meant it. Respect, gratitude, and devotion toward a teacher do not necessitate mindless acquiescence to any request a teacher may make of us. Here the advice of Swami Radha, one of the most respected female spiritual teachers of recent times, is especially pertinent:

> Disciples should not do anything that goes against their conscience. They need to use discrimination, and for female disciples that is often a stumbling-block. Women have learned to listen to their fathers, their male teachers, their professors, their male doctors, and they do not use enough discrimination. Aspirants should study and find out what is involved in spiritual life and not just race ahead looking for acceptance by a male as if the guru by virtue of his title will automatically make them spiritual.[14]

A woman named Sara told me:

> I concluded that my studying with him and receiving his blessing did not require that I become his consort. I find fulfillment of my sexual needs elsewhere, and I expect him to do so too with someone appropriate. I just wish he could openly adopt one woman into this role, instead of engaging in the kind of sneaky, surreptitious fondling that seems to have been going on in his quarters.

Unquestioning submission to requests for sexual favors, or to any other form of exploitation by a teacher, is no guarantee of accelerated progress on the path. Indeed, it may profoundly wound us and hinder our advancement in life and on the spiritual path. Our responsibility is to ask ourselves if we feel more liberated, joyous, or enlightened as a result of this experience. If not, then it is our responsibility to take appropriate action. We need not be powerless victims.

John Welwood distinguishes between submission and surrender:

> To understand the value of commitment to a genuine master, we need to distinguish between mindful surrender, which can be enlivening, and mindless submission, which is a deadening flight

from freedom. . . . For many people today, the idea of surrender implies losing intelligence or individuality to another person and taking a weak, submissive, "one down" position. True surrender, however, is never enslaving, but rather is a genuine step toward empowerment, the discovery of one's own most genuine power.... The recent critics of narcissism in our society tend to see all involvement with spiritual masters in this light, failing to distinguish between submission as a developmentally regressive retreat from maturity, and genuine surrender, which allows people to move beyond egocentricity to a fuller realization of their being. . . . With a genuine spiritual master, surrendering means presenting oneself in a completely honest, naked way, without trying to hold anything back or maintain any facade. . . . Being in the presence of a true master is a rare opportunity to let down all one's pretence, to unmask and simply be as one is.[15]

In a story that encapsulates the transformative potential of testing, a man named Karl gave this account of a test that led to thorough self-examination and enabled him to unmask in his teacher's presence:

Darshan with my teacher was so intense because he was so unpredictable. One day I approached him and he began yelling at me, cursing me, and accusing me of doing all these things I hadn't done. I said, "Guruji, no, I didn't do these things." He slapped me a couple of times hard on my back and told me to go away and come see him tomorrow. I went back to my room frightened that I had committed some terrible act, but I couldn't figure out what it was. I was very upset because I didn't know why my teacher had turned on me suddenly. I had no idea what I had done wrong. I searched myself and thought, "I know I didn't do these things he accused me of, but have I done anything else that might have hurt anyone?" I had done a thorough moral inventory when I went through A. A., but now in my mind I went through different periods of my life and I saw various instances of discord with others. I could think of a number of people I still had issues with. Later on that evening I called up some of them and talked for a long time. I felt really sorry about some of the thoughtless, insensitive things I had done. But I also felt a lot of compassion for myself. I saw how I had been motivated by fear and ignorance, lust and jealousy. And I just felt tremendous love for everyone. By the time I was finished that night I felt totally clear with everyone. I was peaceful because my conscience was clear. I felt more self-love than I ever had. And that feeling continued to the next day when I went back for darshan. I was very open and delicate because so many of my imperfections had been brought into the open. I knew my teacher might still be mad at me and start yelling again. I understood. I had many impurities that I was sure he was aware of. But I loved him, and I loved myself. In that frame of mind I came before him. He got up out of his seat and rose to embrace me. We hugged for a long time. He whispered in my ear, "Your essence is completely pure." He smiled at me with a golden warmth. And that was the last time he ever spoke to me.

Surrender is not an easy lesson to learn. Indeed, surrender can be a battleground that causes us to face all our fears and resistance. We may think we know what is best for us, but life often has different ideas. We cling tightly to our attachments and concepts, refusing to surrender, until life pushes us to the limit and we have no choice but to accept the way things are. Often we reach the point of acceptance only when we have been so thoroughly squashed by the pain of life that we feel as if it will shatter us. Yet, when we surrender in moments of suffering or disappointment, we are often met by an unexpected response—a descent of peace or a flood of inner ecstasy that seems senseless and absurd. How can we feel this way when things are so terrible? It does not make sense. When we surrender at such moments, our hearts open to the presence of an intelligence greater than ourselves.

Surrender is a threshold we are all called upon to cross sooner or later. The fruit of our surrender is serenity. We experience inner peace when we let go and allow things to be as they are, without judgment or resistance. We learn to trust the goodness of the path, coming to believe that we are being shown, through all events, a way to wholenes. We trust the unfolding of our karma and stop struggling. We are who and what and where we're supposed to be.

There is an innocence and purity in the eyes of the spiritual apprentice—who has faced the fires of testing with courage, and who now offers up the powers and talents of the self to the service of all life. The student now becomes receptive to the greatest gift the teacher has to offer: the mystery of grace.

# *Notes*

1.  A. Schimmel, *Mystical Dimensions of Islam* (Chapel Hill, NC: Univ. of North Carolina Press, 1975), p. 101.
2.  H. Guenther, *The Life and Teaching of Naropa* (New York: Oxford Univ. Press, 1963), p. 80.
3.  G. Feuerstein, *Holy Madness* (New York: Paragon House, 1991), pp. xxiii, 3, 204.
4.  R. Gale, personal communication.
5.  H. I. Khan, *The Complete Sayings of Hazrat Inayat Khan* (New Lebanon, NY: Sufi Order Publications, 1991).
6.  P. D. Ouspensky, *In Search of the Miraculous* (New York: Harcourt Brace and World, 1949) pp. 351–56. According to Kevin Langdon, a longtime student of the Gurdjieff teachings, the point of the "stop exercise" is to create favorable circumstances for self-observation, to witness ourselves in between the physical postures we ordinarily assume, and to gain greater understanding of our habitual intellectual, and emotional activities. This exercise forces a confrontation with whatever is arising in that moment.
7.  *The Science of Yoga: The Yoga Sutras of Patanjali,* translated by I. K. Taimni (Wheaton, IL: Theosophical Publishing House, 1961), pp. 142–42.
8.  *Shankara's Crest Jewel of Discrimination*, translated by S. Prabhavananda & C. Isherwood (Los Angeles: Vedanta Press, 1975), pp. 80–1.
9.  M. & J. Arguelles, *The Feminine: Spacious as the Sky* (Boston: Shambhala, 1977), p. 46.
10. L. Llalungpa, *The Life of Milarepa* (Boston: Shambhala, 1978).
11. *The Science of Yoga: The Yoga Sutras of Patanjali,* translated by I. K. Taimni (Wheaton, IL: Theosophical Publishing House, 1961), p. 127.
12. H. I. Khan, *The Complete Sayings of Hazrat Inayat Khan* (New Lebanon, NY: Sufi Order Publications, 1991).
13. M. Eckhart, "The Talks of Instruction." In *Meister Eckhart: A Modern Translation,* translated by R. B. Blakney (New York: Harper & Row, 1941), pp. 15–16, 115–17, 121–22.
14. S. Radha, "Dispelling Illusions: The Guru-Disciple Relationship," *Ascent*, Spring, 1992, p. 8.
15. J. Welwood, "On Spiritual Authority: Genuine and Counterfeit." In D. Anthony, B. Ecker, & K. Wilber (Eds.), *Spiritual Choices* (New York: Paragon House, 1987), pp. 296–97.

# Grace and Guru Yoga

The void Mind-Essence is my Guru's body;
My Guru is Dorje Chang, with the Wisdom-Body;
My Guru is Tilopa, with the Six Miraculous Powers;
My Guru is Naropa, with the Net of Myriad Spells;
My Guru is Marpa, to whom I owe the greatest debt.
They sit ever upon my head as my glory;
If you have a pair of clear and sincere eyes
You will see them as real Buddhas.
If with sincerity and faith you pray to them,
The rain of grace will ever fall upon you,
If you offer practice and devotion,
The treasury of Accomplishments will be opened to you.
*The Hundred Thousand Songs of Milarepa* [1]

At a certain stage, the relationship between student and teacher ceases to be a relationship of instruction between two individuals. As the student opens to meet the enlightened mind of the guide, he or she has glimpses of expanded consciousness. By inwardly merging with the teacher's awareness through internal attunement, the student has an experience best described as sacred—profoundly peaceful, holy, or numinous. In the company of the guide, a spiritual presence reveals itself, so that the student now feels tangibly, if mysteriously, blessed. And while the student cannot definitively explain or comprehend the mechanism by which this self-disclosure of the Sacred occurs, intuitively it seems clear that the teacher is the catalyst and agency of the experience. Now awareness of the all-pervasive Spirit or divine presence is conveyed and revealed through the teacher's contagious influence. Georg Feuerstein writes:

The enlightened teacher communicates Shiva-Shakti or Consciousness-Power, by his or her mere existence. He or she is in fact not different from that Reality because he or she no longer suffers from the presumption of being a finite being with a body and mind that is ultimately separate from other beings. An enlightened person lives as, and out of, the fullness of the single Reality. Therefore, his or her sheer presence has transformative power, which is of advantage to those who can attune themselves to it. . . . The teacher's communication of that which is Real has a purifying effect on the disciple who receives this spiritual transmission. And that is its whole purpose. The teacher's transmission can have very different effects in the disciple. It can lead to utterly blissful states or violent emotional reactivity, feelings of well-being or episodes of illness. Regardless of the effects, the primary function of spiritual transmission is to intensify the disciple's whole life.[2]

It is because of this transformative influence that all schools of yoga in India recommend that a spiritual aspirant seek out the company (*satsang*) of an illumined being who rests constantly in an expanded state of consciousness.

In the company of the God-realized master, the practitioner is continuously exposed to the realizer's spiritualized body-mind, and by way of "contagion" his own physical and psychical being is gradually transformed. . . . For this spontaneous process to be truly effective, the disciple must consciously cooperate with his guru. He accomplishes this by making the teacher his focus of attention. This is the great principle of sat-sanga. The word means literally "company of the True" or "relationship to the Real." Sat-sanga is the supreme means of liberation in guru-yoga. And since the guru has from ancient times been deemed essential to yogic practice, sat-sanga is at the core of all schools of Yoga. It would not be wrong to say that all Yoga is guru-yoga.[3]

## Gifts of Spirit

As a consequence of contact with a teacher we may experience a descent of peace or spiritual power. As we are purified, and as our tranquility deepens through meditation, then the *guru tattva*, the principle of revelation of grace, begins to operate with greater intensity. At this stage of spiritual apprenticeship we experience mysterious but tangible gifts of Spirit. These experiences inspire us, fill us with devotion to the teacher, and strengthen our commitment to seek enlightenment.

Such experiences are more likely to occur if we are under the influence of a great teacher, not an ordinary one. Indeed, one way we discern that we have truly found an awakened teacher is as a consequence of experiences of grace, subtle guidance, and inner blessings. Our subjective experience is that a being who serves as a conduit of grace has somehow transcended ordinary human limitations, yielded to the will of the universe, and become a lightning rod of Spirit.

Now we are initiated into a great mystery, which is that as we actively seek God, the ground of existence, formless source-consciousness—through devotion, one-pointed attention, and protracted struggle to diminish the power of competing desires—then we meet a response, Spirit's answer to our longing, the self-disclosure or revelation of the divine presence. This is the mystery of grace. Let me recount a personal experience to illustrate this further.

## Unfathomable Grace

There is a day celebrated every year in India called Guru Purnima, which is traditionally a day of celebration akin to our Mother's Day, except that its purpose is to honor the guru. It is said traditionally that on Guru Purnima the guru showers blessings on all devotees. In the summer of 1976, I took a long bus ride to visit my teacher for this occasion. However, on this Guru Purnima I had a very unpleasant reaction to the ashram and the thousand or so other visitors and residents who were present. I was preoccupied with various personal problems and wanted some attention from my teacher. Instead, Muktananda ignored me all day, and I began to wonder why I had even bothered to come.

Later that evening I returned home to New York City, several hours' drive from the ashram. I went to bed, sadly bemoaning the fact that no blessings had been showered on me. I slept soundly for several hours. Then at about three a.m. I awoke suddenly, sensing a presence hovering above me that I can only describe as a cloud of bliss. A soft but powerful current of energy descended into my body, electrifying every cell. For about twenty seconds I was bathed in ecstasy. All I could do was to lovingly receive this visitation of the sacred, the numinous Spirit, the holy. I was completely in awe. Then, suddenly, the energy vanished.

In the weeks that followed I pondered this experience constantly, trying to figure out what had happened as well as how to bring it back! Some weeks later, I traveled to visit my teacher again. The day I arrived, he strode into a room where many hundreds of students were seated. When he sat down, he looked straight at me and said, "The grace of the guru is truly unfathomable!" He lifted up his sunglasses so his eyes were visible like bright suns, and looked directly at me for several long moments. His statement had deep significance for me, for I realized I could never fathom the mysterious energy that had visited me by any act of conceptualization. I came to understand that, having received such a gift of grace, the appropriate response is faith and continuing receptivity. Rather than trying to explain this experience with my rational mind, I was being instructed to live in devotion—not to a person, but to that energy or presence that revealed itself on that summer night. I began to understand that the true guru is not the physical person of the teacher but rather the agency for the bestowal of grace. I saw that my task was to make myself, and my life, a vessel worthy of holding further infusions of that ecstatic presence.

I was profoundly moved by this experience and filled with gratitude. My teacher had revealed the presence of the great mystery, the invisible Beloved. It was my personal burning bush episode, a moment when gentle lightning struck and it had absolutely nothing to do with my volition or will. There is a stage of evolution where we feel ourselves existing in relationship to a transcendent Other that is infinite and undefinable. For me, this was that moment.

When this infusion of grace occurred I had just finished a course in religious studies in which I had read a little book called *The Idea of the Holy*, by Rudolph Otto. Contemplating my experience, I realized that I had just encountered what Otto called the holy, the numinous:

> The numinous is . . . felt as objective and outside the self. . . . [To describe the numinous], there is only one appropriate expression, *mysterium tremendum*. The feeling of it may at times come sweeping like a gentle tide, pervading the mind with a tranquil mood of deepest worship. It may pass over into a more set and lasting attitude of the soul, continuing, as it were, thrillingly vi-

126

brant and resonant, until at last it dies away and the soul resumes its "profane," non-religious mood of everday experience. It may burst in sudden eruption up from the depths of the soul with spasms and convulsions, or lead to the strangest excitements, to intoxicated frenzy, to transport, and to ecstasy. . . . It may become the hushed, trembling, and speechless humility of the creature in the presence of—whom or what? In the presence of that which is a *mystery* inexpressible and above all creatures. . . . Conceptually, *mysterium* denotes merely that which is hidden and esoteric, that which is beyond conception or understanding, extraordinary and unfamiliar.[4]

In its appearance as the *tremendum*, the numinous has the characteristics of *awefulness*, *overpoweringness*, and *urgency*. The experience of the divine presence induces awe and fear. And it is overpowering, having the qualities of "might, power, absolute overpoweringness.... [T] here is the feeling of one's own submergence, of being but 'dust and ashes' and nothingness. And this forms the numinous raw material for the feeling of religious humility."[5] As *mysterium*, the numinous is felt to be wholly Other, inducing "blank wonder, an astonishment that strikes us dumb, amazement absolute."[6] The mysterium also has the quality of fascination, entrancing us, and transporting us into "dizzy intoxication."[7]

Otto says that the experience of the numinous also has the qualities of energy, vitality, passion, will, force, movement, excitement, activity, and impetus. The sudden infusion of numinous power into our bodies ignites internal sparks of life-force, the heat of the awakening kundalini, the heaving and writhing internal serpentine movements of self-liberating consciousness, bursting our small vessels and returning to its inevitable freedom. The aspirant who receives this infusion of the light is visibly affected, becoming filled with awe and gratitude, and alive with the reverberations of this visitation. Often inspired creativity, non-ordinary states of consciousness, or metanormal capacities begin to manifest in one who has had such a numinous encounter.

## Grace and Self-effort

The student who experiences the bestowal of grace and the eruption of numinous Spirit, may now begin to wonder about the relationship between grace and self-effort in contemplative practice. Is the experience a result of our effort, or is it totally a gift, completely independent of one's efforts and strivings? Did my longing for the experience of the great Mystery have any relationship to its occurence? A model that I have found useful in sorting out these issues was set forth by sociologist of religion Dick Anthony, who identified two major approaches to spiritual growth.[8] One is what he calls a *charismatic* approach, in which the teacher is viewed as a source of power, wisdom, or grace that can be transmitted to the student, who only need be open to receive it. The second approach is what he calls a *technical* orientation to inner growth, in which practicing contemplative techniques is thought to lead directly to illumination and enlightenment, without requiring a teacher's grace or subtle influence.[9] In a technical approach, the teacher's job is simply to instruct the student in methods such as prayer, meditation, or yoga. After that, it is up to the student to practice these techniques with discipline and intensity.

Those who favor a charismatic approach often contend that no genuine spiritual advancement is possible through a purely technical approach, that spiritual practices only gain the power to lead the aspirant toward enlightenment or Self-realization because of the investiture of energy bestowed when an enlightened teacher initiates the student. Those who favor a technical approach contend that a charismatic emphasis gives the teacher too much power and responsibility for the student's growth, and also makes the student vulnerable to flaws in the teacher's character. If the teacher is viewed as the necessary agent of transformation, then the spiritual apprentice's progress on the path may be severely hindered if the teacher proves to be an impure or imperfect vehicle for the transmission of truth.[10] In the technical approach progress is solely dependent on the student's effort in practicing techniques of self-transformation such as meditation or breathwork. There is no external agency that assists.

The technical, technique-oriented approach to spiritual growth is founded in the awareness that the teacher's blessings will not do it all. To grow toward enlightenment takes sustained effort as well as grace. Ultimately we learn to incorporate both surrender and self-effort in our quest for inner freedom. Right effort is that which enables us to abide in enlightened awareness. We actively focus the mind and practice disidentification from the ever-changing contents of thoughts, emotions, physical sensations, desires, and attachments. We begin to rest naturally in our real nature, as Consciousness, the silent witness, unconditioned, mindful awareness. We abide in, and as, the field of consciousness itself—blissful, vast as space. The goal of the spiritual path—transcendence of the false sense of self and the realization of the Self—is attained by recognizing the oneness of one's own mind with all-pervasive Consciousness. A teacher can show us the way, teach us the doctrine, and embody the enlightened state, but ultimately we stabilize ourselves in this state through our own effort and spiritual practice.

According to Swami Lakshmanjoo, a great teacher of Kashmir Shaivism, liberation comes when "the grace of Lord Shiva is showered on you, or when your God consciousness is liberated by the vibrating force of the teachings of your master." However, Swami Lakshmanjoo explains that the deeper stages of meditation "can only be accomplished through one's will and concentration."

> Even the Guru's grace will not help a seeker unless he is determined and fully devoted to maintaining awareness and concentration. . . . The spiritual aspirant who waivers and becomes disturbed gains nothing. . . . In the *Tantraloka* it states that if the master is elevated, and if the disciple is endowed with complete qualifications, then the master can assist his disciple. But on the other hand, if the disciple is not really qualified, then the master cannot properly help or elevate him. [11]

The teacher can serve as an important catalyst for the accelerated spiritual evolution of the student, and is to be revered and honored for revealing a path to truth. But the teacher's assistance will be of no benefit if the student does not strive intensely to practice meditation, yoga, or other disciplines. Quieting down the mind by practicing meditation reveals our original and essential nature, the clear mind, the God within us. In Buddhist terms, self-purification through meditation and prayer allows our intrinsic clarity and spacious awareness to awaken—our Buddha nature. Active self-purification centers us and refines our awareness so that we become receptive to mysterious inner blessings. The more sincere effort we make, the more grace flows toward us—not only from our own teacher, but also from all the saints and Buddhas and siddhas. Self-effort and receptivity to grace are both necessary and are eternally wedded on the path of the spiritual apprentice.

The disciple's dedication to spiritual practice is like a magnet that draws the enlightening influence of a great teacher and of formless Spirit. As the aspirant becomes established in the discipline of abiding as the Self, or unconditioned awareness, an invisible conduit opens that puts the disciple in contact with a universal power. One-pointed pursuit of liberation through meditation and Self-inquiry, coupled with an attitude of internal receptivity, elicits the bestowal of grace, the self-disclosure of the divine.[12]

Traditions vary in the degree of emphasis they place on these two poles of self-effort and grace. Some lineages such as Zen Buddhism downplay the emphasis on receiving grace and blessings. In Zen it is understood that the teacher can show us the way, but we must travel this road on our own, by painstakingly purifying our minds (through sitting meditation) and our actions (by adhering to precepts and codes of moral conduct), or through intense effort to grasp the meaning of a koan. Zen is not a devotional path and features no deities. Self-effort is essential to progress.

In contrast, the mystery of grace is a central feature of the Christian faith. Catholics believe that the spirit of Christ flows down through the Pope to the cardinals, bishops, and priests and that this grace is then dispensed down to the faithful through the sacraments, especially Baptism and the Eucharist. The symbolism of these rites is worth examining briefly. According to Mircea Eliade:

> [T]he Eucharist is reminiscent of the cult agapes practiced in Mediterranean antiquity, especially in the Mystery religions. Their goal was the consecration, and hence the salvation, of the participants through communion with a divinity. . . . The convergence with the Christian rite is significant; it illustrates the hope . . . of a mystical identification with the divinity. . . . Every believer accomplishes mystical union with Christ through the sacrament of baptism. . . . Baptism not only insures the new life of the believer but accomplishes his transformation into a member of the mystical body of Christ.[13]

The language of these rites is filled with themes of incorporation: In Baptism, the individual is absorbed into the body of the church, while through the Eucharist, the individual symbolically takes Christ into his or her own body. The passage just cited evokes themes that are pertinent to spiritual apprentices from every religious and spiritual background: the longing to merge with, or experience full identification with a spiritual teacher, to take the teacher inside, to absorb the teacher, and to make oneself like the teacher. We long to experience oneness with a great teacher who is a conduit for grace, and to become the enlightened awareness that the teacher *is*. We want to awaken in ourselves the same radiance, refined character, and serene wisdom. In this stage of spiritual apprenticeship we experience mystical identity with the teacher, who embodies the enlightened state, and who is for us literally the way to liberation.

## *The Guru Is One's Own Mind*

As the psychic tie between teacher and disciple grows stronger, we sense that the teacher knows us fully and witnesses our thoughts and actions. We sense that our spiritual teacher is very close to us, recognizes our soul, and is familiar with our inner thoughts and feelings. Think for a moment of the story of the sheikh with the lamb's bladder recounted earlier, in which the teacher responded to the student's innermost thoughts and longings. The ability of the spiritual teacher to examine the essential character of the aspirant is much described in Sufi texts:

> [T]hey tell about the *firasa*, "cardiognosia" (soul-reading), of a master. "Beware of the *firasa* [discernment] of the faithful," it was said, "for he sees by God's light." Innumerable stories are told about a sheikh's insight into a disciple's heart; he was able to tell his secret wishes, hopes, and dislikes, to understand signs of spiritual pride or hypocrisy the very moment the [student] entered his presence.[14]

Muktananda showed me many times that he had access to my innermost thoughts and emotions. For example, when I was eighteen years old, I spent several months living in one of his ashrams (spiritual communities) in upstate New York. One day I had an argument with my parents on the telephone. They thought I had been brainwashed and abducted into a dangerous cult, and they insisted that I leave the ashram and return home. I refused adamantly. I told no one about this incident. Later that afternoon, Muktananda entered a room where over eight hundred people were seated. I was sitting a good distance from him and off to his side, well out of his immediate line of sight. He sat down and began to speak, saying, "There was once a young man who loved to meditate. His parents were scientists and skeptics and told him that he was a fool to waste his time meditating. But the young man was very intelligent and handled the situation very well, not like these young men these days, who when they get to be eighteen years old start telling their parents to shut up and go away and not bother them!" Then Baba turned in his seat and gave me his most stone-faced, Shiva-like stare. He was intense!

Two years later I was staying in Muktananda's ashram in Ganeshpuri, India. After several years of austerity and a pure lifestyle, I began to experience a resurgence of old desires. One afternoon I lay on my bed in the dormitory fantasizing about smoking grass with a young woman I was attracted to back at home. The following day I gathered up my courage and got on line to ask Baba a question about an unrelated matter. There was a man in front of me on the line who was visibly dazed and disoriented. It turned out that he was a diabetic who was not taking his insulin shots, and that this accounted for his strange demeanor. But before this fact was discovered Baba asked him repeatedly if he had been taking any drugs. "Did you smoke hashish or take *bhang* in town?" he asked the man. Then Baba looked at me and told me to look through the man's shoulder bag. "See if there are any drugs in there," he said. I didn't find anything in the bag. A few minutes later, after he had answered my other questions, Baba pointed his finger at me and said, "And don't chase drugs!" I felt there was no place to hide, no place where he did not inwardly see me and know what was in my heart.

Swami Muktananda had reached a level of consciousness where he knew what I thought, felt, or experienced because he was one with my own Mind. He had transcended identification with the individual body, thoughts, and feelings, and was established in the state of the Self, which is the root of every mind—the universal consciousness from which individual consciousness springs. Through these experiences, I realized that I am always seen by the Guru, who is none other than the God within me. As Ramana Maharshi used to say, "Guru, God, and Self are one." Having my teacher demonstrate knowledge of my inner life gave me an enduring sense that I am always seen in the eyes of Spirit. When I turn my mind and heart within, I feel that the current of grace is open, and that my prayers are heard and often meet with an instantaneous response, a wave of peace. Moreover, realizing the oneness of the guru with the Self within me supersedes the fact that the personality of my teacher may have imperfections.

## Psychic Attunement of Teacher and Student

Spiritual apprenticeship engages us in a relationship not just with a person who instructs us but with a presence that transforms us. The teacher is not just a teacher, because that implies someone separate from ourselves teaching us something that we do not know—when in truth, the teacher embodies that fullness of awareness that is our *own* nature. Through deep meditation, the spiritual apprentice forges an inner link with the teacher, proceeding farther into the space where student and teacher both share one consciousness. Boundaries between the student and teacher now become more fluid.

In the Sufi tradition of spiritual instruction it is recognized that spiritual guidance is an alchemical process that occurs through a blending or interpenetration of psychic boundaries. The consciousness of the student and teacher meet in inner space where ultimately there is no separation. This interior contact opens both teacher and student to deeper expansion into Spirit. In the early stages of Sufi training, the student listens to the teacher's words, reflects on them, recognizes their truth, and assimilates them by practicing these teachings. Later, the student experiences a state known as *fana fi' sheikh* ("annihilation in the master"), which is often described as a state of transcendence of the ego and merger with the consciousness of the teacher. Richard Gale explains:

> The real point here, more than a sense of union with the teacher, is to experience the *stage* of the teacher. You don't deify the teacher. It's more the *maqam*, the station of a teacher, that level the teacher is stable in. There are states of consciousness that can be broader than our *maqam*, states of expansion, ecstasies of different levels. But the *maqam* is where the teacher is stabilized in awareness. We are concerned with that level the teacher is at, and what one is trying to do is to discover oneself in that station.

> So it is really annihilation in the station where the teacher is sta-
> bilized.[15]

A notable feature of Sufi spiritual instruction is that not only do students attune their awareness to that of the teacher, but the teacher also consciously attunes to the student in meditation in order to vibrationally uplift the aspirant on inner planes. Through these meditations, the teacher becomes deeply familiar with the character and evolutionary stage of the student, prescribes specific practices to aid the student's unfolding, and closely supervises these practices. The teacher's attunement to the student implies that the teacher accepts a solemn responsibility for the student, and makes conscious efforts on behalf of the student's inner freedom. Annamarie Schimmel writes:

> The master watches every moment of the disciple's spiritual growth;
> he watches him particularly during the forty-day period of medi-
> tation that became, very early, a regular institution in the Sufi path....
> The sheikh interprets the murid's dreams and visions, reads his
> thoughts, and thus follows every movement of his conscious and
> subconscious life.... The strong relationship between sheikh and
> *murid* is exemplified in the technique of *tawajjuh*, concentration
> upon the sheikh.... One speaks in Turkish of *rabita kurmak*, "to
> establish a tie" between master and disciple. The sheikh, too, would
> practice *tawajjuh* and thus "enter the door of the disciple's heart"
> to watch him and to guard him every moment.[16]

The spiritual apprenctice comes to feel this inner tie more and more reliably, and feels the teacher subtly protecting and guiding from within. As this psychic connection with the teacher grows, the student's conscious invocation of the teacher's image and presence becomes the foundation of a most transformative practice.

## Meditation on the Teacher's Form

The student can use the potent influence of an enlightened being as a means of transformation through meditations involving visualization of, and inner union with, the teacher. According to the Yoga Sutras (I.37), a yogi can attain steadiness of mind by fixing his or her attention on a being of purity who is free of attachment.[17]

Because of his realization, the guru is considered to be an embodiment of the divine itself. This "deification" of the God-realized master must not be misunderstood. He is not God in any exclusive sense. He is, rather, thought to be coessential with the transcendental Reality. That is to say, he has abrogated the ordinary person's misidentification with a particular body-mind. He abides purely as the transcendental Identity of all beings and things.[18]

In his book *Play of Consciousness,* Swami Muktananda wrote a detailed account of this practice.[19] He described how he focused all of his attention on his guru Nityananda, mentally installing the guru inside his own body—until he began to identify with him fully. He described how practicing this meditation on the guru's form and inner state he began to act, feel, and perceive as his guru did. Through meditation on the teacher's expanded, joyful condition, he said, the student becomes one with the teacher and achieves the same state of consciousness. The practitioner of guru yoga gazes at the teacher's physical form, meditates on a picture of a beloved spiritual master, or inwardly invokes mental images of the teacher, and imagines seeing the world through the teacher's eyes and meditating, as the teacher does, on the bliss of pure consciousness. In this manner, the aspirant feels the living presence of the teacher within.

The awakened teacher is, in truth, one's own Self, and not separate from one's own consciousness. Meditation upon the teacher enables us to absorb the teacher's state of consciousness and to identify with it fully. Some Western psychologists might view such a practice of meditation on the guru as a dangerous exercise in dissociation, or regressive dependency on an idealized figure. Yet such a practice is explicitly described in a number of traditions and prescribed as a means of awakening. For example, in Sufism students are transformed by learning to observe enlightened qualities—like mercy, radiant joy, and patience—in the teacher and consciously absorbing these qualities into themselves. Sufi teacher Atum Kane writes:

> This stage is centered upon incorporating archetypes and qualities into one's personality. . . . [W]hile contemplating the power that moves the universe, you awaken that same power in yourself. The use of *mantras* or *wazifa* promotes the embodiment of a quality in the personality by repeating the sounds which corre-

spond with its vibrational frequency. Perhaps the most valuable
meditation in this vein is that of entering into the consciousness
of a great human being who manifests a particular quality to a
high degree of perfection. The quality ceases to be an abstraction
and one discovers how it can function in a person. The blending
of two opposite qualities is very difficult, but can be experienced
by meditating upon the sovereignty and humility found in Christ
or the combination of detachment and compassion present in
Buddha. Reflecting [on] the lives of such beings shows how these
qualities functioned in very concrete situations, and can be related to the problems one faces. . . . The key meditation [at this
stage] is that of the Ideal Being. Creative imagination inspired by
one's longing for an ideal forms a being in whom one can discover one's vision of perfection in human form.[20]

In this practice, the path to enlightenment is to consciously identify
with a person who has already attained that state, an awakened being
who embodies and models all enlightened qualities. If we aspire to become a great businessperson and closely observe the conduct, habits,
and acumen of a successful businessperson, we are likely to become
like this person. If we wish to become a great musician or tennis player,
we fix our minds on those who have achieved greatness in these fields,
closely observing their technique. Then we practice and imitate as best
we can. So it is if we wish to become an enlightened, serene, awakened
being. We find someone who has attained this stature, contemplate this
person's qualities of freedom, illumination, and joy, and strive to internalize them. We observe and meditate upon the teacher's state of consciousness until it becomes our own. There is no more direct way to
freedom. Invoking internal images of the teacher, we merge our minds
into the clear light of the Atman Sun.

While I cannot explain the mechanism by which this occurs, the
practice of meditating on an enlightened teacher seems to magnetize
the power of grace that flows through such a being so that it enters the
student and begins to transform the latter's consciousness. Indeed, we
start to perceive the guru not just as an individual person who is physically present, but as a powerful energy that lifts us up, that gives us
inner wings, that allows our spirit to take flight. The guru is that which
comes to meet our aspiration and reveals the light within us. With continuing experience of this mysterious energy of blessing and guidance,

we come to realize that we have become disciples not just of a human teacher, but of the grace-bestowing power of formless Spirit. Increasingly, we become disciples of the Light.

When I arrived at the Ganeshpuri, India ashram in May 1978, I gave myself wholeheartedly to the discipline of work, chanting, and meditation. I contemplated something Muktananda often said, which was that as the student attunes to the teacher's enlightened awareness, the grace of the divine begins to flow effortlessly to that student. Quite spontaneously I began to practice guru yoga, the meditation on the guru's form. After quieting down my mind in meditation, I mentally visualized Muktananda, feeling that I was seeing through his eyes, walking in his body, laughing with his laughter, filled with the same ecstasy and joy I saw in his eyes. This practice was extremely potent for me. For days I walked around ecstatic, expanded, and in love with the Atman in everyone. In meditation, both thought and breath were suspended for long periods. I witnessed waves of thoughts and emotions but was untouched by them, as I merged into expansive and thought-free awareness, serene and unwavering. There was only consciousness, pulsating everywhere, alive and vibrant in all beings. I experienced my own presence as the peaceful witness.

For several weeks I practiced emptying myself of all but God. I quietly repeated the mantra *So'ham*, which means "I am that, I am consciousness, pure awareness." I tried to remain immersed in Self-awareness while rising in the morning, walking, eating, working, talking, and meditating. I maintained this state for several weeks, continuing the practice of inner identification with the guru. A deep peace filled up the space where before I had experienced only anxiety and agitation.

One day, I sat in Baba's courtyard, gazing at him while also resting in meditation. He wasn't doing anything special, but his very presence conveyed power. He sat reading the newspaper and making frequent use of an orange plastic back-scratcher that he kept near his seat. As devotees came before him, I watched him blissfully greet everyone as one and the same Being, as vibrations of the divine presence. Then he sat silently in a timeless emptiness. I focused on him while simultaneously recognizing him as my own Self. Suddenly, Muktananda looked me over and seemed to thoroughly examine my state of consciousness. His gaze was full of light. Our eyes met in a place of silent recognition of our oneness. My heart felt like liquid and expanded outward to be one with him. He looked at me with great love, nodded his head several times, and said "*Bahut achha*. Very good." For days afterward I was exultant as I recalled, over and over again, this meeting of minds with my teacher. It was a moment I will always remember.

## Perils and Promise of Guru Yoga

There are those who will say that it is courting disaster to imagine ourselves merging as we gaze into some exalted guru's eyes. It is true: The practice of merging inwardly with a teacher could make us vulnerable to loss of boundaries and discrimination. Merging with the teacher can appear in healthy or unhealthy forms, as I will discuss at length later on. Guru yoga can be a dangerous practice for those without an adequately differentiated sense of self, who may be receptive to the teacher's magnetism yet unable to perceive the teacher's imperfections of character. But identification with the teacher's enlightened mind does not require that we relinquish our own capacity for discrimination. We may cease to invoke the presence of a teacher whose actions do not seem enlightened. And inward merger with the teacher is not the same as inviting the teacher to violate our boundaries.

In optimal psychological health, our boundaries and sense of self are both resilient and fluid, well differentiated, yet fully transparent to the light of Being. Ideally, we maintain a clear sense of who we are as individuals, while also becoming established in dimensions of our being that are universal and transpersonal. Meditation on the enlightened presence of a great teacher can be one way to contact this transpersonal dimension of existence. We have had time to observe the teacher's character and have come to trust the teacher's intention. Now we allow ourselves to absorb and identify with the teacher's awakened consciousness, to perceive the light that shines in the teacher's eyes, and to drink it in without paranoia or fear of exploitation. With this attitude we reverently observe the teacher.

To deepen my understanding of guru yoga I have found it helpful to consider the distinction, articulated by Lama Govinda, between the Hindu concept of *shakti* (power) and the Buddhist concept of *prajna* (wisdom):

The concept of *Sakti*, of divine *power*, of the creative female aspect of the highest God (*Siva*) or his emanations does not play any role in Buddhism. While in the Hindu Tantras the concept of power (*sakti*) forms the focus of interest, the central idea of Tantric Buddism is *prajna*: knowledge, wisdom. To the Buddhist *sakti* is *maya*, the very power that creates illusion, from which only *prajna* can liberate us. It is therefore not the aim of the Buddhist to acquire power, or to join himself to the powers of the universe, either to become their instrument or to become their master, but, on the contrary, he tries to free himself from those powers, which since aeons kept him a prisoner of *samsara*. . . . The attitude of the Hindu Tantras is quite different. . . "United with the *Sakti*, be full of power," says the *Kulacudamani-Tantra*. "From the union of *Siva* and *Sakti* the world is created." The Buddhist, however, does not want the creation and unfoldment of the world, but the coming back to the uncreated, unformed state of *sunyata*, from which all creation proceeds. . . . The becoming conscious of this *sunyata* is *prajna*: highest knowledge. The realization of this highest knowledge in life is enlightenment, i.e., if *prajna* (or *sunyata*), the passive, all-embracing female principle, from which everything proceeds and into which everything recedes, is united with the dynamic male principle of active universal love and compassion, . . . then perfect Buddhahood is attained.[21]

In the context of Hindu yoga, meditation on the enlightened spiritual teacher sometimes turns into an attempt to "suck shakti" from the teacher, who is seen as emanating "rays" of power that can be absorbed by devotees. The student can become addicted to the teacher's shakti, and feel weak and diminished without periodic infusions of this power. A dependency on the magnetic power of the master may be created. In Buddhism, however, prajna is emphasized; thus, the Buddhist approach to guru yoga stresses the practitioner's identity with the teacher's wisdom mind. It is not a question of absorbing shakti from the teacher. We are not seeking power through our practices. We seek wisdom and compassion. These qualities awaken in us as we contemplate the mind of the enlightened ones. Let us look at the Buddhist practice of guru yoga more closely.

## *Tibetan Guru Yoga*

The practice of meditation upon an enlightened being is strongly emphasized in Tibetan Buddhism, where guru yoga is considered one of the essential practices that leads to inner awakening. In this practice, the aspirant invokes, supplicates, and meditates upon the illumined Buddha Padmasambhava, Guru Rinpoche—the teacher who established Buddhist teachings in Tibet, the Buddha whom Guatama Buddha had predicted would be even greater than himself.

> Guru Rinpoche is the lord or protector of all sentient beings because all turn to him for refuge. . . . Beings afflicted by poisonous emotions and accumulated karma who turn their minds toward him will receive his compassion and his blessings.[22]

By examining Tibetan Buddhist guru yoga in detail we will see how meditation on the qualities of an awakened being can be a potent means of transformation for the spiritual apprentice. In perhaps the clearest exposition of guru yoga ever written, *The Wish Fulfilling Tree*, the venerable Lama Dilgo Khyentse Rinpoche states:

> Guru yoga, the union with the nature of the guru, forms the foundation for all practices, and there are many different techniques for its practice. . . . There are outer, inner, secret, and most secret methods. . . . The outer method . . . is to visualize the guru dwelling above our head and to pray to him ardently with fierce devotion. The inner method is to realize . . . that our own body, speech, and mind are inseparable from the wisdom body, speech, and mind of the guru. . . . The secret method is to meditate upon the guru in his *sambhogakaya* form, the body of divine enjoyment. The most secret method introduces us to the natural state of awareness. . . . On the absolute level, the teacher is one with the very nature of our own mind, which is itself the essence of Buddhahood.[23]

Khyentse Rinpoche explains the stages of guru yoga as follows: We begin with visualizations of a pure Buddha field and of a vast assembly of yogis and Buddhas; and of Guru Rinpoche above our heads, dressed in elaborate garb, wearing a lotus crown. We visualize ourselves as his consort, Yeshe Sogyal, fully devoted to Guru Rinpoche and able to receive his teachings and his stream of blessings. Then, we offer the Supplication and Prayer with Seven Branches:

1) *Prostration* to Guru Rinpoche, the antidote to pride. 2) *Physical offering* of water bowls, flowers, incense, lamps, and food, as an antidote to greed and miserliness; and *mental offerings* of whatever we cherish most, including our own body, spouse, property, and money. 3) *Confession of all negative actions* of body (killing, stealing, sexual misconduct), speech (lies, gossip, slandering others, angry and hurtful words), and mind (envy, wish to harm others, adherence to false views) that hinder progress toward enlightenment. 4) *Rejoicing in virtue*, finding joy in the accumulation of merit by others, without envy or attachment—the antidote for jealousy and hatred. The practitioner cultivates positive actions (through prostrations, circumambulations of sacred sites, and offerings to the community of practitioners) and *samadhi*, one-pointed awareness of the absolute. 5) *Requesting the turning of the wheel of dharma*, the antidote for ignorance. The aspirant requests teachings and rejoices when the teacher gives them. One's own teacher is identified with Guru Rinpoche. 6) *Requesting the teacher to stay in this world* until all sentient beings have been rescued from the wheel of samsaric existence. 7) *Dedicating the merit of the practice* to the benefit of all sentient beings, that they might attain liberation.

At the subtlest level of guru yoga practice, the practitioner visualizes himself or herself as a yidam deity, realizing that "one's body, speech, and mind have always been inseparable from the body, speech, and mind of Guru Rinpoche."[24] Thus, the essence of the practice is to generate oneself as a deity so that Guru Rinpoche's mind is recognized to be "undifferentiable from your own."[25] Buddhist philosopher and psychologist Rick Amaro, a long-time practitioner of guru yoga, explained the significance of this practice to me as follows:

> In guru yoga you're fundamentally generating devotion to the teacher's mind as phenomenal reality, the world of appearance. The Buddhist *mahamudra* or *dzogchen* level of understanding is that the world as it appears is the teacher, and is your own mind, inseparable. There's not one hair's breadth difference between the phenomenal world and my mind. The awareness dawns that I am the phenomenal field of presence, beneath the appearance-awareness distinction. Buddhists say that awareness is inseparable from appearance. And vice versa.[26] But beneath the distinction between appearance and awareness is the field of presence. Guru Rinpoche *is* the field of presence, which is also one's own Bud-

dha nature. We supplicate him in the practice of guru yoga to inhabit this field of presence fully, so we can welcome the world as our own mind and relate to it with friendliness and compassion without distinction. Then we leap into space fully, and overcome the primordial fear of space that inhibits us from opening to the world. We become more fearless with space, and recognize that our own mind is inseparable from space. Further, we recognize that space is *luminous*. Recognizing this luminosity of space-awareness awakens in us openness, clarity, and wonder. So by supplicating Guru Rinpoche we supplicate our own *dharmakaya* mind, our original, primordially pure awareness.

The significance of the figure of Guru Rinpoche deepens with further contemplation. According to Chogyam Trungpa, Padmasambhava, who first appeared as a child on a lotus flower in the center of a lake, represents our "primordial innocence," a "fresh and sparkling" quality of awakeness in which there is no duality; he is the symbol of a playful, exploratory approach to life that is open to miraculous events, including a sudden flash of enlightenment.[27] Padmasambhava represents "complete and total openness that makes us able to transcend hope and fear. With this openness we relate to things as they are rather than as we would like them to be. That basic sanity, that approach transcending hope and fear is the attitude of enlightenment."[28] Trungpa also finds rich symbolism in Padmasambhava's efforts to introduce highly complex Indian Buddhist doctrines to the somewhat simpler, agrarian population of Tibet in the eighth century. The perspective of Padmasambhava "is not the point of view of sentient beings trying to attain enlightenment, but the point of view of an enlightened person trying to relate with sentient beings. . . . The approach here is to recognize oneself as being a Buddha already."[29]

In guru yoga, we view the figure of Guru Rinpoche, or our own beloved teacher, as the living Buddha, the embodiment of fully expanded consciousness. Contemplating the qualities of such a being, we ourselves become Buddha, an awake Being. And the mysterious presence that revealed itself to us earlier, which was experienced as existentially Other, and greater than ourselves, is now recognized to be our own nature—the radiance of what we already are. Attuning to the teacher's wisdom mind, the spiritual apprentice finds a doorway to inner freedom, and reaches out to join the heart of the infinite.

# *Notes*

1. *The Hundred Thousand Songs of Milarepa*, translated by G. C. C. Chang (New York: Harper & Row, 1962 ) pp. 158–59.

2. L. Sannella, *The Kundalini Experience* (Lower Lake, CA: Integral Publishing, 1987), pp. 123–24.

3. G. Feuerstein, *Yoga: The Technology of Ecstasy* (Los Angeles: Jeremy Tarcher, 1989), p. 25.

4. R. Otto, *The Idea of the Holy* (New York: Oxford University Press, 1950), pp. 11–13.

5. Ibid., p. 20.

6. Ibid., p. 26.

7. Ibid., p. 31.

8. D. Anthony, "The Anthony Typology: A Framework for Assessing Spiritual and Consciousness Groups." In D. Anthony, B. Ecker, & K. Wilber (Eds.), *Spiritual Choices* (New York: Paragon House, 1987), pp. 82 ff.

9. Separation from a teacher with a technical orientation is usually somewhat less problematic than with a charismatic teacher. The charismatic teacher is viewed as essential to the evolution of the student, whereas in the technical approach, the student is believed to reap benefit from the techniques alone, since these are seen as the essential source of transformation.

10. D. Anthony, "The Anthony Typology: A Framework for Assessing Spiritual and Consciousness Groups." In D. Anthony, B. Ecker, & K. Wilber (Eds.), *Spiritual Choices* (New York: Paragon House, 1987), pp. 82 ff.

11. J. Hughes, *Self Realization in Kashmir Shaivism: The Oral Teachings of Swami Lakshmanjoo* (Albany, NY: State University of New York Press, 1994), p. 32.

12. In noting the importance of effort, it is also important to recognize that self-effort is no guarantee of liberation in this lifetime. We cannot know when our efforts will come to fruition. We learn to continue our efforts unceasingly, without concern for when we will experience a dramatic breakthrough or mystical experience. Ultimately, effort and discipleship become a way of life, an end in themselves. We stop thinking about reaching some distant destination. The path and the goal are the same— to realize and abide in our own present nature. Conversely, a person can become enlightened without appearing to have done any practice at all. Perhaps the most famous example of this is Ramana Maharshi's spontaneous enlightenment at age sixteen. Undoubtedly his sudden and permanent realization of the Self was the fruition of arduous efforts in previous lifetimes.

13. M. Eliade, *A History of Religious Ideas*, Volume 2 (Chicago: Univ. of Chicago Press, 1982), pp. 342, 347–8.

14. A. Schimmel, *Mystical Dimensions of Islam* (Chapel Hill, NC: Univ. of North Carolina Press, 1975), p. 205.

15. R. Gale, personal communication.

16. A. Schimmel, *Mystical Dimensions of Islam* (Chapel Hill, NC: Univ. of North Carolina Press, 1975), pp. 103, 237.

17. I. K. Taimni, *The Science of Yoga* (Wheaton, IL: Quest Books, 1961).

18. Ibid., pp. 22–23.

19. S. Muktananda, *Play of Consciousness* (South Fallsburg, NY: SYDA Foundation, 1974), pp. 38 ff.

20. A. Kane, "The Art of Spiritual Guidance." In J. M. Spiegelman (Ed.), *Sufism, Islam, and Jungian Psychology* (Scottsdale, AZ: Falcon Press, 1991).

21. L. Govinda, *Foundations of Tibetan Mysticism* (New York: Samuel Weiser, 1969), pp. 96–7.

22. D. Khyentse, *The Wish Fulfilling Tree* (Boston, Shambala, 1988), p. 56.

23. Ibid., pp. 8–9.

24. Ibid., pp. 70–1.

25. K. S. Rinbochay, *Tantric Practice in Nying-Ma*, translated and edited by J. Hopkins (Ithaca, NY: Snow Lion Press, 1982), p. 179.

26. As Padmasambhava himself said, "As a thing is viewed, so it appears." W. Y. Evans-Wentz, *The Tibetan Book of the Great Liberation* (New York: Oxford Univ. Press, 1954), p. 232.

27. C. Trungpa, *Crazy Wisdom* (Boston: Shambhala, 1991), pp. 25–30.

28. Ibid., p. 18.

29. Ibid., p. 34.

# Glimpses of the Goal

Through unmistakable learning and contemplation, he should enter the gate of Mahayana and Vajrayana, and practice them diligently with great determination; then finally, he can please his guru with his real experiences of Enlightenment, which are produced step by step through his devotion.

*The Hundred Thousand Songs of Milarepa*[1]

There are numerous signs that the spiritual apprentice is advancing on the path toward enlightenment, knowledge of the Self, the elevation of consciousness into Spirit. One sign is the emergence of positive virtues: patience, kindness, desire to serve other beings, human and non-human; the quieting of obsessive desires; absorption in meditation; serenity; acceptance and equanimity under all conditions; renunciation of the transitory, and abiding in the unchanging light of consciousness.

Another important sign of progress is a notable change in daily life attitudes and behaviors. The aspirant's daily life becomes filled with tranquility and mindfulness, and one learns to maintain peace of mind under difficult circumstances. A man named Lonnie, a longtime Buddhist meditator, told me this story, which exemplifies how the student may now begin to live as a more enlightened being, here and now:

One night in New York a very large black man approached me near the Bowery and demanded money. His breath reeked of booze and his eyes were bloodshot. His shoes were torn and his clothes were ragged. He was easily six foot five and I was scared of him. He stared at me with menacing eyes. I could have walked away quickly but I felt a composure in my body that I remembered from the practice of meditation. I took a breath and for a brief moment I saw in his eyes the eyes of Mahakala, the Tibetan deity of time, usually depicted as a wild demon—a ferocious black deity that helps bring us to enlightenment. I felt compassion for this suffering sentient being. I gave him two dollars and looked him in the eye and I noted how cold it was and asked him if he had a place to stay indoors for the night. The man's demeanor softened. He looked sad for a moment, then said it had been a long time since anyone had expressed concern. He was genuinely grateful for the money. At that moment I felt that my spiritual practices were truly worthwhile because I was seeing real changes in my actions.

## Equality Vision, Acceptance, and Contentment

The spiritual apprentice also develops equality vision, seeing the same divinity, pure light, or Buddha nature in everyone. A story is told about the great yogi and Advaita Vedanta philosopher, Shankara:

> One morning, when he was on his way to bathe in the Ganges, he met a *Chandala*, a member of the lowest caste, the untouchables. . . . For a moment inborn caste-prejudice asserted itself. Shankara, the Brahmin, ordered the *Chandala* out of his way. But the *Chandala* answered: "If there is only one God, how can there be many kinds of men?" Shankara was filled with shame and reverence. He prostrated himself before the *Chandala*.[2]

I learned a similar lesson once at a party where a man named Joe talked to me incessantly and began to annoy me so much that I started to ignore him. Later, a rather prominent and popular sperson named Dave arrived, and I rushed over to speak with him. Dave did not remember me at all, and while polite, was not all that interested in speaking to me. I was brushed off exactly as I had brushed off Joe. I had treated Joe with disrespect, failing to recognize him as an embodiment of Spirit. Later I saw him again and spoke with him at length, seeing his luminous essence. We became fine friends.

Related to equality vision is acceptance and detachment. We accept whatever comes in life with the detachment of Lord Shiva, the great ascetic, who accepts whatever is placed in his begging bowl— sometimes sumptuous feasts, sometimes scraps of rotting fruit.

Yet we are not completely passive and resigned. We learn to use the powers of will with determination and develop understanding of the law of karma—the awareness that we form our future through our every action. We accept our responsibility for what we have created in our lives, and strive, through every act, to create a better future for ourselves and others. We become free of greed and any desire to do harm. A man named Bradley told me this story:

> I was living down in Mexico because I was wanted in the U. S. for a crime. I had embezzled some money and now I was on the lamb. Then one day the bag holding all the cash was stolen from my hotel room, and I had only a few pesos to my name. The scales had been balanced. I was detached because I saw the perfection of it. Eventually I went to stay with some friends in a village. Someone loaned me some money and I rented a bungalow. Everything was quite comfortable. Then a teenager in the village got hit by a car and had his face torn up pretty badly. He desperately needed surgery, but his family had no money. I gave them all the money I had so they could pay for the operation. That was probably the one really good thing I'd ever done for another person in my life. Several weeks later the police tracked me down and had me sent back to the U.S. Somehow my lawyer arranged a plea bargain that enabled me to pay a fine, repay the money, do some community service, and cooperate with the police, but no jail time. In my heart I felt certain the only way I'd gotten off so easily was because I had helped that kid. That was about the time I started to get some inkling of this thing called karma.

## Glimpses of Enlightenment

A simple formula for the spiritual apprentice is: Do your practice, meet the teacher's awakened consciousness, and you will be transformed. The student who has proceeded this far is likely to experience glimpses of an awakened state. Spiritual guides teach powerful methods that can transform the student's consciousness, methods that can awaken a state of perfect purity and radiance, and that lead us directly to the experience of enlightenment, liberation, or Self-realization. Meditative disciplines polish the mirror of the mind so that awareness grows clear and unobstructed—so that one perceives the clear reflective space of the mirror, rather than the ever-changing images reflected in it. We wake up in moments of breakthrough beyond conditioned perceptions of the world, into a state of freedom.[3] In a timeless moment the ground shifts and the seeker becomes aware of the light that is alive in everything. Time stands still. We perceive the sacredness and oneness of all life. The spiritual apprentice is now seized with the vision of the Beloved, Source of all, the One Being, whose beauty pervades all creation. It was such an experience that led William James to write:

> I remember the night, and almost the very spot on the hillside, where my soul opened out, as it were, into the Infinite, and there was a rushing together of the two worlds, the inner and the outer. It was deep calling unto deep—the deep that my own struggle had opened up within being answered by the unfathomable deep without, reaching beyond the stars. I stood alone with Him who had made me, and all the beauty of the world, and love, and sorrow, and even temptation. I did not seek Him, but felt the perfect union of my spirit with His. The ordinary sense of things around me faded. For the moment nothing but an ineffable joy and exaltation remained. It is impossible to fully describe the experience. . . . I have stood upon the Mount of Vision since, and felt the Eternal round about me.[4]

In such moments, the ripples of the mind subside so that one perceives that presence that underlies the constant change of forms, the witness and ground of all existence. One is illumined by the light of all-pervading Consciousness. A long-time meditator named Michele said:

> I had a vision of white light in meditation one day. It was staggering. Then I realized I could see that light everywhere around me with my eyes wide open. It was my own emanation. A few days later I saw my teacher. She smiled at me and said, "It's beautiful, isn't it? White light everywhere!" And she laughed.

In the *Crest-Jewel of Discrimination,* Shankara described the experience in these words:

> Now I shall tell you the nature of the Atman. If you realize it, you will be freed from the bonds of ignorance, and attain liberation. There is a self-existent Reality, which is the basis of our consciousness of ego. That Reality is the witness of the three states of our consciousness, and is distinct from the five bodily coverings. That Reality is the knower in all states of consciousness—waking, dreaming, and dreamless sleep. That Reality sees everything by

its own light. No one sees it. That Reality pervades the universe. It alone shines. The universe shines with its reflected light. . . . Its nature is eternal consciousness. . . . It is the knower of pleasure and pain and of the sense-objects. . . . This is the Atman, the Supreme being, the ancient. It never ceases to experience infinite joy. It is always the same. It is consciousness itself.

With a controlled mind and an intellect which is made pure and tranquil, you must realize the Atman directly, within yourself. Know the Atman as the real I. Thus you cross the shoreless ocean of worldliness, whose waves are birth and death. The Atman is indivisible, eternal, one without a second. . . . Its glories are infinite. . . . It is the witness of the mind. . . . It is the inner Being, the uttermost, everlasting joy.[5]

The spiritual apprentice now approaches the gates of enlightenment, the goal that was sought from the beginning of the path. The seeker has entered the temple of the eternal presence, the Truth whose praises have been sung by mystics throughout the ages. The experience of enlightenment was lucidly described by John White:

The perennial wisdom is unchanging; truth is one. That is agreed on by the sages of all major religions and sacred traditions, all hermetic philosophies, genuine mystery schools and higher occult paths. Enlightenment is the core truth of them all. Even more broadly, it is the essence of life—the goal of all growth, development, evolution. It is the discovery of what we ultimately are, the answer to the questions: Who am I? Why am I here? Where am I going? What is life all about? . . . . Paradoxically, the answer we seek is none other than what we *already are* in essence—Being, the ultimate wholeness that is the source and ground of all Becoming. *Enlightenment is realization of the truth of Being.* Our native condition, our true self is Being, traditionally called God, the Cosmic Person, the Supreme Being, the One-in-all. . . . We are manifestations of Being, but like the cosmos itself, we are also in the process of Becoming—always changing, developing, growing, evolving to higher and higher states that ever more beautifully express the perfection of the source of existence. . . .

The truth of all existence and all experience, then, is none other than the seamless here-and-now, the already present, the prior nature of that which seeks and strives and asks: Being. *The spiritual journey is the process of discovering and living that truth.* It amounts to the eye seeing itself—or rather, the I seeing its Self.

In philosophical terms, enlightenment is comprehending the unity of all dualities, the harmonious composite of all opposites, the oneness of endless multiplicity and diversity. In psychological terms, it is transcendence of all sense of limitation and otherness. In humanistic terms, it is understanding that the journey is the teaching, that the path and the destination are ultimately one. In theological terms, it is comprehending the union of God and humanity. In ontological terms, it is the State of all states, the Condition of all conditions that transcends the entire cosmos yet is also everyday reality, since nothing is apart from it or ever can be.

When we finally understand that Great Mystery, we discover our true nature, the Supreme Identity, the Self of all. That direct perception of our oneness with the infinite, that noetic realization of our identity with the divine is the source of all happiness, all goodness, all beauty, all truth.[6]

In some traditions, such as Chinese *Ch'an* Buddhism, enlightenment is said to occur suddenly. Edward Conze wrote:

> Enlightenment according to Hui-Neng and his successors is not a gradual, but an instantaneous process. . . . The Ch'an masters did not intend to say that no preparation was necessary, and that enlightenment was won in a very short time. They just laid stress on the common mystical truth that enlightenment takes place in a "timeless moment," i.e., outside time, in eternity. It is an act of the Absolute itself, not our own doing. One cannot do anything at all to become enlightened. To expect austerities or meditation to bring forth salvation is like "rubbing a brick to make it into a mirror." Enlightenment just happens without the mediacy of any finite condition or influence. . . . It is not the gradual accumulation of merit which causes enlightenment, but a sudden act of recognition.[7]

The parting of the clouds that gives us glimpses of an expanded state is often quite sudden. I experienced a spontaneous moment of illumination one day while visiting Harbin Hot Springs. After soaking for a long time in the steamy hot pool, I proceeded to the freezing cold plunge. I was breathing deeply. As I sat in the cold pool I assumed a meditative posture, gazed at the green beauty all around me, then turned my attention inward. I spontaneously began to practice guru yoga, repeating the mantra Guru Om while envisioning the form of Bhagavan Nityananda, the great south Indian siddha. In my inner eye I saw his dark body and how he sat totally absorbed in meditation. I became very still. Suddenly, a powerful energy rushed up my spine and out through the top of my head. My consciousness began traveling up the ladder of Being into dimensions beyond form. Some ten minutes later I returned to body consciousness, exhilarated and drenched in light.

The spiritual apprentice who practices on a regular basis the potent disciplines of self-transformation taught by the teacher begins to experience a variety of non-ordinary states of consciousness. A woman named Phyllis gave this account:

> I lived with my teacher for several years in a community. I rarely left the grounds. I was focused solely on the final adventure of consciousness—the quest for Self-realization. I meditated four or five hours a day, did my job, and rested quietly. That was my existence. I spoke very little. As I got more and more absorbed in meditation my teacher showed greater interest in me. He would look at me from time to time and I knew he was monitoring my progress. One day I saw a beautiful beam of golden light project from his eyes into mine. Afterward I went into a very deep meditation where I saw a tiny blue dot that scintillated with blue-white light. After that I meditated even more intensely. I had experiences of traveling to other planes of existence where I saw visions of great masters like Ramakrishna, Shirdi Sai Baba, Jesus, and Shakyamuni Buddha. Once I had a vision of White Tara; she held up her hands in blessing. My teacher's energy and my own meditation had made my mind clear so I could now perceive other planes of existence.

Such moments of illumination arise spontaneously and so impact some individuals that they become fully dedicated to repeating and deepening the experience, through disciplined efforts to cleanse the body, mind, and heart. The aspirant discovers what has always been present but only now is clearly seen—a non-dual state in which there is no sense of separation. We are one with the totality; our field of presence encompasses all phenomena with limitless compassion. We are released from the bondage of self-preoccupation into the freedom of divine contemplation. This awareness may break through in transient episodes or may become more constant. The student now directly perceives the infinite and all-pervasive ground of existence, and is filled with determination to live that vision ceaselessly.

Some disciples reach a stage of maturity in which they dwell constantly in an enlightened state. A woman named Jill, who has meditated and lived by her guru's teachings faithfully since 1962, said:

> I cannot say whether or not I have gone to the farthest stages of
> the Path but I can say in truth that I see only God, all the time,
> alive everywhere, pulsating in my heart, and shining in the face
> of every being, shimmering in every leaf and flower. My quest
> has been fulfilled. I think of my teacher with reverence and love,
> yet I am not fixated on him. I learned from him to look within
> myself to find peace.

Let us examine two more accounts by students who experienced awakenings. Joseph, a long-time practitioner of Transcendental Meditation, reported:

> The first time I went on retreat I became very emotional. Once I
> just burst into tears and I didn't have any idea why. Then I experi-
> enced a settling down in the body and in the space of the mind.
> Thought became quieter and ceased to be so prominent. It ceased
> to fill the mind. I would meditate to a certain place and then stop.
> There was a feeling of an obstruction. Then one day during medi-
> tation it broke. It felt brittle like ice or glass. When that inner ob-
> struction broke I fell through into infinite space. I felt like I was
> suspended above a body of water with no end. The bliss and plea-
> sure of this experience were indescribable. I felt a vibration mov-
> ing up through my toes and through my whole body. Then I felt
> myself falling farther into the water until there was nothing. Sheer
> vastness. Eventually I resurfaced. Some time had passed that I
> couldn't account for. I had experienced pure consciousness with-
> out an object of attention. Later on, during this same retreat, I
> found myself altered in my waking state. I wasn't in contact with
> things anymore. Everything seemed really far away from me.
> There was an unreality to things that previously had seemed real
> and tangible. I had a sense of empty, intangible, dreamlike phe-
> nomena that were taking place that I had no relationship to. I was
> the witness of all phenomena. My relationship to the mind and
> body had shifted so that it was no longer who I was. I rested in a
> very deep stillness. This persisted for several days.
> Once at a retreat I became aware of someone making a loud
> moaning sound. I was somewhat annoyed by this and thought to
> myself, "That person shouldn't be doing that." But he or she per-
> sisted. I began to be really annoyed because I was having a deep

meditation, and this noise was disturbing me. I didn't appreciate that. Then as I came out of meditation I realized that I was the one making this noise. I had no idea it was me. My body was moaning and moaning and I was drooling all over myself. I had lost body awareness. The bliss was almost unbearable. It was like an orgasm, only thousands of times more intense. And it was everywhere in the body, not localized in one place.

Joseph had directly perceived the Atman or Self as witness, and as consciousness without form. His experience of merging his awareness into the stillness of Being was ecstatic, immeasurably blissful. Similar themes appear in this account by a man named Stuart, who described his experiences on the spiritual path:

I met my teacher Swami Kripalu when he came to America in 1977. I saw golden light around him. I cried in his presence all the time. I had eye contact with him and received transmission. All my contact with him was inspiring. If I could find someone else more moving than he was I would follow that person. I have never found anyone else like him. I gave up my job to follow him across the country in 1977. I had shaktipat experiences that changed my consciousness and my basic body sensations for months. I had experiences I was graced with, that I did not earn through meditative efforts of any kind. They were given. Ongoing states of bodily pleasure. Tingling, seething feelings throughout my body. A writhing sensation in the cells, in the base of the spine and the throat, and constant ecstatic quivering in the tongue that has never gone away for the past twenty five years.

I did practices to cultivate these experiences. The most radical thing I did was to take vows of brahmacharya. Yoga took hold. I remained celibate for ten years. I got up at four or five in the morning and practiced hatha yoga, meditation, pranayama, and chanting before I went to work. During chanting I found myself crying a lot for no apparent reason. It felt good. For a two month period after I moved to California I wasn't working and I did a lot of yoga practice at that time. I got to the point where I didn't want to speak. I could have given up speaking. A lot of my experience has been in the throat and heart area. I was experiencing the *khechari mudra*, a yogic process in which the tongue reaches up inside the palate toward the brain. It brings about a transformation of the larynx and tongue. The tongue stretches back and up spontaneously. It would happen spontaneously during chanting or meditation or while practicing asanas. I felt like Romeo stretching up to

Juliet in the pineal gland in some balcony scene; it had the feel of some very romantic ardor, longing.

My practice plateaued for a while. Only after I finished school did I have the time to practice intensely again. I did as much as I could. Then in 1984 or '85, I did a long yoga retreat with Baba Hari Dass. After that I experienced a nine-month period of enlightenment in which I just enjoyed being. Being was enjoyable. Vision was enjoyable. The sound of things was enjoyable. I thought to myself, "I am enjoying my Self." Later, during a long period of fasting, physical purification, pranayama, japa, and hatha yoga, all of a sudden my body started to have a thrill. My whole body, every cell was thrilling, quivering with joy. It was extraordinary. That went on for about a day and a half. Then it filtered away, despite my efforts to keep it. I have had other subtle experiences involving the cranial vault. I close my eyes and feel this cathedral-like ascending space. I had a number of experiences of the hormones of the pineal gland scintillating in this spiraling, sparkling descent into the space of the closed-eye darkness. I was amazed by that radiance. I thought, "This is the glimmer of infinity."

These startling experiences are peak moments of the path of spiritual apprenticeship, major turning points in our journey of evolving consciousness. They are to be savored, celebrated with gratitude, and integrated into our lives. As our consciousness expands, we experientially replicate the claims of mystics throughout all ages—claims that there is an all-pervading unity, and that we are, in our essence, one with the entire universe. We enter realms of experience sometimes called transpersonal because they far exceeds the limits of the personality as we ordinarily know it.

According to Stanislav Grof,[8] experiences of transpersonal dimensions of consciousness have some central features: These experiences transcend our ordinary conceptions of time and space: We may travel to places other than our present physical location, and events from the remote past and distant future can be experienced with great clarity. The distinction between microcosm and macrocosm is transcended. We realize that the part contains the whole; each of us is a microcosm containing the macrocosm. Time slows down, or accelerates, flows backward, or ceases to exist. One transcends the sharp distinction between matter, energy, and consciousness; matter disintegrates into patterns of energy. One experiences identification with other people, with other species, or with the earth itself. Transpersonal experiences demonstrate the arbitrary nature of all physical boundaries; the existence of nonlocal connections in the universe, and the possibility of communication through unknown means (as in telepathic communication); also, memory without a material substrate—the ability to experience memories of events we have not directly experienced with our senses, such as memories of past lives; and the realization that consciousness exists in all living forms, even inorganic matter.

> These experiences clearly suggest that, in a yet unexplained way, each of us contains the information about the entire universe or all of existence, has potential experiential access to all its parts, and in a sense *is* the whole cosmic network, as much as he or she is just an infinitesimal part of it.[9]

It is in discovering these transpersonal dimensions of existence that we grow toward enlightenment.

## Intensification of Practice

At first, states of illumination are momentary. But ultimately the aspirant longs to be established in an expanded condition all the time. Glimpses of the goal are not enough. We continue to practice ceaselessly in order to reach the final goal. John White reminds us:

> Enlightenment . . . is an endless process—not simply a one-time event. True, there are quantum leaps in awareness that mark the spiritual path. . . , but one white-light experience does not a mystic make, nor a saint. Even the most spiritually elevated people have found there are states of being beyond their present level of development.[10]

Glimpses of expanded consciousness motivate the seeker to continue disciplined practices to accelerate and deepen the experience of enlightenment. A major sign of progress on the path is a hunger for Self-realization and a lessening of the strength of other desires. The aspirant at this stage burns for awakening, and experiences an intensified desire to practice mindfulness, to abide as formless awareness. We use whatever method we learned from the teacher, and practice it as close to perfection as we are able, until our minds and heart become clear and jewel-like. With deeper commitment to this process, all physical, emotional, attitudinal, or subtle, energetic impurities and limitations are consumed until the spiritual apprentice climbs toward the highest summits of freedom.

Sometimes every cell of our bodies aches for liberation, for release into the unconditioned freedom of Spirit returning to awareness of its own radiance and omnipresence. Spiritual practice becomes a focal point of our daily lives.

> I raise my hands in prayer
> as I drink the inner sun
> from the cup of inner longing
> my everyday gesture of praise
> to the light that surrounds me everywhere.[11]

At this stage we eliminate distractions, developing dispassion and detachment from desire. We are not unfriendly toward pleasures and good times, but we recognize that ordinary human fulfillments are fleeting and bring no lasting fulfillment, peace, or satiation of desires. Peace arises as we dwell in a state of calm receptivity, with senses steady and quiet mind. We no longer need to fill every moment with the urgent search for information, stimulation, or conversation. We become still. At long last we find peace.

With this awareness comes a spirit of renunciation. Renunciation does not mean total renouncing of the world, the senses, the body, and the need to work in society. What ultimately needs to be renounced is dualistic perception and attachment to the transitory. Renunciation means cutting through mental chatter, fluctuating emotions, elusive objects of desire, fixed agendas and conceptions. Shankara says:

> When renunciation and the longing for liberation are present to an intense degree within a man, then the practice of tranquility and the other virtues will bear fruit and lead to the goal. Of the first steps to liberation, the first is declared to be complete detachment from all things which are non-eternal. Then comes the practice of tranquility, self-control, and forbearance. And then the entire giving-up of all actions which are done from personal, selfish desire. Then the disciple must hear the truth of the Atman,

## Dream Darshan of Swami Muktananda

In February 1999 I had a powerful dream darshan of Muktananda Baba, a dream that helped me heal and resolve my feelings about him. In the dream, Baba appears before me. I am so happy to see him! He looks small, old, but immensely powerful. His head is shaved. His eyes are partially closed and his awareness is drawn inward. He does not gaze outward or interact with me, but he allows me to view him. In his presence, I see him. In his presence, I feel a magnetic pull into the divine presence. I merge into Consciousness, the self-revealing light of the divine. In the dream, I intuitively know that he has suffered with the consequences of his actions, that he has been undergoing penance and purification. I have the awareness that he is reconciled with himself for his actions, that I am reconciled with him—I have forgiven him; and that he has forgiven me for having doubts and being upset with him.

I am grateful for this dream *darshan*, this glimpse of the teacher.

and reflect on it, and meditate upon it constantly, without pause, for a long time. Thus the wise man reaches that highest state, in which consciousness of subject and object is dissolved away and the infinite unitary consciousness alone remains.[12]

Renunciation also means simplifying our lives so that we can spend more time doing consciousness-enhancing practices such as meditation or breathing. It may also take the form of deepening commitment to self-transformation through rigorous discipline.

My friend Joann spent years as an ordained monk. After her teacher died, she found a job and an apartment, and there she continued her practices of meditation, chanting, and study while living in the world. At a certain point she realized there she had no pressing desires other than to attain liberation. She found a new teacher and moved to a community in the mountains where she is studying Buddhism and doing intensive practices. She has gone for broke, relinquishing all lesser goals and desires. She has given up everything to pursue enlightenment, to follow the Dharma, the path of peace. As she departed for a meditation retreat, I wrote her this little poem:

> As you met each obstacle you never wavered
> You remained resolved to walk your path
> You've chosen the highest destination
> You've never been afraid of Shiva's wrath.
>
> Where others grasp and cling to fleeting shadows
> You fix your mind on timeless realms of peace
> Clear as space, abide in your own nature
> May your love and wisdom endlessly increase!
>
> You are free of aggression and self-hatred
> You are the friend of everyone you meet
> You relinquish attachments as you notice them arise
> May your peace and contentment grow complete.
>
> You are a brave explorer with strong intention
> Liberation is where you fix your gaze
> We bid you go well now on your journey
> Let the fire of sadhana become a blaze!

## *The Goal is Already Attained*

Attachment to the method is very important. Indeed, it accelerates our progress to periodically engage in some spiritual practice with intense discipline—whether it be sitting practice, fasting, breathing, or other methods. Only by fanning the flames of consciousness can we consume our limitations.

I also believe that periodically we need to let go of all our forms, and allow our own inner wisdom and the intelligence of each moment to guide us toward freedom. (See Stage Eight). We seek that state beyond all methods, where our freedom isn't bound by a single way or setting or technique. Our goal is the recognition of our true nature, which has always been liberated. This was the perspective of the great Advaita Vedanta philosophers. In the words of Lance Nelson:

> Liberation is not something that can be brought into existence, as if it were a product of action. Nor is it something that can be acquired. Rather the opposite is true: It has no beginning, and it is eternal. Being our very Self, it is eternally accomplished, eternally attained. Ontologically speaking, we are always liberated....
> [T]here is no bondage, no seeker of liberation, and no one who is liberated. . . . Mukti [liberation] is in truth an atemporal state that has always been ours. . . .To speak of attaining liberation is therefore, figurative.[13]

Indeed, the enlightened mind or Self is already attained. It is not some distant goal but our eternal nature, the very ground of our existence. As Annamalai Swami put it:

> Don't make the mistake of imagining that there is some goal to be reached or attained. If you start to think like this you will start looking for methods to practice and people to help you. This just perpetuates the problem you are trying to end. Instead, cultivate the awareness. "I am the Self. I am That. I am *Brahman*. I am everything." You don't need any methods to get rid of the wrong ideas you have about yourself. All you have to do is stop believing them . . . The Self is always attained, it is always realized; it is not something that you have to seek, reach, or discover.[14]

## *Seasons of Practice*

As months and years pass, we go through many seasons of formal practice. At some stages we become more disciplined—perhaps spending several hours a day practicing asanas, pranayama, mantra repetition, prayer, or meditation. At such times we derive great peace and energy from our practices, so that we begin to feel like a different person. A subtle psychic sensitivity awakens, and we feel streams of energy moving through our bodies, and a deepening inner silence.

We also experience plateaus as other life concerns and pursuits move into the forefront of our awareness. Sometimes the desire to practice wanes and we experience laziness, sloth, torpor, or unwillingness to make the effort it takes to continue a meditation practice. There are also periods when we have a strong desire to practice but are obstructed by other tasks and responsibilities. This is usually a sign that we need to make these activities the focus of our spiritual practice: our job, spouse or kids, our desire to practice a musical instrument, or the need to lend support to a friend. Hazrat Inayat Khan says, "Consider your responsibility sacred."[15] There is nothing that is not part of our spiritual apprenticeship, our training to be fully unfolded human beings. Every event is a meaningful phase in the process of our awakening.[16]

The focus and form of our spiritual practice is ever-changing. We are constantly challenged to evolve into more complete human beings. Spiritual life expands until it overflows from formal practices and encompasses every facet of our lives. A wise practitioner lets the form of practice change over time, rather than trying to keep things always the same, or to recreate some past amazing experience. We need to stay fresh in the living moment. I know many meditation practitioners who despair because they cannot recreate high experiences of meditation they had ten or twenty years ago. The moment has changed. We need to change with it, allowing room for our complexity to develop and express itself. Our next step may be to intensify our practices of meditation or chanting, or it may be to start a business or take up pottery or belly dancing. Thus, we allow seasons of intense practice to come and go, knowing that sometimes the urge to practice will be intense and at other times less intense.

## Continuing to Seek the Teacher's Guidance

As we begin to have stronger inner experiences, the teacher's guidance is as important as ever. We still need to return periodically so the guide can offer more instruction, confirm the validity of our experiences, and explain their significance. This is especially important when we have experiences we cannot understand or integrate without assistance. A notable example is Gopi Krishna, who underwent a spontaneous kundalini awakening for which he was unprepared, resulting in years of anguish, confusion, burning sensations, and agonizing physical pain. He feared many times that he was going irrevocably insane. After many years, Gopi Krishna met a yogi who taught him a yogic breathing technique that quickly brought the wild kundalini symptoms under control. If Gopi Krishna had found the guidance of a teacher sooner, he might have been spared years of suffering.[17]

We may feel stirrings of an urge for greater independence from the teacher. We realize that the truth is inside us, so that is where we wish to focus our attention. But we are still keenly aware that the teacher was the match that lit our flame, and for this we are grateful.

## Devotion

> [The guru is like] a wish fulfilling tree granting all the qualities of realization, a father and a mother giving their love equally to all sentient beings, a great river of compassion, a mountain rising above worldly concerns unshaken by the winds of emotion, and a great cloud filled with rain to soothe the torments of the passions. In brief, he is the equal of all the Buddhas. . . . To have full confidence in him is the sure way to progress toward enlightenment. . . . Whether or not we achieve realization depends entirely upon our devotion to the guru.
>
> *Dilgo Khyentse Rinpoche, The Wish Fulfilling Tree*[18]

An aspirant who has received both the teacher's consistent, steady, reliable guidance and the mysterious but tangible blesings of Spirit, begins to experience a spontaneous uprising of devotion. Sometimes this devotion is expressed openly through joyous songs of praise or by bowing respectfully to the teacher. One student began constantly repeating his teacher's name and felt her presence with him always, protecting, guiding. We may also experience devotion as a willingness to serve and do the teacher's bidding faithfully. We become Hanuman in service of our Rama. Devotion shouldn't be something we force on ourselves or exhibit because of group pressures to act blissed out. It spontaneously arises within us as an expression of love and gratitude toward the teacher.

Once in Ganeshpuri, I became very discouraged. I didn't feel that my spiritual practice was proceeding well or bearing fruit. My health was bad, my energy was low. My meditations were barren. I was lost and didn't know what direction my life was taking. I had doubts about finding a job and a career. At one point, a week-long chant of the mantra Om Namah Shivaya was held in the ashram. On the final morning Muktananda was expected to arrive in the temple to celebrate the conclusion of the celebration. I stayed up all night so I would get a good seat up near Baba's throne at the front of the room. I chanted and meditated through the dark hours of the morning. At sunrise the temple filled with devotees. The place was packed. Right before Baba arrived, one of his assistants came over to me and told me to move to a seat much farther in the back, so that some very important honcho could sit up front. For a moment I was crushed, absorbed in my melodrama of disappointment. I had waited all night so I could sit close to my teacher, and now this unjust and arbitrary pandering to ashram VIPs had snatched this opportunity from me.

Then I began to get absorbed in the chanting. I closed my eyes and dissolved into the sounds of the mantras. With my eyes still closed I began to speak to my teacher inwardly. (By now I knew he heard all my thoughts). I said, "Baba, I don't know who I am or where I'm going in life or or what I'm supposed to do next. All I know is that I honor you, I trust you, and I love you. You have shown me that you know me. I honor you for that. I believe in the transmission of spiritual energy that has been bestowed and I trust that it will unfold in an appropriate way and lead me toward awakening."

At that moment I opened my eyes and Baba was looking right at me. His gaze was full of love, concern, and compassion. I looked down for a moment, but he did not avert his gaze. He kept looking right at me so I would know with certainty that he knew what was happening inside me. In that moment I felt more connected to him than I ever had. I knew that the cord between us was strong, and I felt what Victor Mansfield calls the "telepathic link" between the student and the guide.[19]

At that instant, I felt deeper devotion for my teacher arise. Until then there was always something self-conscious and half-hearted in my feelings of devotion. Now I sensed my teacher's stature and his ability to guide me from within, at any distance. It didn't matter how close to him I was sitting. He was with me always and everywhere.

I felt a tremendous weight lift off me. Whereas moments earlier I had been miserable, now I felt happy just seeing him. Now I remembered why I was sitting here in a white marble temple in monsoon-drenched India staring at a seventy year-old Indian man in a silk lungi. As I joined in the rousing finale of the chant, I was transported out of my problems into a state of devotion, not only to my teacher but to the formless, all-pervasive awareness that connected us as one.

Many people have serious reservations about the idea of devotion to a teacher because it encourages us to view the teacher through the lens of idealizing projections and makes us vulnerable to exploitation and an unwillingness to look realistically at the teacher's human faults.[20] Regarding the topic of devotion and guru worship, David Frawley has made these insightful comments:

> Many of our problems with gurus come from our misunderstanding of guru worship. We create a personality cult around the guru, rather than using the guru as a vehicle for worshipping the divine. When gurus are worshipped, it is not their human side that should be honored but the Divinity working through them, the Divine guru. Guru worship can be one path of spiritual growth, but it is not the only path. In knowledge approaches (*jnana yoga*), the guru has the role of an instructor. In devotional lines (*bhakti yoga*), the guru is usually subordinate to the chosen form of God for worship. While for some great gurus, like Ramana Maharshi or Anandamayi Ma, guru worship appears appropriate, few gurus are of this stature.[21]

When we come in contact with a being who is worthy of our devotion, we may express it through tears of gratitude, or by inwardly remembering the teacher's influence in our lives. We may also express devotion by singing or silently repeating the name of our chosen form or symbol of the absolute—Great Spirit, Yahweh, Shiva, Allah, Ram. The many names of God become alive with shakti as our repetition of these sacred words becomes imbued with our longing for union with the eternal presence.

Devotion can feel a little uncomfortable at times because it may look strange to other people. I remember how once my mother walked in on me while I was chanting and meditating in my room wrapped in a saffron shawl covered with Sanskrit print, while in front of me on the floor was a photo of the rather rotund, almost entirely naked, and ecstatically blissful form of Bhagwan Nityananda. My mother was in shock; she could not fathom what she had done wrong in rearing me that I had grown up to worship pictures of dead yogis!

True devotion is ultimately directed not just to a teacher but to our own enlightened consciousness, the Self, the God that dwells within us. This is the non-dual understanding of devotion. There is no separation between ourselves and universal Being, the light that shines in all. As we saw in the last chapter, by contemplating the qualities of a teacher, we awaken our own potentials, which begin to manifest in us in their totality as we mature.

There are also stages in which it can serve our transformation to maintain the dualistic attitude of a lover in devotion to the beloved. Ramakrishna once said, 'I don't want to become sugar, I want to taste sugar.' We experience the joy of relationship with an invisible Friend who loves and guides us, and wants nothing more than our freedom. Devotion is conscious relationship with transcendent Being, which responds when we voice our intent, our joy, and our longing. That presence manifests compassion for our condition, and demonstrates the intention to liberate us. Through devotion, we fan its light, invoking it with prayer, mantra, silence, song, and effort to see it alive in every being and occurrence.

Devotion may deepen as a consequence of illuminations that occur in moments of great suffering, at moments when we feel the solace of the invisible. One night I was upset about a loss and very bitter with my fate. As I sat in meditation I realized that something had been taken from me and something else was being given in its place. I closed my eyes tightly in pain and said, "So, is that what you have in mind! You want me to let go of what I want so you can give me what?—your presence? Is that the bargain?" As I said these words my eyes flooded with tears and there was a surge in the crown of my head and my whole body was blanketed by peace. And at that moment a voice within me said, "Exactly."

## Integration and Vocation

The spiritual apprentice becomes conscious of the Being that is present always and everywhere—the One that lives and breathes and unfolds in every form and occurrence. We have touched the shores of Self-realization, catching glimpses of the truth that always exists, beyond the veil of ignorance. As we grow in consciousness, increasingly we bow our heads before the light of Spirit; in innumerable forms we see its face. We have traveled far with the guide, who has shown us how to set ourselves free. But soon the time will come for us to travel to new lands where even our teacher will be left behind. We see our own way clear now, and it is soon to be our time to be aflame.

One of the disciple's major tasks at this stage is to begin to ground expanding awareness in constructive activity. We have been illumined by the light of consciousness. But we also experience enlightenment as the revelation of our own work in life—the way in which we are to manifest as instruments of Spirit in the world.[22] This may mean developing a talent with color, fabric, law, medicine, childrearing, music, photography, or business. It may mean following a calling to work for social change or in a field of scientific inquiry. Or it may mean awakening psychic capacities or pursuing metaphysical studies. Each of us is called in different ways into the field of human and planetary service.

As we progress on the path we become more well-balanced, making use of all our faculties (physical, emotional, intellectual, artistic, and spiritual), constantly attempting to refine our character. The spiritual apprentice strives for the deepest integration of ego and Self. Ego is not to be transcended but wedded to the radiant consciousness of the Self, the silent, transpersonal witness. We utilize the ego to fulfill the purpose of our unique incarnations as individuals. The task now is refinement of our work in the world. By developing a vocation, we construct a sacred vessel of spirit, preparing ourselves to contain and express the inner light through our life's central projects. Here is where we may begin to need to set our own course, sometimes separate from the teacher. We learn to recognize the signs that our innermost being is speaking to us, and know that we are best served in our development when we listen to this interior voice and knowing—which leads us forward toward an integration that is uniquely our own. Our work is to mold ourselves into the embodiment of our own image of incarnate Spirit. And for this we may need to leave the teacher's form behind. The teacher points the way, but we find our own way home.

# *Notes*

1. *The Hundred Thousand Songs of Milarepa*, translated by G. C. C. Chang (New York: Harper & Row, 1962), p. 116.

2. *Shankara's Crest Jewel of Discrimination*, translated by S. Prabhavananda & C. Isherwood (Los Angeles: Vedanta Press, 1975), p. 4.

3. Arthur Deikman called this the deautomatization of consciousness—the dishabituation of awareness that enables us to shift out of our usual, conditioned perceptual frameworks into a mode of perception that is more vivid, sensuous, and animated. All spiritual practices such as meditation are ways of systematically deconditioning awareness, breaking down our ordinary state of mind and making us receptive to new modes of perceiving and knowing. We see more of reality because our minds are less clouded. According to Deikman, mystical experiences and expanded states of consciousnes can be understood in terms of perceptual expansion, the awareness of new dimensions of the total stimulus array, so that aspects of reality previously unavailable enter awareness. We see the world with new eyes, new freedom. A. Deikman, "Deautomatization and the Mystic Experience," *Psychiatry* (29:324–88, 1966).

4. W. James, *The Varieties of Religious Experience*, cited in F. C. Happold, *Mysticism: A Study and an Anthology* (Middlesex, England: Penguin, 1963), pp. 138–39.

5. *Shankara's Crest Jewel of Discrimination*, translated by S. Prabhavananda & C. Isherwood (Los Angeles: Vedanta Press, 1975), pp.52–4, 91.

6. J. White, *What is Enlightenment?* (New York, Paragon House, 1985), pp. xii–xiv.

7. E. Conze, *Buddhism: Its Essence and Development* (New York: Harper & Row, 1975), p. 204.

8. S. Grof, *Beyond the Brain* (Albany, NY: State Univ. of New York Press, 1985).

9. Ibid., pp. 44–5.

10. J. White, *What is Enlightenment?* (New York, Paragon House, 1985), pp. xv.

11. Excerpt from one of my poems.

12. *Shankara's Crest Jewel of Discrimination*, translated by S. Prabhavananda & C. Isherwood (Los Angeles: Vedanta Press, 1975), pp. 36, 42–3.

13. L. Nelson, "Living Liberation in Sankara and Classical Advaita." In *Living Liberation in Hindu Thought*, edited by A. O. Fort & P. Y. Mumme (Albany, NY: State Univ. of New York Press, 1996), pp. 19–20.

14. D. Godman, *Living by the Words of Bhagavan* (Tiruvannamalai, India: Sri Annamalai Swami Ashram Trust, 1995), p. 259–260.

15. H. I. Khan, *The Complete Sayings of Hazrat Inayat Khan* (New Lebanon, NY: Sufi Order Publications, 1991).

16. This idea is discussed at length in my book, *Astrology and Spiritual Awakening* (Berkeley, CA: Dawn Mountain Press, 1994).

17. G. Krishna, *Kundalini, The Evolutionary Power in Man* (Boston: Shambhala, 1970).

18. D. Khyentse, *The Wish Fulfilling Tree* (Boston, Shambala, 1988), pp. 11–12.

19. V. Mansfield, "The Guru-Disciple Relationship: Making Connections and Withdrawing Projections." Unpublished paper. Available on the internet at this address: www.lightlink.com/vic/guru.

20. These themes are discussed at greater length under Stage Seven.

21. D. Frawley, "All Gurus Great and Small," *Yoga Journal,* March–April, 1997, p. 34.

22. See G. Bogart, *Finding Your Life's Calling* (Berkeley, CA: Dawn Mountain Press, 1995).

# Separating From a Spiritual Teacher

The one with clear eyes will tell you to align your sight, with his finger and the head of the crow seated on the tree. Then, look beyond the finger and the crow, the moon is sighted. But if you hold onto the finger or the head of the crow, can you see the moon? Most teachers keep their students holding the finger and thus both are satisfied. As ego becomes inflated, the finger is worshipped and the new moon is forgotten. Only the selfless one says to go beyond and declares himself a mere indicator, a humble messenger not to be held.

*H. W. L. Poonja, Truth Is*[1]

Everything in life is cyclic: All things begin, develop, change, and eventually come to an end. We find a teacher, we study with that teacher, and eventually we need to move on, even if we love that teacher deeply and carry him or her with us wherever we go. Our needs in the life cycle change. There are times to be a disciple, devotee, or spiritual apprentice, and times when it is appropriate to do something else with our lives. In many cases, external training under the guidance of a spiritual teacher ends. Either we lose interest and move on, or we leave having absorbed the teaching, and having our feet set firmly on our own spiritual path.

Our relationship with a spiritual teacher tends to become a focal point in our lives, or a period of our lives. But it is also one of those experiences that we often try to freeze into permanence, failing to recognize it as a *phase*. When we find the teacher, we experience ecstasy and gratitude. We surrender to the teacher from a place beyond the mind. We feel a cord of love connecting us. But sometimes we must part ways, even if we feel profound and undying gratitude for the teacher's guidance and uplifting influence.

Some students will never leave their teachers. A student whose desire for enlightenment, God-realization, or self-transcendence is powerful enough may remain with a teacher steadfastly despite the considerable inner tensions often generated during the process of testing discussed earlier. One student remained devoted to his teacher even after accidentally finding the supposedly celibate teacher in bed with another student:

> I've learned not to question. His wisdom and spiritual power cannot be denied, so as far as I'm concerned, he can do whatever he wants. I'm past the point of trying to understand him or judge him according to the standards of ordinary morality. I've surrendered. The only thing I want is enlightenment and he's the only person I've ever met that I believe can lead me toward that goal. He is not an ordinary human being. I could view his actions as a sign that he is morally deranged and a fake. But I prefer to view his strange behavior as a way he tests students to see who is really serious and who is not. The serious, committed devotee will stay with the guru no matter what he does.

While some students are this unshakably devoted to their teachers, equally common are instances where the student-teacher relationship runs astray, often resulting in great confusion, bitterness, or despair for the disciple. Many spiritual apprentices, who have previously experienced surrender and devotion, eventually feel an overriding need to leave their teachers. I have found this to be true for many students who have had positive experiences with their teachers, as well as for those who leave feeling that a teacher has disappointed, injured, or betrayed them in some way.

Many difficulties and complications in student-teacher relationships arise, or become evident, at that moment when students attempt to individuate, to leave the teacher's immediate company, and to pursue their own life projects. While many traditions recommend a more or less protracted period of association with a spiritual teacher, there usually comes a time when students either have become disillusioned with the teacher or have assimilated from the teacher all that they can for the moment, have other affairs or interests to attend to, and begin to want to be on their own. Of course, students may leave feeling the blessing, love, and continuing internal influence of the teacher. In such instances their separation, whether permanent or temporary, can be undertaken with mutual goodwill, affection, and respect. However, it is also common for the exhiliration, gratitude, and joy that students felt earlier to turn sour, leaving a lasting residue of anger or bitterness.

Such was the case with Robert, a young man who had spent eight years as a student of a teacher who emphasized surrender and obedience. After some time he had become one of the teacher's personal attendants. During this time he loved the teacher very much and felt privileged to serve him, feeling that he was being transformed by his close proximity with such a highly evolved being. His departure from the teacher's spiritual community came in the aftermath of allegations of financial and sexual misconduct. Robert sought counseling for help in exploring his feelings of anger and betrayal, and in readjusting to life outside this teacher's community.

There were aspects of discipleship that had been distressing to Robert long before the events that hastened his departure. In fact, after the first several years of discipleship, Robert had considered leaving his teacher to pursue his own calling to become a novelist. Robert had largely abandoned this work during the period of his discipleship, and the teacher had always spoken derisively of his ambition, saying that Robert was entertaining this fantasy as a way of bolstering up his ego in the face of the teacher's "fire of ego-destroying grace." Robert had suppressed his creative urge and remained a loyal devotee. Now, in the aftermath of his departure, Robert alternated between angry defiance toward his teacher, a determination to succeed on his own, and paralyzing feelings of fear, worthlessness, and guilt. Robert's case, to which we will return momentarily, illustrates the dilemma that students can face in leaving a spiritual teacher and reestablishing an independent life.

## Emotional Conflicts in Spiritual Apprenticeship

Psychologist Daniel Levinson views the relationship between a mentor and novice or apprentice as inherently conflictual, because the novice is subject simultaneously to feelings of admiration and respect, and feelings of resentment, inferiority, and envy towards the mentor. In Levinson's view, mentor-student relationships often end with conflict and bitterness because of the inherently ambiguous role of the mentor, who is a transitional figure—both parent and peer—who must eventually be left behind by the novice in order to fulfill the developmental task of "becoming one's own man."[2] Levinson writes that often,

> The mentor who only yesterday was regarded as an enabling teacher and friend has become a tyrannical father or smothering mother. The mentor, for his part, finds the young [person] inexplicably touchy, unreceptive to even the best counsel, irrationally rebellious and ungrateful.[3]

Spiritual apprentices are especially prone to inner tension at this stage, for, on the one hand, they yearn for the good father or mother who will make them feel special; while on the other hand they may perceive the mentor as a bad parental figure, dictatorial, and manipulative. I believe that this tendency to split the perception of teachers is a central factor in the conflict experienced when the time arrives for the student to separate from the teacher. Levinson's analysis also suggests the essentially paradoxical nature of all mentoring relationships, which involve a temporary dependence of the novice upon the teacher. This dependence, however, is undertaken to allow the novice to ultimately emerge transformed and independent. A similar insight was expressed by transpersonal psychologist Ken Wilber in the context of a discussion of relationships with spiritual teachers:

> Virtually all authentic Eastern or mystical traditions maintain that the guru is representative of one's own highest nature, and once that nature is realized, the guru's formal authority and function is ended.... Thus, once the student awakens to his or her own equally higher status as Buddha-Brahman, the function of the guru is ended and the authority of the guru evaporates. In Zen, for instance, once a person achieves major satori (causal insight), the relationship between *roshi* and disciple changes from master and student to brother and brother (or sister-brother, or sister-sister)—and this is explicitly so stated. The guru, as authority, is phase temporary.[4]

While it is easy to understand that discipleship is phase-temporary, a developmental stage to be passed through, it is quite another, more difficult matter, to actually go through the process of separation from a teacher, or to assume the stance toward the teacher of an equal.

## *The Case of Otto Rank*

A relevant historical example of the complex dynamics of mentorship and apprenticeship is the relationship between the great psychologist Otto Rank and his teacher, Sigmund Freud—which led to a predicament that Ira Progoff describes as "a disciple's dilemma."⁵ Freud had put Rank through college and graduate school, introduced Rank into the circle of his closest associates, and helped establish him in the psychoanalytic profession. Now, however, after years of receiving encouragement, guidance, praise, financial assistance, and professional favors from Freud, and after making many important contributions to the field of psychoanalysis, Rank began to feel a need to differentiate and distance himself from his mentor. Matters came to a head in 1924, when Rank published *The Trauma of Birth*, where he first set forth his own psychological theory. I will quote liberally from Progoff's account:

> Increasingly Rank found that it was his intellectual rather than his artistic energies that were being called into play, and a major part of his personality was thus left unfulfilled. . . . Nonetheless, his strong personal attachment to Freud—an attachment verging on dependence—and his sense of gratitude for favors received in the past prevented his breaking his connection in a deliberate or abrupt way. . . . But . . . the net effect of the book [*The Trauma of Birth*], and perhaps its unconscious intention, was to precipitate his separation from Freud. . . . Rank [later] made the acute observation that one of the aftermaths of a creative act is an attack of guilt feelings, remorse, and anxiety. . . . In making this point, Rank may well have been describing his own experience, for we know that when *The Trauma of Birth* drew strong attacks from the Freudian circle Rank was on the verge of retracting his views. The thought of being cut off from Freud became exceedingly painful for him, for he feared the isolation and ostracism it might bring. . . . [The result of publishing this book] was to upset his accustomed position as the loyal disciple of a revered master. . . . Rank had much for which to be grateful, and his attachment to Freud was deep indeed. But how could he develop the artist in himself and fulfill his own need for creativity while remaining a

loyal disciple? . . . His devotion to Freud . . . conflicted with the necessary unfoldment of his own individuality, and his act of self-liberation in writing *The Trauma of Birth* was followed by a sense of remorse that took many forms over the years and from which Rank never fully recovered. . . . [Although Rank moved away from Freud's circle in Vienna] it was much easier to separate himself from Freud geographically than psychologically. The man and his teachings remained at the center of a continuous struggle in which Rank was forced to engage within himself. . . . Freud, who had been his protector, was now his psychic adversary.[6]

Here we see the depths of the conflict one may face when standing at the crossroads between continuing allegiance to a mentor, and the need to set forth on one's own independent journey. This passage accurately describes issues that are also pertinent to many teacher-student or guru-disciple relationships. Progoff also makes the significant observation that not only did Rank have an extremely strong personal attachment to Freud, but Freud was also quite attached to Rank and was eager to avoid defection by such a close and devoted disciple. This example demonstrates that to understand the problematic aspects of spiritual apprenticeship we need to consider how the same dynamics of *transference* and *countertransference* that operate in the context of psychotherapy may also be present in student-mentor or guru-disciple relationships.

## Developmental Readiness for Discipleship

The passage just cited described the student's conflict between feeling unfulfilled as a disciple and feelings of gratitude, attachment, and dependency toward the mentor. Progoff also noted the fear of ostracism by the teacher and the teacher's circle of followers and the feelings of guilt and remorse that are precipitated by the student's impulse to separate or express his or her individuality. In addition, there are several other basic psychological and cultural issues that have a bearing on "the disciple's dilemma" in our current context.

First, it is important to consider the role played by unresolved childhood issues a person may have regarding individuation and separation from parental figures. In the dance of discipleship, the teacher comes to play many roles for the student: mentor, friend, trickster, and, most notably, parent. Not surprisingly, some students reenact old parent-child scripts and interactions with their teachers, just as many clients do with their psychotherapists. Thus, students who revolt against the teacher's authority may be acting out unresolved childhood or adolescent issues. Similarly, students who have never adequately resolved issues of separation or differentiation may hang onto the guru's feet long past the time when discipleship has actually served their development.

However, such parallels need not imply a reductionistic interpretation of the nature of spiritual apprenticeship. For example, some observers try to reduce discipleship simply to unhealthy dependency, unresolved family of origin issues, and psychological or emotional deficits. Such explanations are a quintessential example of what Ken Wilber calls the "pre-trans fallacy"—the confusing of issues and stages of consciousness from early childhood, prior to the formation of the ego, with later transpersonal stages of development in which one transcends ordinary ego consciousness.[7] People become involved in mentoring relationships at different stages of their lives and for different purposes. While some may become students of spiritual teachers in an attempt to avoid the developmental tasks of individuation and adulthood, for others discipleship is an appropriate, even a necessary, step in maturation. Clearly, as transpersonal psychologist Jack Engler has shown, spiritual practices in general and the spiritual teacher-disciple relationship in particular, while intended to lead the student toward transegoic, transpersonal stages of evolution, may become complicated by unresolved egoic, or even pre-egoic, issues and concerns—for example, disturbances in the ability to sustain interpersonal relationships.[8] But these tendencies do not negate the fact that countless seekers throughout history have pursued the path of spiritual apprenticeship and attested to its efficacy. In short, it would be inaccurate to reductionistically pathologize discipleship.

At the same time, it seems reasonable to suggest that those considering commitment to a spiritual teacher should have already successfully traversed some of the fundamental egoic stages of human development (as outlined, for example, by Ken Wilber) and achieved a certain degree of adult maturity and strength as an individual.[9] Such a person can seek a spiritual teacher as an outgrowth of a genuine longing for spiritual awakening, freedom from the limitations of ego-centered awareness, and evolution into transpersonal stages of consciousness. Without prior resolution of developmental tasks related to social adjustment (work), individuation (identity), and relationships (love), such concerns may begin to override the deeper purpose of spiritual apprenticeship, which is to lead the seeker beyond egoic consciousness into transegoic realms, the experience of enlightenment. The need to resolve such "unfinished business" is one primary reason many students feel they must separate from their spiritual teachers.

This is not to imply that there are, or should be, strict developmental prerequisites for discipleship. Discipleship and spiritual practices do not have in many respects the same goals, methods, or outcomes as psychotherapy.[10] However, nearly everyone who approaches a spiritual teacher probably has unresolved egoic concerns that need attention, and these days such concerns might better be addressed in psychotherapy than through discipleship.

## The Confusion of Discipleship and Psychotherapy

There are two major implications of the confusion of psychotherapy with training under a spiritual teacher. First, many Western students of spiritual teachers have the hope or expectation that their teachers will fulfill the role of psychotherapist. This obscures the fact that a spiritual teacher's concern is generally not with strengthening a student's sense of self, improving relationship skills, or working through difficult emotions—the traditional province of a therapist. Rather, it is to reveal the reality (e.g., *Atman*, *sunyata*, God, pure consciousness) beyond, or prior to, the disciple's identity structure and thought forms. Therefore, those who approach spiritual teachers looking for the kind of care and support a therapist might offer are setting themselves up for disappointment, and misunderstanding the purpose of spiritual apprenticeship and the role of the spiritual teacher.

The second implication of the contemporary interface of therapist-client and guru-disciple relationships relates to the impact of therapeutic models on our conceptions of teacher-student interactions. The growth of Western psychotherapy has included the evolution and widespread adoption of ethical codes for therapists' behavior toward clients that have had an impact on how we believe spiritual teachers should behave toward their students. Indeed, many contemporary Westerners have come to expect spiritual teachers to abide by standards of ethics and behavior similar to those of other contemporary professionals such as doctors, psychologists, and counselors.

These issues have been raised by numerous recent instances in which students have confronted their spiritual teachers with purported abuses of their position. Some teachers faced with such situations have denied the charges outright, justified their actions as crazy wisdom teachings, or contended that their students were enacting adolescent types of rebellion against a parental surrogate. Others have defended themselves on the grounds that their rebellious students were failing to properly understand and honor the sanctity of the spiritual teacher's position in traditional spiritual lineages, where trust in the teacher's methods and fundamental good intention are assumed, and where the teacher's actions, motivations, or apparent abuses of power are rarely, if ever, questioned.

It is also possible that the nature of the spiritual teacher-student relationship may be changing as this tradition is revived in our era. While equality and a cooperative spirit were not prevalent features of traditional discipleship, contemporary students of spiritual lineages and practices increasingly demand that their teachers treat them as equal partners in a democratic process of spiritual training or community living. Whether Americans inheriting a tradition of democracy and individualism can hope to achieve spiritual illumination through nondemocratic forms of traditional discipleship demanding obedience and surrender without considerable discomfort is still an open question.

At the same time, the tradition of spiritual apprenticeship could be strengthened in our culture by teachers able to better adapt to the Western cultural context—by treating students with nonpossessive warmth, by respecting their independence, by showing a willingness to scrutinize, and in some cases correct, their own behavior, and by relinquishing their demand for absolute surrender of the student.

Having briefly described the influence of unresolved developmental issues, the blurring of the distinction between discipleship and psychotherapy, and some cultural assumptions regarding the authority of spiritual teachers, let us now examine the influence of basic transference dynamics that often cloud the perceptions and experience of both spiritual teacher and disciple.

## *Transference Dynamics in the Student-Teacher Relationship*

One of the major contributions of modern psychology to our understanding of human consciousness and behavior has been to develop insight into the phenomenon known as transference—in which relationships with others are colored by emotions, themes, and perceptions deriving from earlier relationships, especially the earliest relationships with parents or parental figures. Transference phenomena seem to be a part of all close human relationships; we rarely see others accurately but rather view them through the filter of our fears and expectations, based on past experience of important people in our lives. According to psychoanalytic theorist Heinz Kohut, there are two main types of transference: mirroring and idealizing.[11] The mirroring transference is the hope and expectation that others will be constantly available to see, acknowledge, and validate us, whereas the idealization transference is the tendency to perceive others as perfect and worthy of our esteem and utmost trust. Satisfaction of our needs for both mirroring and idealization is essential to healthy psychological development. To build self-esteem we need to be seen and mirrored by others and reassured of our importance to others; and to develop clear personal goals and ambitions we need idealized others whose qualities we can emulate.

Kohut has also described a third kind of transference characterized by a desire to feel a sense of "twinship" or alikeness with another person. This "alter-ego" transference may be very significant in those cases where discipleship proceeds smoothly and the student comes to feel a deep sense of identification with the teacher. It may be one of the mechanisms operative in the effectiveness of techniques in which the student meditates upon the teacher. In the present context I will focus on the mirroring and idealization types of transference, since these more commonly lead to complications.

## Mirroring Transference and Discipleship

In the mirroring transference we seek "empathic resonance" from another person. By being consistently, accurately, and sensitively received by another person, we learn to feel real, accepted, and valuable to others, and thus, in turn, to ourselves. In mirroring relationships we do not perceive others in their actuality and otherness (in what Martin Buber termed a mature "I-Thou" relationship) but rather as what Kohut calls "self-objects," extensions of the self that we use to bolster our own self-esteem and sense of specialness.

In the teacher-student relationship, teacher and student mutually mirror one another. The student often receives mirroring from the teacher if, as in Rank's case, he becomes important and valuable to the teacher, and receives the latter's affirmation, attention, and praise. Similarly, the spiritual guide may strongly experience a mirroring transference with the disciple, basking in the novice's admiration, devotion, and love—although presumably there are teachers who have transcended such needs.

According to Mario Jacoby, the person who serves as the mirroring self-object can be either undervalued or overvalued. When students receive extensive mirroring, they may overvalue the guru or spiritual teacher, who becomes essential to their internal equilibrium and self-esteem, and without whom they may feel empty, depleted, lost, or depressed. Thus, my client Robert, whom I described earlier, felt confused, disoriented, and worthless after leaving his teacher. In a sense, Robert had been overvaluing the "guru self-object." Conversely, as he realized that the teacher had seemed to favor other disciples and that he did not enjoy the teacher's exclusive love, Robert became enraged and began to angrily devalue the teacher.

However, these dynamics can be transposed. For teachers also may be subject to overvaluing the mirroring self-object, feeling that the love and attention of students are essential to their own well-being. Similarly, a teacher may become jealous or enraged and may devalue a student if the latter shows signs of lessening devotion or competing allegiances to other teachers or loved ones. Indeed, unconscious transference needs may account for the rigidity with which some spiritual teachers demand exclusive devotion. Thus, it is important to consider the extent to which the teacher may receive narcissistic gratification from relationship with students. In some cases a student may be psychologically more mature than the teacher, which can cause a student-teacher association to end in a hurtful, painful way.

Discipleship is a two-way relationship, in which both partners must act responsibly and consciously. Some contemporary psychotherapists have recognized the need to receive training in meditative disciplines to increase their compassion and their stillness of mind in order to best facilitate healing for their clients. Similarly, perhaps more spiritual teachers would benefit from examining their own personal needs for mirroring, admiration, and idealization from their students. This might even one day be considered part of the necessary training for those performing the role of spiritual teacher.

## Idealization and the Shadow in Discipleship

According to Jacoby (summarizing the views of Heinz Kohut), in idealization transferences one person projects archetypal images of perfection, omnipotence, and omniscience upon the other, whose perfection is equated with one's own perfection through a psychological process of fusion.[12] In childhood this idealization of others is considered a necessary precursor to the eventual development of one's own goals and ambitions. Similarly, the disciple's deep devotion and tendency to view the teacher as perfect and all-knowing may in part be founded upon this kind of idealization. Kohut and his colleague Ernest Wolf have written,

> Ideal-hungry personalities are forever in search of others whom they can admire for their prestige, power, beauty, intelligence or moral stature. They can experience themselves as worthwhile only so long as they can relate to selfobjects to whom they can look up. In most cases . . . the inner void cannot forever be filled by these means. The ideal-hungry feels the persistence of the structural deficit and . . . begins to look for—and of course he inevitably finds—some realistic defects in his God. The search for new idealizable selfobjects is then continued, always with the hope that the next great figure to whom the ideal-hungry attaches himself will not disappoint him.[13]

Through gradual disappointments—similar to those by which a child's idealizations of a parental figure are modified—we learn to modify distorted perceptions of others, and to perceive them more realistically—that is, as individuals possessing a mixture of both good and bad qualities, rather than as being either all good or all bad. According to Kohut's theory, only when such idealizing perceptions of others are gradually modified can we begin to modify our own grandiosity and arrive at a more realistic assessment of our ambitions, talents, and value. Ideally, students of spiritual teachers are able to recognize their idealizations of their mentors, to contain the disappointments of these idealizations that inevitably arise, and to accept their teachers as human beings with a mixture of good and bad characteristics.

Unfortunately, this developmental process frequently does not unfold in such an optimal manner. In such cases a very different scenario may ensue, in which the disciple may begin to negatively "idealize" the teacher, viewing him or her as the embodiment of absolute Evil. Donald Sandner discusses this phenomenon in his essay on "The Split Shadow and the Father-Son Relationship," observing the tendency to project both the positive and negative characteristics of our own bipolar shadow.[14] The unconscious, unintegrated, positive characteristics of the self "tend to be represented by superior, noble, heroic, spiritual or religious figures."[15] These are the figures who become the objects of our idealizations. Conversely, the negative pole of the shadow complex (containing culturally undesirable qualities and personal characteristics that we have repressed) tends to be projected in such a way that we perceive others as evil, aggressive, lustful, hateful, menacing, or sinister.

This perspective sheds some light on why Robert's positive idealization of his spiritual teacher had turned into a negative, devaluing attitude toward a figure he now perceived as cruel, greedy, dishonest, authoritarian, and manipulative. Similarly, this may help clarify Otto Rank's predicament; as Progoff put it, "Freud, who had been his protector, was now his psychic adversary."[16]

Thus, while to some extent accurate perceptions of the teacher's actual shortcomings may be involved, the dramatic reversal of the disciple's affection may partially be the result of projecting first the positive and then the negative facets of his or her own shadow upon the teacher.

## An Archetypal Perspective on Spiritual Apprenticeship

An illuminating perspective on the student-teacher relationship can be derived from psychologist James Hillman's comments about the archetypes of the Puer and the Senex.[17] Hillman has noted the coexistence and interrelationship between the archetypes of Youth and Maturity, known as Puer and Senex. More specifically, the Messiah aspect of the Puer — the aspect of the self that is filled with a sense of infinite possibilities and personal mission and is subject to psychic inflation— constellates the complementary figure of the Wise Old Man. The Wise Old Man (or Wise Old Woman) is a symbol of perfection, psychic wholeness, and the internal guiding function of the Self, from whom the Puer-Messiah derives a sense of stability, power, and recognition. In the course of maturation, the Puer-Messiah is transformed through the emergence of the Puer-Hero—the archetype of youth heroically actualizing the Puer-Messiah's visions, goals, and sense of personal mission. However, the Puer-Hero corresponds internally not to the beneficent Wise Old Man, who came forth to guide and befriend the Puer-Messiah, but rather to the figure of the Old King of Power—symbol of power and social authority. In Hillman's view, the Old King of Power is a psychic image of both external and internalized social forces that obstruct the Puer-Hero's growth. It is a symbol of the reality principle, the disapproving father, the competitiveness of the marketplace, the world that does not immediately welcome and applaud the Puer-Hero's ambitions and achievements. In fact, the Old King of Power represents everything that seems to actively try to thwart the Puer's ambitions. Thus, the Puer-Hero must fight to overcome the figure of the Old King in order to emerge as a man or woman of power and achievement in his or her own right.

Here we observe the essential paradox in the internal world of the Puer-Disciple. The individual derives inspiration, strength, and comfort by associating with the Senex-Mentor when the latter is perceived as a benificent, helpful, wise figure. But the Puer-Novice's attempts to actualize the dreams and possibilities envisioned with the Old Wise Person's help also constellates a perception of the teacher-guide as a representative of all social norms, conventions, expectations, and institutional structures that appear to actively obstruct the novice's self-actualization, and against which he or she must therefore struggle.

In Otto Rank's case, these dynamics were evident in his increasing boredom in his position as Freud's follower (as Progoff put it, "A major part of his personality was thus left unfulfilled") and his yearning for new freedom and new channels of self-expression. Something within the disciple knows that it may not be possible to fully accomplish his or her own goals while remaining in a position of inferiority, deference, or servitude with respect to the mentor or spiritual guide. In many cases the student's individuation will eventually force a separation from the teacher, and relinquishment of the role of the loyal disciple. Of course, this process is considerably easier if the teacher is able to tolerate, encourage, and respect the autonomous development and individuation of the student, allow the articulation of an independent point of view, and the accomplishment of the tasks of the student's own life project.[18] Indeed, a teacher's degree of skillfulness and sincere good intention toward students is made apparent in how he or she reacts to, and hopefully encourages, the student's natural need to graduate from the teacher.

## Separation, Guilt, and Self-Appointment

A spiritual apprentice may feel a profound identity crisis and sense of loss looming when contemplating separation from a teacher. The need to let go of an accustomed identity as the loyal follower of a great teacher may produce profound uncertainty and anxiety. Although the period of spiritual apprenticeship is often a period of "liminality" (i.e., transitional suspension between worlds, social roles, or periods of life[19]), ending a relationship with a spiritual teacher may induce a frightening sense of being "betwixt and between." This possibility is more likely when the student is not separating with a clear sense of an individual purpose or destiny that necessitates the separation, but rather out of an angry, negative reaction to the teacher-mentor— full of projection of unresolved parental issues or the negative traits of his or her own shadow. However, even in cases where the novice knows that the time has come to stand independently and to forge an independent pathway, he or she may experience considerable guilt, anxiety, and remorse regarding separation from the teacher.

Otto Rank noted that the impulse to separate, to individuate, and to create is always attended by feelings of guilt—which often derive from fear of injuring or destroying a parental figure.[20] Recall how Rank's feelings of gratitude toward Freud and his fear of ostracism and isolation caused him to attempt to remain in his discipleship role. Nevertheless, the heroic personality—exemplified in Rank's writings by the artist—struggles against this guilt and wills himself or herself into existence as a creative individual. And just as modern artists have had to appoint themselves artists in the face of social disapproval or ridicule, so too the growth of the creative personality almost always requires severing symbiotic ties in an act of "self-appointment."[21] Similarly, students may need to overcome the guilt of separation and learn to feel worthy of being independent, even if they continue to acknowledge a spiritual teacher's influence and authority.

It is important to recognize the extent to which teachers may exacerbate students' feelings of guilt by their actions or statements. For their own conscious or unconscious reasons, teachers may seek to keep the novice within the community of close devotees. Discipleship, like psychotherapy, involves a very human kind of relationship—notwithstanding beliefs that a true spiritual teacher is more-than-merely-human. Therefore, the motivations of the teacher as well as the student need to be considered to fully understand the dynamics of such relationships.

One man whom I worked with was affiliated with an extraordinarily narcissistic teacher. Dale wrote his teacher a letter questioning his teacher's affairs with two students, his arrogance toward students during classes, and lies he had told Dale directly. The teacher's response was full of scorn, condescension, and seething anger. He belittled Dale, saying, "You never were much of a student. I don't know why I invested so much of myself in someone so unworthy. If you want to learn anything from me you must learn never to question me or my actions." This is actually what this so-called teacher wrote to his student!

As we saw earlier, teachers have their own needs for power, admiration, fellowship, mirroring, as well as financial and organizational needs, all of which may become motivating factors in their efforts to prevent "defection" by their students. While some teachers may be free of such motivations, we should not assume that all are. Most apprenticeships are with teachers who combine both altruistic-benificent and selfish-narcissistic motivations. Wise teachers will recognize these tendencies within themselves and will attempt to prevent them from contaminating the guidance of students.

## Distortions of Discipleship

According to Jungian psychologist Donald Sandner, discipleship or apprenticeship is potentially a process of initiation into a new state of individuated existence through a process of submission, fusion, and re-emergence.[22] Students submit to the teacher's authority, and fuse internally with the mentor in order to derive strength, clarity, and an internal image of perfection around which their own ego ideals can begin to solidify. The completion of the relationship, in Sandner's view, should witness the reemergence of the disciple or initiate as an independent man or woman. However, major distortions in this process can occur. If the disciple remains unconsciously bound to the position of submission to the Father-Master-Mentor, Sandner suggests that the mentoring relationship can devolve into a spiralling sequence of compulsive sadomasochistic acts from which the student can in some cases derive either pleasure or a sense of security.[23] My own observations are that in such cases, the student may adopt a deliberate posture of humiliation, one that can be instilled and reinforced by experiences of being physically or emotionally injured, psychically immobilized, severely criticized, or publicly denounced by the teacher.

In Robert's case, this process was enacted quite dramatically. Long before his departure, the teacher had often embarrassed Robert publicly, castigating him for incompetence, and, on several occasions in private, physically striking him. Robert's response had not been to rebel, but to internalize his teacher's criticisms and to come back for more. He had held out the hope that by continuing to remain under the teacher's guidance he might yet win some great praise, confirmation, or sponsorship from his "mentor" that would enable him to advance spiritually. In the course of therapy, Robert slowly began to recognize how the abusiveness of this relationship was virtually a replica of his relationship with his father—an angry alcoholic who had humiliated and physically injured Robert, and whose approval Robert had always doggedly and unsuccessfully sought. This story grimly illustrates both the potential influence of the student's developmental issues, and the exaggerated form that the relationship between teacher and disciple can take in some unfortunate instances.

## Healing the Wounds of Separation

Robert suffered significant emotional turmoil as a result of his discipleship, and it took him many years to work through his anger and resentment toward his teacher and his feelings of remorse over unfulfilled promises and expectations. What was most helpful to him was to write about his experiences and thereby to begin to discover his own thoughts, feelings, and story. He wrote and eventually published a novel about a spiritual community led by a charismatic teacher.

The student may take a significant step along the road to healing the wound of separation with the realization that, despite the gratitude he or she may feel toward the teacher, the guru's teachings are nevertheless inadequate in certain respects; or that some of the teacher's actions are wrong, destructive, or indefensible. This requires a recognition that although he or she may have taught the student much about spirituality, love, or meditation, the teacher is not necessarily the final authority in all matters. For example, the teacher's instructions about spiritual practice or doctrine may not adequately illuminate other important aspects of our lives, such as sexuality and relationships, the need to find fulfilling labor and pursue other forms of education, or the anger and despair so many of us feel today about ecological destruction and social injustice. We reach an important stage in our maturation when we recognize and accept that we will have to look outside the guru's teaching for guidance in these areas.

As noted earlier, a fundamental sadness or loneliness often arises as we accept our existential aloneness. The spiritual teacher can only go so far with us. Sooner or later the teacher will die, send us away, reject us, or let us down. We may experience disappointment because teachers refuse to give us their approval; or because they are fundamentally inaccessible to us on a personal level; or because we recognize that in some respects the teacher is basically a fool. Other teachers may disappoint us when we discover how cruel they can be and how immature they are in their own emotional and spiritual development.

# The Role of Dreams

In other cases, resolution of the relationship with a spiritual teacher may be facilitated through the spontaneous symbol-producing activity of the unconscious, in the form of dreams. A man who had spent years affiliated with an ashram in which many disciples had taken monastic vows of celibacy and poverty and who was now grappling with issues of separation from the teacher and his desire for sexual life and marriage, had the following two dreams: In the first, he was walking through the ashram and noticed several of the swamis lifting weights, while another swami, a usually austere and very dry monk, was walking hand-in-hand with a woman and wearing an expensive tennis outfit. His guru stood on the roof of the ashram spraying everyone with a hose. In the second dream, he walked into a large meditation hall in which hundreds of seats were arranged facing *away* from the guru's seat at the front of the room. The first dream seemed to say that the dryness of his inner world was ready to receive the waters of life; clearly the tendency here was for the swamis to embrace the life of the body, sexuality, and the company of women. The second dream vividly portrayed his readiness to remain in reverential relationship with this spiritual teacher, but now with his attention more directed away from the guru and out into the world.

A twenty-nine-year-old man named Chris was also aided in addressing these issues by a series of remarkable dreams. Chris was an ardent spiritual seeker, with a particular interest in hatha yoga. He had studied with numerous teachers, but always ended up in some way disappointed. Two of his teachers died without bestowing on him the enlightenment, the approval, or the recognition of his high level of spiritual development that he had sought from them. He was upset to learn that a third teacher was sleeping with students. The instruction of yet another teacher had contributed to a serious arm injury, from which he was still suffering acutely. To make things worse, this teacher had denied any responsibility in the matter. Chris was full of bitterness, cynicism, and disappointment. During this period, he had the following dream:

> A small baby boy with a very large Buddha head is lying on the ground. He appears to be on the verge of an epileptic seizure,

trembling and thrashing about spastically, but his parents are no-where to be found. I try to hold him down while "Ron" [one of the teachers who had disappointed him] sprinkled water on his third eye. Ron says to me, "No, you're not doing it right," and he insists that he should hold the boy down while I sprinkle the water on him. The boy's convulsions become intense and he thrashes around uncontrollably. As he does so I hear the boy's voice angrily exclaiming "You f____ a____, you're supposed to be helping me but you can't even prevent this from happening to me!"The boy begins smashing every bone in his body on the ground, and twists his head so much that his neck breaks and his head falls off. Finally all that remains of his body is one arm bone.

The baby with a Buddha's head seemed to be an image of the enlightenment that Chris had pursued since his youth but that had thus far eluded him. The dream portrayed his disappointment and anger at the inability of his teachers to help him, and his feeling of being blamed for his injury ("You're not doing it right"). The dream also suggests that his potential for achieving an enlightened state of consciousness (the Buddha's head) was being destroyed by the anger, rage, and bitterness toward all of the teachers whom he felt had failed to initiate and sponsor him properly. In this sense, the statement "You're not doing it right" is directed at the gurus who had disappointed him. In addition, the imagery of bodily dismemberment in the dream evoked themes of shamanic initiation. Thus, this dream also seemed to carry the message that he should view his injury (the arm bone in the dream) as a shamanic wound suffered in the course of initiation by an elder—an initiation that, while it had torn him apart physically and emotionally, could indeed lead to his eventual reintegration.

After several months of reflection on this dream and efforts to release his negative feelings toward his teachers, Chris had another dream:

> I am in a lush green meadow, standing near a large, very ancient and beautiful tree. I am observing a vigil here for my dead teacher and father, who is buried underneath this tree. It is a very solemn moment, yet I feel very much at peace.

Chris felt that the burial of his dead teacher and father signified the death of the need for an external spiritual guide and heralded the emergence of his capacity to become his own source of wisdom, vision, and authority. And the appearance of the tree, perennial symbol of growth, maturation, and rebirth, seemed to suggest that he was growing closer to resolution of his issues with spiritual teachers. In his words, "Now, with these men fertilizing my roots, I can become my own father."

## Discipleship as a Culture of Embeddedness

The teacher-student relationship is not an end in itself, although it may remain a continuing source of inspiration and joy. Instead, as both Daniel Levinson and Ken Wilber have suggested, it is a transitional relationship that is intended to lead beyond itself. Psychologist Robert Kegan has characterized human development as a passage through a series of holding environments or "cultures of embeddedness"—such as the symbiotic tie with the mother, the structure of the family, educational institutions, and interpersonal relationships—that nurture and support us, and that let go of us when we are ready to differentiate from them.[24] For Kegan, growth means the emergence from "embeddedness cultures" and the subsequent reappropriation of the objects of that culture. These objects, which were formerly part of the self, are now recognized to be other, apart from the self, yet also an environment with which the differentiated self can be in relationship. Nevertheless, the tendency is for a person to repudiate a culture of embeddedness, such as the family, in the process of separating from it. Kegan notes:

> Growth itself is not alone a matter of separation and repudiation, of killing off the past. This is more a matter of transition. Growth involves as well the reconciliation, the recovery, the recognition of that which before was confused with the self. [25]

Students of spiritual teachers are sustained and nourished by a mentoring relationship but must ultimately emerge from that culture of embeddedness into their own enlightenment or independent functioning in the world. For Otto Rank, the emergence from Freud's circle was the source of a wound that never healed completely. We have also seen the difficulties Robert has faced in completing this process. But such an outcome is not inevitable. Ideally, separating from a spiritual teacher does not require that the teacher be completely repudiated but rather allows the teacher to be maintained as a valued inner part of the student's emergent self. Assuming the mentor is willing and able to relinquish his role of control and authority, and accept the student's independence, a mature relationship between the two can develop. As I tried to suggest in discussing the case of Chris, this also requires that the student recognize that the love, power, wisdom, and other spiritual qualities once thought to be embodied only by the teacher can now be internalized. In such a case, the transformational relationship has achieved its purpose, and the two participants can take their leave of one another with mutual affection and gratitude, free to walk their respective paths without regret. When the disciple is ready, the guru disappears.

## How I Left the Ashram

In 1978 I had a reading by the famous Vedic astrologer Chakrapani Ullal at his home in Bombay, India. He told me, "Your relationship with Muktananda will grow stronger once you leave the ashram and go home. That will be the real beginning of your sadhana and discipleship."

Several events helped me make the transition toward greater independence. First, after some of the profound experiences in Ganeshpuri described earlier, I experienced a sudden setback: While traveling in northern India I contracted typhoid and became quite ill. I was hospitalized when I returned to the U.S., and was dependent on my family to care for me while I recovered for several weeks. Thus I had to confront the reality of who I really was and where I came from, rather than remaining lost in my romanticized fantasy of becoming a swami in India.

> I remember how I came into my body, age twenty
> half dead in a hospital after Montezuma took revenge
> at Akbar's castle in New Delhi.
> I fell suddenly to earth, like Icarus singed
> into the life I tried to flee in ashrams
> where I stood in gaudy Hindu temples
> chanting Sanskrit
> longing to erase my personal history.[26]

Also, my three-year period of celibacy ended when I became involved in several passionate love affairs. It felt great. As I regained my health I began to come alive in the body and felt myself bursting with energy and vitality. At this time I also rediscovered music, song-writing, and poetry.

At one point, I decided I could no longer live near the ashram, because I wanted more time to pursue my interests in music and writing. Also, one of the swamis in the ashram was on my case because I was letting my hair grow long. I was getting more interested in playing guitar and reading Tom Robbins novels than sitting in a temple chanting. It was time to move on. I finally made my escape one morning by hitching a ride with a couple of cute young women from North Carolina.

At this time, I was filled with wanderlust. In *Finding Your Life's Calling,* I described how I departed from New York and spent several years traveling, performing as a street musician in Boulder, Colorado, and living in a tent in the forests of Oregon, Washington, and northern California. I spent days and weeks wandering aimlessly, often unsure where I would sleep each night. During this period of homelessness I often spoke internally to my teacher, and often felt his presence with me. These experiences marked a major transition in my spiritual apprenticeship. For now I began to relate to the guru primarily as an internal presence, one that helped me remain peaceful and unworried despite the uncertainty and loneliness I felt during this time of transition.

At one point, I wrote Muktananda a letter confessing various transgressions of the ashram discipline I had committed. I was living in Colorado, playing music, writing poetry, studying mystical texts, psychology, and astrology, becoming more sexually active, and not meditating as much. I took a few mushrooms and smoked a little weed. I felt some conflict about the fact that I wasn't adhering to a fully yogic lifestyle. But my intuition told me that these activities were not detrimental to my spiritual unfoldment. I was developing my mind, my imagination, my creativity, my capacity to love, my understanding of dreams and the unconscious. I expressed feelings of remorse that I was not fully following his teachings, and that I was no longer living close to him as a direct disciple. I felt my varied activities in music, dreams, and metaphysical studies may have been leading me off the focused path of yoga. He responded by mail that I should continue my current work, viewing this work, as is all work, as service to the Lord. He said, "Your heart is very good. Let go of the past. Renew your dedication to your sadhana."

When I read his response I felt so liberated. I could trust my own inner voice about the direction my life needed to take now. I could allow the form and structure of my life to change. I could be independent, allowing the spiritual energy that had awakened through my teacher's influence, and through my practices of yoga, to unfold in my life—and *creating* something with it. My path was not to renounce the world but to create a spiritual personality in the world. My practice was to live as the Self, to be a unique emanation of universal consciousness. My discipline was to live the natural unfolding of my inner being.

I recalled how several years earlier I was meditating one day in Ganeshpuri in a room right outside Baba's apartment. I heard him come out of his door and walk down the aisle, and I opened my eyes to look at him. Later that day he scolded me, saying that those who look at the guru with external eyes instead of looking within to find the inner light in meditation are nothing but fake yogis. While at the time this occurred I wasn't so happy about being chastised, as I recalled this episode it reminded me that my task now was to meditate and discover the mysteries of my own consciousness, letting go of preoccupation with the teacher's visible, external form.

For me, separating from a spiritual teacher was not an angry, bitter process. I learned from my teacher that I must live my own life. Muktananda actively encouraged me to leave the ashram, to go in peace, and to go out into the world to find my own life, my own calling. He encouraged me to find my destiny. I am deeply grateful that my teacher had the wisdom not to try to bind me to him, to recognize that I was a young man who still needed to find his own way in life. Leaving his physical company was the beginning of a new stage of spiritual apprenticeship in which I would test and practice the teachings I had received, relying on my own judgment, in attunement with the inner spirit of guidance. My teacher guided me to become independent of him, to be self-reliant, and to follow my own path.

## Saying Goodbye

About two years after I left the ashram I went back to see my teacher. I sat quite far back in the meeting hall. But the moment he sat down in his seat he looked at me. He didn't say anything, but he looked me over, neither approving nor critical. His long gaze conveyed the awareness that he had never left me, that he was conscious of my inner struggles, and that he would never leave me. I felt that he truly saw me, and silently witnessed all. Later, I realized the significance of the fact that he looked at me in this way on this occasion. It was as if he knew what I didn't know at the time—that this would be the last time I ever saw his physical form.

His spirit came to me when he left his body. I was living in Colorado at the time. In those days I often practiced meditation in the afternoon and evening but rarely in the morning because I tended to be restless to go about the business of my day. However, one morning I found myself drawn to meditate as soon as I awoke. Without planning to do so, I sat for over three hours without moving. In my mind's eye I saw myself sitting in my teacher's presence in the courtyard in Ganeshpuri, and I felt myself bowing to him respectfully. Soon after I got up from my meditation the telephone rang. A friend had called to inform me that Muktananda had departed this world. This visitation of his subtle presence was his final gift to me.

## When Teachers Fall

Up to this point I have made the assumption that there are both genuine spiritual teachers and charlatans or false teachers. I have also noted that a wise or enlightened person may not necessarily be a skillful teacher, able to handle the complexities of a mentoring relationship effectively and responsibly. Conversely, there are teachers whose knowledge or realization may not be perfect but who nevertheless are masterful, dedicated teachers who benefit others. Mentoring is an art in itself, and some spiritual teachers are more effective than others in their instruction and guidance of students.

There are also teachers who are gifted both in realization and in instructing others, yet whose behavior may not live up to the image they have created of themselves, the ideal they have taught, and the expectations of their students. They may not truly embody the purity, holiness, and good judgment that we have come to expect, or that we have projected upon them. They may fall from a height of spiritual realization into deluded thinking or impure actions, into greed, lust, or sadistic behavior. Many widely respected teachers have fallen in this way. What do we do if we suspect or know that our teacher has committed some form of misconduct, and that our trust and respect have been shaken? How does the teacher's misconduct affect our spiritual apprenticeship? If we believe that the teacher is a necessity for the seeker of truth, then is the seeker who has lost trust in a teacher unable to advance further on the path? In this section I will argue that we can continue to make progress on the spiritual path even if our teachers' actions and character have fallen short of the standards or ideal they claimed for themselves or that we expected from them.

In his book *Grist for the Mill*, Ram Dass described how a teacher of his named Joya became psychologically imbalanced and engaged in deceitful, manipulative behaviors. Nevertheless, Ram Dass asserts that she was the catalyst for a tremendous fire of purification for himself and other students, and was thus an important teacher for him even though her behavior was in some ways tainted:

> These teachings had their positive side. Many underwent incredibly deep experiences of who they really were during an intense sadhana they may not have undertaken without the illusion to draw out the energy and commitment needed to do the work that each must do for himself. . . . The question arises as to whether there is reason to fear taking teachings because the teacher might not be coming from the purest place. I think we need not fear this, for often a student can progress very far, indeed their purification may be greater than their teacher's, because their intention is purer. . . . If your longing for God is pure that will be your strength. Then though you may get lost for a time eventually your inner heart will hear what to do and all the impurities in your world will just become grist for the mill.[27]

We should not be surprised and shocked when teachers fall. Many teachers are not able to handle the responsibilities and temptations implicit in guiding others. They, like us, are just human beings on the Path. Most teachers are flawed, even though they may sometimes be inspired conduits or instruments for spiritual power, or love. They may not be perfect or completely selfless and desireless, but we may continue to hold them in high esteem because we are inspired by their teachings and their effectiveness in liberating others.

Students have a responsibility to honestly face the teacher's dark side, and to develop maturity in spiritual apprenticeship by continuing to cultivate enlightened awareness regardless of the teacher's conduct. Even if our teacher has misbehaved, we need not abandon the principles of spiritual life our teacher imparted to us in more lucid moments. We need not abandon the Path. We have to trust that the whole process of spiritual apprenticeship has been authentic, and that we have indeed had many valuable experiences along the way.

While we are wise to be concerned about the virtues or the misdeeds of a spiritual teacher, it is helpful to consider the process of spiritual apprenticeship in terms of a human relationship subject to the cyclic phases of devotion and disillusionment that are found in any relationship between two people. It is an intimate relationship, full of dangers and complexities. It can permanently change our inner substance. The teacher begins to live inside us and becomes a part of ourselves. We absorb the teacher's most enlightened qualities, yet we also now see the teacher more clearly and honestly as a human being.

## Facing the Teacher's Dark Side

Nothing is more uplifting than the presence and influence of genuine spiritual masters. They are rare and precious. They turn our minds and hearts toward the light of consciousness within us. They guide us on the path of meditation, and illuminate us through both doctrine and direct transmission of awakened consciousness. Such a teacher's presence brings peace to the hearts of others and inspires students to transform themselves through transformational disciplines.

A true teacher is not an ordinary person whose knowledge can be bought easily in the marketplace, in a bookstore, or at a weekend workshop. A fully expanded being, a saint or *siddha,* can actually awaken our latent spiritual energy and our capacity for expanded states of awareness. Such a liberated teacher is a source of love, wisdom, and grace.

Some rare teachers possess personalities that seem to be flawless. Sometimes an enlightened being will be a saintly person with a pleasant and kind disposition, with no visible desires, moral flaws, or shadow. There are a few great personages, such as Paramahansa Yogananda, Hazrat Inayat Khan, or the current Dalai Lama, whose reputations have survived public scrutiny over time and whose lives and actions appear to be genuinely stainless. Such beings are both spiritually illuminated and personally integrated. Their personalities are clear and unobstructed. They are not pursued by scandal or allegations of misconduct, and their good reputation is almost universal.

However, there are other teachers who seem quite neurotic, who use unorthodox, outrageous tactics, who do not conform to our expectations of purity and humility, and who act in ways that others find shocking or reprehensible: crazy wisdom teachers. Such teachers defy our conceptions of how a holy man or woman should behave, making impossible demands on students or exhibiting insatiable appetites. Crazy wisdom can also take relatively benign forms, such as that evident in the story of the sheikh with the lamb's bladder.

As I noted earlier, some of those claiming to be crazy wisdom teachers often counter critics by stating that their sexual escapades, financial exploitation of students, and binges of drug and alcohol use are actually ways of testing students and uprooting their ego attachments and conceptual limitations.[28]

As I also noted earlier, many of us have limited and erroneous conceptions of gurus and discipleship, expecting a teacher to be a parent or a therapist. The true guru is a physician of the spirit who alchemically transforms the student's whole life. One of the teacher's tasks is to shake students loose from their habituated perceptions so that they become free. Sometimes teachers do this through the outrageous behaviors associated with crazy wisdom. Feuerstein explains:

> In its most radical manfestation, holy madness or crazy wisdom transcends the mind and the ego-function; it is a specific expression of the disposition of enlightenment itself. . . . Enlightenment is the shattering of all mental constructs about existence. . . . It is the awakening from the dream in which we mistake our metaphors for the real thing. . . . Holy madness, or crazy wisdom, exists to serve such an awakening; it has no purpose or value beyond that. . . . The crazy-wise adept is a trickster par excellence. Such an adept plays his or her role as "disappointer" of deep-laid conventional notions with gusto. . . . To show that all taboos are human-made and to point beyond them to Reality is the mad adept's self-appointed task. . . . It is natural enough that we should feel offended by some of the escapades of crazy-wisdom mas-

ters. But instead of taking the easy option of righteous indignation, wholesale condemnation, or angry retaliation for our offended sensibilities, our first obligation is to cultivate the light of understanding, including self-understanding.[29]

In a few moments I will consider the possible meanings of a teacher's strange actions. However, at this juncture we must also consider the possibility that what is claimed to be crazy wisdom teaching is in fact inappropriate conduct. Teachers may fall into traps they had not foreseen, even if their strange actions are attributed to crazy wisdom. Sangye Drolma told me, "Teachers can always fall until the moment they die. Sufism acknowledges that you can always lose your state, your level of spiritual attainment. In Christianity you can't be considered a saint until you are dead and your life has been thoroughly examined."

## *Transcendental Denial*

A spiritual apprentice needs to be prepared to realistically perceive the teacher's human flaws or improper conduct, and to not ignore or whitewash these. According to Katy Butler, many Western students of spiritual teachers engage in "devotional or transcendental denial," the denial of the teacher's human limitations.[30] Butler sees this at the root of many situations where teachers are obviously engaging in destructive or addictive behaviors that students refuse to acknowledge or question; at the very least, they do not say anything openly to avoid causing trouble. Butler attributes such behavior to an effort by Westerners to imitate the cultural emphasis in Asian countries such as Japan on acceptance of hierarchy and avoidance of open conflict.

> For the Japanese, witholding one's personal feelings in order to maintain the appearance of harmony within the group is seen as virtuous and noble. . . .This attitude is part of the structuring of Japanese social relations—it has a place there. But when imported under the banner of enlightenment and overlaid on an American community, the results are cultish and bizarre. [31]

Butler notes that in Asian societies, the behaviors of spiritual teachers are circumscribed by vows and obligations to their community or monastery—which constitute systems of reciprocal obligation. In

America, however, such social controls do not exist in the same way. Here personal freedom and individual choices are favored, rather than shared social ethics and mutual obligation. In Butler's view, the tendency of Western students to engage in an exaggerated form of Asian deference toward teachers is combined with an equally exaggerated form of American licentiousness on the part of teachers, a combination that in many instances proves disastrous.

Lest anyone think that I am biased in raising these issues, I will use my own teacher as an example. Toward the end of his life, rumors began circulating that my teacher was not celibate, as he proclaimed himself to be, and that he had been having sexual relations with many women and adolescent girls.[32] For this he has been widely criticized. Feuerstein, for example, wrote, "A fallen angel of considerable stature was the late Swami Muktananda. . . . The rumors of sexual exploitation that reached the public after his death did much to disenchant many of his followers and left countless others suspicious and confused."[33] Feuerstein adds: "There is a clear distinction between a teacher who preaches one thing and lives another and a teacher who openly teaches in crazy-wise fashion." As this statement implies, what was most upsetting about Baba's behavior was not just that he wasn't celibate but that he lied about it. He didn't live what he taught. He also involved young girls, which most Americans find morally unacceptable.

I will neither defend Muktananda nor attack him, but I will try instead to share as honestly as I can the process I have gone through in sorting out my reactions. I was shocked when these stories were made public. Indeed, the entire community of his students was in upheaval, and many left immediately. Others responded with outright denial that such rumors could be true. Since Muktananda was an enlightened being, how could he have committed such actions, which were totally contrary to his teaching about the importance of renunciation of desire and sexual abstinence or moderation on the path of kundalini yoga? Others responded by proclaiming the fall of a great guru, seduced by the easy availability of nubile young women and the opportunity to exercise power over others. From this perspective, Baba's entire career as a teacher had been a sham, and he had been irreversibly corrupted by his own desires and improper actions. And following the argument put forth by Peter Rutter in his important book, *Sex in the Forbidden Zone,* sexual relations between two people involved in any relationship where there is a clear differential of power and status (such as the relationship between doctor and patient, psychotherapist and client, or teacher and student), almost inevitably end up hurting the client, patient, or student because trust is betrayed; the safety of the relationship is disturbed, and the student or patient ends up feeling discarded and used.[34] By virtue of the fact that his actions may have directly caused harm or distress to his students, Muktananda failed to live up to the most sacred responsibilities of his role as a spiritual teacher.

Others took the position that, if the stories were true, then Baba must have been giving special tantric initiations to these women, who should consider it a great privilege. The women displayed a great variation in their accounts and personal reactions. One woman cited by Liz Harris in her *New Yorker* article, "O Guru, Guru, Guru" says that the sexual contact between Muktananda and his female devotees was clearly abusive, while another, after recounting intimate details of their encounter, stated, "All I know is that I was in a state of total ecstasy, and whatever happened had nothing to do with sex."[35]

I recently spoke with Master Charles, one of Muktananda's closest disciples. He told me:

> A fact that is not very widely known is that Baba never hid anything from the people close to him. We were told about it and he explained that this was his way of celebrating the divine in all forms. What many people don't grasp is that a master is coming from a non-dual state of being, so his or her perceptions are non-dual. The disciple is coming from a dualistic paradigm of good and bad, right and wrong. Baba had a non-dual understanding of celibacy, which was that celibacy meant perceiving no one and nothing as separate from the Self, the one Source that lives in all and everything. For him celibacy meant refraining from dualistic perceptions. He was not having a relationship with anybody. He was worshipping the One present in every form as his own Being. Most people could not grasp this non-dual understanding.

Eventually I found myself taking a middle ground between these various positions. The consistency and sheer number of reports from women who claimed to have had sexual liaisons with Muktananda made it appear likely that the allegations were true. To insist that these allegations could not possibly be true strikes me as a perfect example of the transcendental denial that Butler noted. For me, the real question is, What does it mean that he did this? Does this behavior negate entirely his contributions to humanity as a spiritual teacher? While any illusions I had about him being a perfectly pure yogi who transcended desire were shattered, I feel that I can still honor him as the teacher who awakened and guided me on the path. No purpose can be served by trying to deny that my teacher appears to have been involved in sexually exploitative behavior. Nevertheless, since he continued to have a transformative influence on others, it is difficult for me to view him as a complete fraud. Studying with Muktananda served my growth greatly; for me, he was a powerful catalyst of transformation. I've never met anyone else like him, and my personal experience with him was positive and uplifting. Yet I also recognize that for others he was the cause of disillusionment, emotional pain and feelings of betrayal. The reality is that some of his actions caused suffering, not liberation, for others.

All of us have loved ones like parents, spouses, children, and friends. And sometimes our loved ones get in trouble—trouble at work, in school, with the law. This is the time when we really demonstrate our love, when we stand by them knowing full well that they made mistakes. That is how I feel about Muktananda.

Like many of his other students, I passed through periods of sadness and confusion after learning of the claims against my teacher, as well as the reprisals that some students suffered when they attempted to discuss these matters openly. I personally have a strong streak of righteous indignation about the idea that my teacher was engaging in sexually abusive or exploitative activities. Intuitively, this seems wrong.

In her book *The Chasm of Fire*, Irena Tweedie recounted how her teacher crushed her ego, ignored her, and humiliated her. Her kundalini awakened furiously and her body was filled with heat. She began to have intense kriyas in which she had visions and experientially relived all manner of perversities and sexual experiences—whether involving human, animal, animate or inanimate objects. The mania was so intense inside her that she felt she was going crazy. Her teacher was extremely fierce and worked with her on transforming her experiences of sexuality, but he did it without any sexual contact at all with his student. Her story demonstrates that a teacher can work very deeply with a student without blurring and violating boundaries.[36]

# The Need for Open Discussion

There's no way to discuss these issues without arousing strong feelings and reactions. I offer these comments because I know that many students and ex-students of teachers embroiled in controversy about sexual, financial, or other transgressions are grappling with similar concerns. Many have been deeply hurt in such situations. The lack of open discussion within the community of a teacher embroiled in such controversy is one of the most upsetting aspects of the experience of discovering a teacher's dark side, and may hasten the end of our formal involvement with a spiritual group or organization. Members of respected spiritual communities such as the San Francisco Zen Center, the Vajradhatu Buddhist community, the Kripalu Ashram, the Himalayan Institute, and the Ananda Expanding Light community have all had to grapple with similar difficulties in recent years. In several widely publicized incidents, students confronted teachers, and invited discussion and dialogue. I know of one spiritual teacher who was pressured to enter Alcoholics Anonymous, and who put his life back together with the support of caring students and friends. Apart from this one instance, I am not aware of a single case where a teacher has been sufficiently chastened that he or she has openly admitted wrongdoing, expressed genuine remorse, asked to be forgiven, or vowed to improve future conduct. Indeed, in most cases I am aware of, teachers have responded defensively and defiantly. In several cases these teachers were eventually forced to leave communities they had founded.

People who try to discuss allegations are often silenced, harshly ushered out of the group, harassed, or threatened with physical harm. As we saw earlier, in some spiritual groups, members are subjected to strict control of their behavior, emotions, thoughts, and access to information. Under such conditions it becomes most difficult for anyone to express their misgivings, to demand answers, or to speak the truth. One of the most positive things that has happened in several recent instances where groups purged themselves of a teacher's influence has been that, in the end, everything finally came out into the open. I believe allegations of misconduct should be discussed openly. Suppressing dialogue serves no one's understanding. Expressing anger toward a teacher doesn't mean that a teacher can no longer be loved or valued, any more than it means this when a child is angry with a parent. It is not unhealthy to feel angry and disappointed. It *is* unhealthy to not be permitted to express, or work through, these feelings.

This is one of the sad things about many of the controversies involving teachers accused of misconduct. Often the teachers do not meet directly with students to openly discuss their concerns, to listen to their complaints, or to receive their reprimand. We need to give teachers a chance to learn from their mistakes. And they need to show a willingness to do so.

Perhaps teachers from the East also need to be better educated about the Western sense of morality. For example, in America we have a relatively open ethic about sexuality compared to many other countries, but we have our own cultural conceptions of when someone is mature enough to engage in adult sexual relationships. We also have an intolerance for dishonesty and violation of relationships of trust. Peter Lamborn Wilson has offered this eloquent commentary:

> The gurus arrive here (actually or psychologically) from traditions which contain strong anti-sexual codes—combined in some cases with social customs that mitigate the religious laws through tacit tolerance of deviance. Our society, by utter contrast, has a *code* of tolerance and a *discourse* of "freedom,"along with a social praxis of horrified rejection of all deviance and even of all pleasure. The guru's first temptation therefore will almost certainly be a sexual one—but once he's arrived at a good esoteric excuse for disciple-boffing, he may as well go all the way and cheat and lie and steal as well—all in the name of his "transcendence" of mere religious and moral codes. The rejection of petty morality might perhaps be defended as spiritual revolution, except that the freedom *never* extends to the guru's disciples. . . . Let me be clear: personally I do not disapprove of sexual intercourse nor of "deviant" desire and pleasure. I do, however, disapprove of hypocrisy, power-tripping, and the self-aggrandizement of self-proclaimed avatars. I can even imagine erotic love as an integral aspect of spiritual/pedagogic companionship, but only on condition of its open consensuality. I reject (for myself) the moral/sexual codes of outdated and reactionary ideologies, but I accept (for myself) the best ethics I can imagine, based on a perception of the other as an aspect of the self, so that my desire to some extent depends on the other's desire and not on the other's loss. If I can do this for

myself, then I can demand of anyone who claims to be able to reach self-realization that he too follow this minimal ethics of mutuality. 37

An obvious question that arises is whether or not the student actually benefits from such secret "initiations." For further insight, let us listen to the voice of one student who directly experienced these kinds of intimacies with a teacher. June Campbell has given an illuminating account of her long-time role as the secret consort of the Tibetan lama, Kalu Rinpoche. Campbell concluded that the system of Tibetan tantric practice was built upon the subjugation of women. In Tibetan culture, she says:

> Women were excluded from the sacred domain, except under conditions laid down by men, and "tantra" was used as a means of polarizing male and female as opposites. As a result, women and their role in the system had to remain hidden. . . . [T]o have an actual sexual consort is considered the most important ingredient in the path of tantra. That's where so much of the confusion and ambivalence and misogyny come into play because you have both: the emphasis on male monastic society, and at the same time, the need for women, but without the acknowledgment of the role women play. . . . My relationship with Kalu Rinpoche was not a partnership of equals. When it started, I was in my late twenties. He was almost seventy. He controlled the relationship. I was sworn to secrecy. What I am saying is that it was not a formal ritualistic relationship, nor was it the "tantric" relationship that most people would like to imagine. . . . [P]eople rationalize these acts as beneficial. . . . I've got no doubt now that when a male teacher demands a relationship that involves secret sex, an imbalance of power, threats, deceptions, the woman is exploited. You have to ask, "Where does the impulse to hide sexual behavior come from?". . . Of course, there are those who say they are consensually doing secret "tantric" practices in the belief that it's helping them become "enlightened". . . . That's up to them, and if they're both saying it, that's fine. But there's a difference between that and the imperative for women not to speak of the fact that they're having a sexual relationship at all. What's that all about if it's not about fear of being found out? And what lies behind that fear? These are the questions I had to ask.38

As I read this account I do not get the impression that Campbell felt she was liberated by her experiences as tantric consort to her spiritual guide. While I remain open to other evidence suggesting that such arrangements could lead the student to the highest freedom, the evidence of this one account does not support that belief. Ultimately, regardless of whether the teacher intends this as crazy wisdom instruction, if the student is not liberated by the teaching then it is not an expression of what Buddhists call "skillful means." And I firmly believe that it is the teacher's responsibility to use skillful means in the guidance of students.

## Confronting Misconduct

> When you know for yourselves: These things are not good, these things are faulty, these things are censured by the intelligent, these things, when performed and undertaken, conduce to loss and sorrow—then do you reject them.
> *Guatama Buddha*[40]

Those considering entering into an association with a spiritual teacher are always advised to do so cautiously and with their eyes open. As the Dalai Lama has stated in recent years, it is best if we test a teacher thoroughly before accepting this person as our guide. And if the teacher does or says something that we strongly feel is ethically wrong, it is our responsibility to say or do something about it. For example, Buddhist teacher Jack Kornfield traveled to India to confront an Asian meditation teacher who had committed acts of sexual misconduct, informing him that he would no longer be welcome as a teacher in the United States until he publicly acknowledged that his behavior was improper.[41]

Sangye Drolma has offered these comments on situations where a teacher is accused of misconduct:

> Some people think that a teacher can be enlightened without being moral. But we do not need to throw away our judgment. Discrimination is the name of the game. It must continue throughout our relationship with a teacher. Sufism and Christianity both say the jury is out until after a teacher is dead. As the immortal Yogi Berra said, "It ain't over till it's over." There are teachers who have so much power and wisdom and claim to be enlightened

and then fall flat on their faces. These teachers often have a total lack of awareness of the consequences of their sexual behavior and fool themselves into thinking it is okay to do it and to lie about it. Power without love and wisdom is nothing. If a teacher openly admits, "Yes, I would give a tantric initiation to some students of the age of consent," then some of us might be able to live with that. Instead they violate our trust and sexually exploit students. This is hypocrisy. You have to use the same moral standards for an enlightened being as you do for a normal person. Enlightenment is no justification for sociopathic behavior.

If you feel a teacher is acting improperly, it is your right to speak up and voice your feelings and let your teacher respond. Recall the example of Doug and Lama Z from page 80. If you feel you are not safe to speak for fear of rejection, intimidation, or retaliation by the teacher or the teacher's followers, reconsider your association with the teacher.

I once spoke to a teacher about some concerns I had about his methods. Students were getting injured in his hatha yoga classes and I felt that he was overly aggressive in his instructions. He reacted defensively, as if my feedback and concern were an attack upon him. His reaction told me much about the man's character, and it soon became clear that I could no longer study with him.

We may reach a point where we no longer trust a teacher's judgment. It is my experience that the best way to regain trust in a teacher is to have an open conversation about any doubts and misgivings. It is when we are unable to communicate directly with the teacher that we may feel the most confusion and anger. Our willingness to listen to our own intuition and inner voice is essential to our spiritual evolution. We need to listen to it now if it tells us that something is amiss.

## Continuing Our Practices

Someone once asked Ramana Maharshi, "If the Guru happens to turn out to be incompetent, what will be the fate of the disciple who has implicit faith in him?" Maharshi's response: "Each one according to his merits."[42] When we become spiritual apprentices we make a commitment that goes beyond devotion to a particular teacher. We become disciples of the Path, the eternal way of initiation and unfolding of spiritual awareness that seekers have walked since time immemorial. Even if a teacher stumbles or falls, as disciples we have made a commitment to cultivate enlightened qualities of awareness and conduct; and we focus on trying to fulfill our commitment to the essence and spirit of discipleship, even if our teacher has not proven to be a perfect model. We can honor teachers for what they have conveyed to us, realistically assess their character, and accept both their achievements and their limitations as instruments of truth and instruction. Increasingly, we become disciples of the universal teacher, the great lineage of all awakened beings. This becomes our primary commitment.

If we abandon all practices at this point, disgusted with the teacher, then we were probably never committed to begin with. This becomes the perfect excuse we need to stop practicing. But now may also be the moment to become more committed practitioners.

I personally believe that other masters from subtle planes come to the assistance of students whose teachers become embroiled in controversy but who may still sincerely wish to proceed toward enlightenment. During a period when I was experiencing doubts about my teacher's integrity, I sat to meditate one day. I felt the presence of Sri Yukteswar, guru of Paramahansa Yogananda, and heard his voice speaking to me. Yukteswar's instruction was to remain steadfast in discipline, in aspiration, and in longing for God. I was to remain a disciple, regardless of whatever my teacher had done.

In some cases it is helpful to enact self-created ceremonies of severance or completion of a relationship with a teacher.[43] I know several people who have found it very cathartic and healing to burn pictures of their teachers. Others may need more extensive exit counseling to work through conflicted feelings about the teacher. My own ceremony of resolution of my inner crisis regarding my teacher involved installing pictures of other great beings on my altar, such as Yukteswar, Nityanada, Shirdi Sai Baba, Inayat Khan, and Aurobindo, along with pictures of my Baba. All of these beings evoke in me devotion and dedication to the process of spiritual awakening. These pictures remind me that I am under the care of an undying lineage of awakened beings, who support and guide my progress on the path.

At a certain point, preoccupation with the issue of the teacher's ethics diverts attention from the necessity for us to continue our own spiritual practice, regardless of how a teacher has behaved. What matters most is that we focus our attention on the pure consciousness that is our goal. Of course, there are times for us to repudiate not just a teacher but also the entire doctrine and way of life he or she teaches. However, if the teachings and practices we have learned are authentic they will withstand the tests of time. They will be based in traditions and lineages that outlive the personality of the individual teacher. Recall how earlier, during the stage of initiation, the spiritual apprentice took refuge in the teacher and the lineage, the Buddha and the Sangha—becoming a link in an unending chain. Now is the time when we need the power and wisdom preserved in our lineage to sustain us through our period of doubt and confusion. Connection to a reliable practice lineage can be a very helpful refuge in cases where a teacher has become imbalanced. For example, senior Tibetan Buddhist lamas played an important role in guiding the Vajradhatu Buddhist community after the downfall and eventual death of their teacher, Osel Tendzin.[44]

When we are struggling with feelings of betrayal by a spiritual teacher, it is important to express the rage or indignation we feel. But we must also face our illusions and come to see the teacher as a human being, who is capable of error. We wake up from the illusion that the teacher is infallible. In some cases we seek another guide more worthy of our devotion. At this point we may not wish to throw ourselves headlong into another intensely devotional relationship with a teacher, but we can reaffirm our quest for enlightenment by focusing our attention on those who convincingly and consistently embody that ideal. Our spiritual apprenticeship continues, even if we have several guides and mentors along the way.

## Phases of Discipleship

To move forward toward the continuing unfoldment of our spiritual journey requires an understanding of the phases of spiritual apprenticeship. If a teacher turns out to be an impostor and a charlatan, we may need to work through feelings of betrayal and anger toward the teacher as that phase of the student-teacher relationship comes to an end. Many people get stuck at this stage of angrily repudiating the teacher, or in feeling that all spiritual teachers are charlatans. This attitude is not freedom or liberation; not all teachers are charlatans. With the proper understanding we can resume our dedication to spiritual practice free of bitterness and regret. We can also reconnect with the longing for truth that impelled us to seek a spiritual teacher in the first place. In this way, we become true disciples of the inner light. We rekindle our commitment to the truth within us. A sincere spiritual seeker will not be deterred in the quest for enlightenment just because the teacher has committed acts of misconduct.

There is a stage where feelings of betrayal and anger toward the teacher may be a healthy response. But eventually we must move on. Ultimately we stop viewing the teacher as responsible for our evolution. Most spiritual guides teach us to unfold our own consciousness through prayer, meditation, yoga, service, and so forth. As we saw earlier, even where a teacher is a source of grace or *shaktipat*, if the student does not do any spiritual practices, actively purifying mind and heart, then no inner awakening will occur.

We recognize that there may be important personal reasons why we need to leave the teacher, such as a need to work on our vocational skills and find better employment, or unresolved issues about our parents that make us uncomfortable in the stance of devotees to teachers. Then we can rededicate ourselves to following a spiritual teaching with sincerity and humility. We come closer to the Truth not by being a slave to the personage of the teacher but by practicing what all great spiritual traditions and gurus teach us: to harmonize ourselves by balancing our bodies, taming our restless minds, doing daily tasks with love and inner peace, and plunging within to experience the riches of the ocean inside us. The spiritual apprentice at this stage is asked to live in accordance with the highest spiritual teachings and ideals, even if a particular teacher has not always done so. The best remedy for the disillusioned student of a teacher who has become embroiled in controversy is to become a more dedicated practitioner of one's chosen contemplative discipline.

A spiritual apprentice needs to understand that mystical experience and insight is no guarantee of a teacher's personal integration, moral integrity, or healthy personality. Enlightenment is not equivalent to moral integrity, or artistic or literary talent, or skill as a teacher. These are all achievements that must be reached on their own terms.[45] The student's task now remains the same as before: to awaken knowledge of the Self, the radiant consciousness within.

If the student has truly learned from the spiritual guide, then the separation from the teacher is really no separation. They are ultimately one. Yet they are also two—separate, distinct manifestations of the divine, with their own destinies and lives to unfold.

The path of spiritual apprenticeship often leads away from the teacher's physical company to the challenges of learning to live as enlighted awareness. This is the task of a lifetime, yet it unfolds in its own time and in its own way once a spiritual teacher has sparked our interest in liberation and directed our efforts toward the realization of enlightened consciousness.

Separation is a crucial phase even for the disciple who remains devoted and committed to the teacher. Dilgo Khyentse Rinpoche, the venerable Tibetan Buddhist lama, told Sangye Drolma, "You don't need any more initiations. You don't need any more teachings. You know what you need to do. Now go do it." Sangye Drolma explained this instruction to me: "You have to go away from the teacher to practice. He had explained everything to me. I knew everything I needed to know. Now it was up to me."

My own spiritual life deepened immeasurably when I left my teacher, when I continued to grapple with my mind in meditation, when I learned to listen to my intuition, and when I continued to practice hatha yoga regularly to liberate my own internal energies. I began to trust my inner nature and the course my life was taking, a path comprised of my interests in yoga, meditation, psychology, dreams, and music. My awareness focused less on Baba and more on the Self, the silent witness consciousness. I sought out new teachers and I found the guidance that I needed from within.

## Notes

1. H. W. L. Poonja, *Truth Is* (Huntington Beach, CA: Yudhishtara, 1995), p. 61.
2. D. Levinson, *The Seasons of a Man's Life* (New York: Ballantine, 1978), p.101.
3. Ibid., p.147.
4. K. Wilber, "The Spectrum Model." In D. Anthony, B. Ecker, & K. Wilber, (Eds.), *Spiritual Choices* (New York: Paragon House, 1987), pp. 257, 249.
5. I. Progoff, *The Death and Rebirth of Psychology* (New York: Julian Press, 1956).
6. Ibid., pp. 188 ff.
7. K. Wilber, *The Atman Project* (Wheaton, IL: Quest, 1980).

8. J. Engler, "Therapeutic Aims in Psychotherapy and Meditation." In K. Wilber, J. Engler, & D. Brown (Eds.), *Transformations of Consciousness* (Boston: Shambhala, 1986).

9. K. Wilber, *The Atman Project.* (Wheaton, IL: Quest, 1980).

10. See J. Needleman, *On the Road to Self Knowledge* (New York: Knopf, 1976); J. Welwood, "Reflections on Psychotherapy, Focusing, and Meditation," *Journal of Transpersonal Psychology 2* (1980), pp. 131–42; J. Welwood, "On Psychotherapy and Meditation." In J. Welwood (Ed.), *Awakening the Heart: East-West Approaches to Psychotherapy and the Healing Relationship* (Boston: Shambhala, 1983); and G. Bogart, "The Use of Meditation in Psychotherapy: A Review of the Literature," *American Journal of Psychotherapy, 45* (1991), pp. 383–412.

11. H. Kohut & E. S. Wolf, "The Disorders of the Self and Their Treatment: An Outline," *International Journal of Psychoanalysis, 59* (1978), pp. 413–25.

12. M. Jacoby, *The Analytic Encounter* (Toronto: Inner City Books, 1984).

13. H. Kohut & E. S. Wolf, "The Disorders of the Self and Their Treatment: An Outline," *International Journal of Psychoanalysis, 59* (1978), p. 421.

14. D. Sandner, "The Split Shadow and the Father-Son Relationship." In L. Mahdi, S. Foster, & M. Little (Eds.), *Betwixt and Between: Patterns of Masculine and Feminine Initiation* (LaSalle, IL: Open Court, 1987).

15. Ibid., p.180.

16. I. Progoff, *The Death and Rebirth of Psychology* (New York: Julian Press, 1956), p. 189.

17. J. Hillman, "Senex and Puer." In J. Hillman (Ed.), *The Puer Papers* (Dallas, TX: Spring Publications, 1979).

18. *Finding Your Life's Calling: Spiritual Dimensions of Vocational Choice* (Berkeley, CA: Dawn Mountain Press, 1995).

19. V. Turner, *The Ritual Process* (Chicago: Aldine, 1969).

20. E. Menaker, *Otto Rank: A Rediscovered Legacy* (New York: Columbia Univ. Press, 1982).

21. Ibid., p.35.

22. D. Sandner, "The Split Shadow and the Father-Son Relationship." In L. Mahdi, S. Foster, & M. Little (Eds.), *Betwixt and Between: Patterns of Masculine and Feminine Initiation* (LaSalle, IL: Open Court, 1987), p.184.

23. Ibid., pp.182, 184. It should be noted however, that Sandner's remarks were made in the context of a discussion of male-male initiation. It is quite possible that the dynamics of female-female initiation or female-male initiation may be considerably different.

24. R. Kegan, *The Evolving Self* (Cambridge, MA: Harvard University Press, 1982).

25. Ibid., p. 129.

26. From my poem Awakening the Flesh.

27. R. Dass, *Grist for the Mill* (Santa Cruz, CA: Unity Press, 1977), pp. 71–72.

28. G. Feuerstein, *Holy Madness* (New York: Paragon House, 1991).

29. Ibid., pp. 213, 215, 228, 229.

30. K. Butler, "Encountering the Shadow in Buddhist America," *Common Boundary,* May–June, 1990.

31. Ibid., p. 18.

32. W. Rodarmor, "The Secret Life of Swami Muktananda," *CoEvolution Quarterly,* Winter, 1983.

33. G. Feuerstein, *Holy Madness* (New York: Paragon House, 1990), p. 142.

34. P. Rutter, *Sex in the Forbidden Zone* (New York: Fawcett, 1991).

35. L. Harris, "O Guru, Guru, Guru," *The New Yorker*, November 14, 1994, p. 97.

36. I. Tweedie, *The Chasm of Fire: A Woman's Experience of Liberation Through the Teachings of a Sufi Master* (Rockport, MA: Element Books, 1993).

37. P. L. Wilson, *Sacred Drift* (San Francisco, CA: City Lights, 1993), p. 106.

38. J. Campbell, "The Emperor's Tantric Robes: An Interview with June Campbell on Codes of Secrecy and Silence," *Tricycle*, Winter, 1996, pp. 40, 42–43.

39. N. Norbu, *The Crystal and the Way of Light* (New York: Viking, 1988).

40. L. Stryk (Ed.) *The World of the Buddha* (New York: Grove Press, 1968).

41. J. Kornfield, *A Path With Heart* (New York: Bantam, 1993).

42. R. Maharshi, *Talks with Sri Ramana Maharshi* (Tiruvannamalai, India: Sri Ramanasramam, 1984), p. 241.

43. V. Hine, "Self-Created Ceremonies of Passage." In L. C. Mahdi, S. Foster, & M. Little (Eds.), *Betwixt and Between: Patterns of Masculine and Feminine Initiation* (La Salle, IL: Open Court, 1987).

44. K. Butler, "Encountering the Shadow in Buddhist America," *Common Boundary*, May–June, 1990, p. 18.

456. A. Bharati, *The Light at the Center* (Santa Barbara, CA: Ross Erikson, 1976).

# Finding the Teacher Within

At times you will think of your Guru.
Whenever such yearning arises
Visualize Him upon your head
And for his blessings pray.
Visualize him sitting
In the center of your heart,
And forget Him never.
But you should know that ever your Guru
Is delusory and dream-like.

The Guru who indicates the true knowledge from without is your Outer Guru;
The Guru who elucidates the Awareness of Mind within is your Inner Guru;
The Guru who illuminates the nature of your mind is your Real Guru.
I am a yogi who has all three Gurus,
Is there a disciple here who wishes to be faithful to them?
   *The Hundred Thousand Songs of Milarepa*[1]

Those who have pursued the path of spiritual apprenticeship this far are likely to have been greatly changed. We have received the teacher's guidance and mysterious blessings, we have made sustained efforts in spiritual disciplines, and we have grown to be independent. If we have resolved the emotional complexities of the student-teacher relationship and remain committed to our practice, we should now begin to experience the fullest awakening of our powers and potentials. This includes unfolding of our capacity for deep meditation and expanded consciousness, as well as the emergence of our creativity, the discovery of our life's work, and the unfolding of all our multi-level capacities as human beings.[2] As the great Indian sage Sri Aurobindo taught, the goal of the spiritual journey is integral development—which includes, not negates, our every faculty as individuals. The goal is not transcendence of the material world and physical body in samadhi states. It is the transformation of the human vehicle into a vessel and instrument of a transpersonal light and power that transcends personal will and desire.

There is more to transformation than amazing visions and energetic phenomena in meditation. We also grow by facing the challenges of building structure in our lives, becoming more effective in the world, developing our relationships with others. As our eyes are raised from the guru's fascinating form, we begin to participate in the ever-expanding activity of divine creativity, which can unfold in countless ways in our lives. This is the liberation that we truly seek—not to be bound to our guide, but to be liberated so we can become who we uniquely are, established in the radiant awareness of the Self, the Spirit within us.

The transition away from the teacher is a delicate moment and is often handled badly—both by the uncertain student in transition and by those teachers and communities entrusted with the responsibilities of spiritual guidance. This is a moment of great opportunity for the student to break through to the next level of development. Unfortunately, as I noted earlier, many students at this stage become frozen in a stance of bitterness, rebellious defiance, and angry denunciation of their former spiritual teachers. If you are such a person, I hope this book demonstrates that there is a way to resolve these feelings and move forward on the spiritual path, with or without a teacher's direct guidance. Separating from a spiritual teacher should not be the end of the path, but rather a new beginning.

We have now reached a stage of spiritual apprenticeship in which our awakening consciousness is expressed in our careers, our relationships and parenting, in how we create community with others, in how we contribute to the evolution of humanity and the Earth. If your destiny is to stay with a teacher indefinitely, you may be transformed. But staying with the teacher is no guarantee of transformation. I have spoken to a number of individuals who reported that spending many years serving a teacher and living in a spiritual community actually thwarted their development by keeping them stuck in menial jobs and subjected to the somewhat arbitrary exercise of authority within communities—which they were told never to question. In many cases their unfoldment was much better served by becoming more independent.

Author Peter Lamborn Wilson has questioned the notion that spiritual growth and realization require the mediation of an external authority such as a spiritual teacher or church. In Wilson's view, the exercise of authority is rarely innocent, but almost inherently implies inequality, betrayal, or the abuse of power.[3] In contrast, Wilson emphasizes the principle of inner spiritual authority, in which we rely solely upon the inner light. He contends that enlightenment is possible without the external authority of a teacher, through what he calls "imaginal auto-initiation"—the internal illumination that occurs through attending to our dreams, visions, and spontaneous inner directives. Two examples of this are the visionary initiation of the great Sufi mystic Ib'n Sina (known in the West as Avicenna) and the visionary initiation of psychologist Carl Jung by an ancient Gnostic teacher known as Philemon.[4] In this chapter I will pursue this idea of internal initiation further and offer some suggestions about how each of us might access, and be guided by, our own inner light.

## Merger and Separation

Our efforts to move on in our development and find the teacher within ourselves may be delayed or thwarted by lingering issues about merger and separation. An emphasis in the student-teacher relationship on merger can take healthy and unhealthy forms. Earlier, I described how inwardly merging with a teacher's state of consciousness through guru yoga can be a direct path to spiritual attainment, especially when we are relatively free of emotional conflicts. However, merging can also be exaggerated by the "ideal-hungry person" (described by Kohut in the last chapter)—who idealizes, and lives vicariously through, a teacher, filling every thought with the teacher, and negating self totally in devotion. Unhealthy merging can also take the form of a more general confusion about how to individuate from a spiritual teacher or community. Indeed, merger with a teacher can become a point of fixation from which a student never emerges.

One man, Ted, could not let go after the death of his teacher and the demise of the spiritual community with which he had been affiliated. Ted missed the ecstasy, the sense of community, the songs and music, the comradeship and fun, and the aura of drama and mystery that always surrounded his teacher. When his teacher died, the community rapidly disbanded, and most of his friends went elsewhere to begin following another teacher. Now Ted was depressed, and his life felt empty and meaningless. Where could he find joy and a new sense of purpose? He needed to find his own life, to move on, and to let go of the past without guilt. I suggested that he bring all of the elements of life in the community that he loved and missed so much into his current life, in his own home. I recommended that he meditate, sing devotional songs, prepare food consciously and peacefully, dance, and pursue other practices that he had learned in the community; and to live each day with the same joy he had experienced there. Why could he not bring alive that same spirit here and now? Was this not what his teacher would have wanted? After several months of this practice, Ted reported that he now felt that there was very little difference or discontinuity between his current life and residence and the time he spent in the community. He felt less distance and separation from his teacher, whose subtle presence he felt in his life again.

The ecstatic Sufi poet Rumi said:

> After being with me one whole night,
> you ask how I live when you're not here.
> Badly, frantically, like a fish trying to breathe
> dry sand. You weep and say,
> *But you choose that.*[5]

## Finding New Teachers

> Gurus are like parents. There are good and bad parents. No parent is perfect. But we cannot dispense with parents altogether because of the failures of some. . . . It is possible for good disciples to transcend inadequate gurus and move on to a better teacher. Not everyone follows the same teacher for life, just as in school we do not stick with the same teacher throughout. Yet we should not discard our teachers carelessly.... Good disciples may grow even through a lesser teacher. Good disciples find what is truthful in the teacher and benefit from it.
>
> *David Frawley, All Gurus Large and Small* [6]

In the Tibetan Buddhist tradition, teachers work together to further the evolution of a student. The disciple usually has a primary, root teacher but may be directed periodically to seek out another teacher for a particular initiation or empowerment. The same model applies in the contemporary experience of spiritual apprenticeship. It is important to have a primary teacher, but we may still need to go to other teachers for further instruction. Over the course of time our needs change. Sometimes we need to have no teacher for a while. At other times we are ready for someone who will both convey new information and perspectives, and who may also serve different psychological needs for us.

In my own life, I reached a point where I needed instruction in several areas. After I left the ashram and began traveling I sought out another teacher, not to be my guru, but to teach me hatha yoga. I wanted personal and in-depth instruction. I was fortunate to find Allan Bateman, who was an impeccable guide for me at that stage. He exuded confidence and gracefulness, and was an exceedingly skillful mentor. He instilled independence in students, never demanded that his opinions be accepted on faith, and insisted that we question him, test everything for ourselves, and reach our own conclusions. "This gives students room to grow on their own," he told me, "and it respects their judgment." He always treated me like an equal and encouraged me to challenge him.

Allan taught me that my path to liberation is through the body. Hatha yoga postures soften physical and energetic blockages and unleash streams of vitality and inner joy. Allan taught me to work deeply with the breath, and to proceed slowly into awareness of every region of the spine, perceiving the subtle movements between the vertebrae while doing each posture. I learned to precisely align the spinal column and to feel the vital force circulating through every muscle fiber. Allan taught me a truly effective, transformative yoga practice, and helped me at several critical junctures on the path.

For example, for a while I was vigorously practicing postures from the book *Light on Yoga* by B. K. S. Iyengar,[7] including the yogic *bandhas* (literally "locks") involving lengthy and repeated contractions of the muscles of the abdomen and anus. Ostensibly, I was trying to transmute my sexual energy and release blocks I felt in my lower chakras. In reality, I was becoming more and more jittery and wired. I went to visit Allan after not seeing him for two years. I went into his studio and warmed up for five minutes. Without my saying a word about what I had been doing, Allan walked up to me and said, "You are a complete mess. Don't do anything to your sexual energy. Practice a full workout of postures without any stress or binding or locking of your energy, and you will open all of the chakras naturally, without any strain." He went on to explain:

> When you lock, you block. You restrict the movement of *prana* (life energy). Why would you want to do that? In Hindu yoga you try to block your sexual energy because it is seen as a reservoir that is exhausted through expenditure. But in Chinese Taoist yoga the principle is to keep energy circulating, knowing that if the reservoir is empty it will fill up again naturally. You never want to block the circulation of energy.

I did not view Allan Bateman as a fully enlightened being, and yet I instantly respected his knowledge, his skill as a practitioner and teacher of yoga, and his general personal demeanor. I didn't have illusions about him and so I have never been disappointed, in eighteen years as his student. He has been an impeccable "helpful guide." Allan taught me how to liberate myself, step-by-step, through the practice of yoga.[8]

Bateman was not the only new teacher I found. For nine months I became the apprentice to a Venezuelan mystic named Andres Takra, a wise and funny man. Son of a prominent Venezuelan family, Andres had been a notorious radical in his country in the 1960s, promoting vegetarianism, communal living, UFO research, and ancient metaphysical teachings before these topics were fashionable. A mystic and scholar, he had been employed for several years as a diplomat stationed in New Delhi, during which time he studied many mysteries. He hired me as his assistant, and I spent my days receiving instruction and devouring his extensive library of spiritual and metaphysical literature. Andres taught me the art of spiritual guidance, training me to assist others using the sacred art of astrology. He taught me tools I could use to help other people, the greatest gift. He and I have an undying friendship.

Once, I had a marvelous darshan with Chogyam Trungpa at a sunrise ceremony in Boulder, Colorado. I was living in a tent at the time and I looked exceedingly scruffy. I had long hair and my clothes were dirty. I was the only person present that was not clean and sharply dressed. I felt many eyes on me, and a keen sense that perhaps I did not belong here. Nevertheless, I was glad to be there, and ultimately I didn't care what others thought of me. I waited my turn and finally got my chance to go before Trungpa Rinpoche to receive his blessing. As I did so, our eyes met, and he treated me with complete kindness, dignity, and respect—with a genuine sense of welcome. He met me with the warmth of Buddha nature, and I felt my own clear Buddha nature in his presence. What a blessing it is when contact with a teacher awakens self-respect and appreciation of our intrinsic goodness.

Later, I studied for four years at the Iyengar Yoga Institute of San Francisco, where I took classes from many wonderful instructors, each of whom further refined my understanding of the transformational power of yoga. There I was trained to teach hatha yoga in the tradition of B. K. S. Iyengar, whose potent book *Light on Yoga* had set me on fire so many years earlier. Judith Lasater was especially helpful to me, teaching me how to learn from an injury—a big setback in my life—and to experience it mindfully. I had been practicing yoga very intensively for several years, reaching new levels of strength and flexibility. Then, one day I injured myself fairly seriously while practicing a back-bending posture. My yoga practice was restricted for almost two years as a result. The injury was slow to heal, and I repeatedly reinjured it by trying to return prematurely to my previous level. Many feelings surfaced in me. I was ashamed because I knew better than to push my body beyond its limits, as I had done. In addition, I was angry because I felt that a teacher I had taken a few classes from had encouraged me to try to exceed my limits. I denied my own responsibility for the injury by projecting the blame onto the teacher. I was also depressed, as I recognized that I would now have to work within certain constraints.[9]

When I started taking Judith's classes, she immediately told me to stop practicing so much. Indeed, she encouraged me to do nothing but meditation, pranayama, and seated relaxation poses for several months.[10] She got me to quiet down so my body could repair itself. She also helped me work through a competitive, grasping, ambitious quality of my practice. Indeed, a factor that contributed to my injury was that I had been secretly imitating another yogi whom I viewed as more advanced than myself. I felt that I should be able to do all the postures he could do and had even given myself deadlines to learn certain very difficult poses. Judith helped me tame this competitive streak, accept my body's limits, practice more quietly and meditatively, and experience inner contentment. Judith rescued me from a serious pitfall, setting me back on the right path.

For several years I corresponded with Dane Rudhyar, the great philosopher, mystic, and composer. He guided me through a difficult transition in my life in which I made the decision to follow the spiritual vocation and profession of an astrologer, despite the social disapproval I experienced in some circles for this choice. I was committed to my path and the form of work that felt to me like right livelihood. But it was painful to be subjected to ridicule. I was uncertain how to cope with the pressures of the world while remaining focused intently on the inner quest. Rudhyar wrote to me these words:

> Yes, being 'in' the world but not 'of' it is very difficult. It is man's supreme power that he can live consistently at more than one or two levels. Polyphonic, counterpunctual living—Caesar *and* God (say the Gospels). Yet there are periods when singleness of purpose and an all-absorbing focus of vision are required to move safely through the rite of passage. Keep on with your work and do not be impatient if the field of transhuman activity and consciousness seems enveloped in mist. Clarity comes only most gradually, and one has to build means of formulation that emerge out of one's own experiences, indeed out of crises courageously and nobly passed through. May you reach in your own time, and with the help of those of who have gone before you, the "other shore." And may peace, deep peace, be with you.

I finally met Rudhyar and gave a talk about the significance of his work on the occasion of his ninetieth birthday.[11] I was present that weekend when Rudhyar gave his final public talk. Though physically frail and experiencing great discomfort, his talk was completely lucid. These were the final words of a great sage:

> He who treads the path is in a way alone, and yet not alone. Our implicit divinity comes to meet us, as we reach towards it. In India it was the guru who was supposed to be a clear lens to give us a feeling, a reflection of what the divine state was. However, if we are individualized enough already, free from biology and our culture, we need not have that kind of physically embodied guru. Yet, we almost always need at first a mentor to dissolve the structure of the individual culture-mind as well as to introduce us to the basic principles of the new mind organization. . . [that incites and gives] strength to our will to metamorphosis. This new mind is only a structural foundation. But it is necessary. In my whole life, I have tried to provide such a foundation in terms which could

inspire the generation following mine. I have done all I could under difficult circumstances, and now it is your full responsibility. The power that held my being as a lens to bring ideas to some focus will be released when I go. Perhaps, when the person that I appear to be is gone, it may be easier to tune up to the wholeness of the spirit, to the freed seed. As it is now, I have stated what I know is my truth, and for me incontrovertibly reality. Do with it what you will, as you will, as you are able to. May you live, think, and *act*, in terms of the wholeness you are. . . . May you act, feel, think, and *have faith*—faith, courage, patience, and endurance. May these be, every day, your companions, as will still be my love and sustainment in whatever state of being I shall be in the years ahead. . . . And now please go, in peace and silence. I bless you all. The whole universe is waiting for you. Be true to yourself.[12]

As Rudhyar spoke these final sentences something extraordinary happened: Rudhyar sat up in his chair and started to radiate light. What I saw, and what others present also witnessed, was that his body was transfigured so that he became luminous. The essential light of Being was shining through him, soon to be liberated from the ninety-year-old shell. This was one of the most moving experiences I have ever had with a teacher.

Right before Rudhyar died, I had a dream about him: I was trying to hold onto him, but he forcefully pushed me away from him, shooing me away like a cat. Since I awoke from that dream I have never had any conflict about holding onto a teacher. I had reached a stage where I no longer needed the visible form of the Wise Old Man.

## Creating Our Own Synthesis

At some point we begin to evolve our own forms of spiritual discipline, ones that are less dependent on the authority of an external teacher, and that are authentic reflections of our unique personal attributes. We can have quite a bit of fun inventing our own disciplines and variations on traditional practices. For example, I like to do what I call the Great Nature Walking Meditation. It is based on the traditional Buddhist walking meditation, in which one gives full attention to the act of walking and all the movements it involves. The Great Nature Walk begins with centering in the serene awareness of conscious physical movement—

rhythmic breathing, the sensation of feet lifting, extending forward, and softly touching the earth. Then one expands the sphere of awareness outward, progressively through each of the senses, registering the odor and freshness of the environment, the sounds, the full, rich tapestry of patterns and forms, the color of leaves and flowers and sky, the texture of tree bark and wildflowers, allowing each of these to be imprinted upon the mind. One is the growing leaf, the inching worm, the barking dog, the scurrying squirrel. You are nature, unceasing growth and evolution, always reaching toward the light.

Another practice that I have found quite powerful is to combine yoga with music. When I practice yoga postures and breathing while listening to uplifting music, my mind grows calm, my inner energy unfurls, and my body moves fluidly through long sequences of poses and becomes supple and alive.

The basic synthesis of spiritual practices I have evolved for myself is comprised of five components: dreamwork, the yoga of integrating unconscious material and subpersonalities; meditation, the yoga of attunement or union with our true nature and essence; hatha yoga, the path of integrating the body, breath, and mind; astrology, the study of cycles in human experience, which I call "the yoga of time"; and receptivity to the mystery of grace, the acknowledgment of the eternal presence of the formless guru.

## Yoga and Self-Liberation

Yoga is the art of self-liberation through freeing the body, breath, and mind of all constrictions and limitations. I have practiced hatha yoga since my youth and it continues to serve as a source of guidance, balance, and clarity. Whenever I am upset or confused, I practice; it soon restores my equilibrium and returns me to a place of inner knowing. From that place of centered calm, my own innate intelligence helps me find the meaning of my present situation, and the answers that I seek reveal themselves from within. The fruit of yoga is not powers and visions, but clarity, poise, serenity, the courage to face life with dignity and confidence. When I practice yoga regularly my consciousness invariably grows calmer, wider, vaster, more joyful. My heart and my creativity expand. While it is important and necessary to receive proper instruction in the techniques, the practices of yoga are transformative without being dependent on the presence of an external teacher.

Hatha yoga is an excellent practice for our era because most of us need exercise, especially a physical discipline that is challenging yet also nourishes the inner Spirit and enhances our realization of the most liberated human qualities. In this practice, we systematically unblock places of constriction, contraction, limitation, discovering both limitless pliability of the body and limitless inner space in which to travel. Our internal body awareness grows more subtle, and we are systematically freed of limitations in our range of motion. For example, right now I have reached a stage where I am aware of a block in the region of my upper thoracic spinal column encompassing the heart, the upper lungs, and the base of the throat. I am practicing postures that open my throat and chest, that restore elasticity to this region, and that relax and deepen my breathing. With this increase in physical strength and flexibility and ease of breathing comes a natural enhancement of my ability to quiet down and turn my awareness inward. I have some of my best meditations after a thorough session of hatha yoga practice.

## *Dreams*

If yoga frees the body and breath of contractions and blockages, then dreams help us become more conscious by revealing information, in symbolic form, from the depths of our being. Dreams are integrative, healing, and prophetic-anticipatory. They help us integrate "subpersonalities," parts of ourselves that may not have been conscious, such as our shadows and emotional complexes. They help us resolve past traumas so that they lose their hold over us. And they portend what is arising within us, the direction our unfolding is taking.[13]

I was guided through the process of separation and individuation from my teachers by a series of dreams. In one, a young infant is being held by his father, who embodies two of my teachers: Swami Muktananda, Allan Bateman, plus a third man named Charles, a Jungian analyst. The message of this dream was that these men represented my own spiritual potential, that the seed of wisdom was within me, and that I would grow up to become my own teacher. The dream also portended a major project I would soon undertake in my life: the blending of traditional yoga with the practice of depth psychology, symbolized by the Jungian analyst. My path was to combine the yoga of meditation, the practice of hatha yoga, and the yoga of the unconscious.

In a second dream I walk through a park where I see a procession of swamis, looking very solemn. I am dressed in punk-looking clothes, a black leather jacket, and a tie-dyed headband. I look like a punked-out hippie dude. The swamis are surprised to see me, a bit shocked at my appearance, and they keep their distance. It is obvious that I am not one of them and will not become one of them. I would not become a renunciate. I would become somebody else.

In a third dream, Muktananda's successor, Gurumayi Chidvilasananda, tells me, "It's okay for you to live your own life." The internal messages from my unconscious mind could not have been any clearer. I had learned a great deal from Muktananda. Now I had to proceed on my own. I needn't feel guilty about finding my own path.

The spiritual apprentice may still feel deep love for the teacher, but by this point everything has changed; new goals and priorities have emerged. There is a phase of spiritual apprenticeship to do intensive practices for hours, days, weeks, or even months at a time. And there is a time to be more active in the world, expressing spirit and participating in divine creativity through our actions and unfolding life-projects. I know many people who complain that years ago they used to have such fantastic meditation experiences but no longer do, often because they are too busy with their families and careers. In my view, nothing has gone wrong, and nothing has been lost. This is simply another moment on the wheel of time. Life brings us new challenges of personal evolution, and these are often the tests of responsibility. Wisdom's way is to keep moving forward, to not cling to the past, to let ourselves change, and to let our form of spiritual practice change as well. Our goal is not only to gain access to our own essential Being, but also to perceive the unique manner in which universal consciousness is seeking to emerge into form, into the world, as us. We need to find our own calling, an intrinsically rewarding activity in which our greatest talents are expressed; in which we find a way to be of service to others, to life, and to the planet; and in which we recognize ourselves to be instruments of a secret, transcendent intelligence seeking to fulfill its intentions through our actions. This is the topic of my book, *Finding Your Life's Calling*.[14]

## Astrology and Inner Guidance

As we seek the teacher within, and a vision of who and what we could become, we can receive reliable inner guidance by meditating upon the planetary symbolism of astrology. The celestial language serves as an impartial teacher, transmitting messages from the mind of the universe, revealing to us glimpses of the divine intention. It is a tool that enables us to lead ourselves forward on the spiritual path, even when a human teacher may be unavailable to us.

> Astrology is the Yoga of Time. It is a form of sacred knowledge that teaches us to live consciously as embodied beings in a temporal world. Study of the birth chart enables us to find our next step in evolution — whether this means choosing a career, forming a relationship, physical or emotional healing, building a business, social activism, or deepening our meditation practice. It can be a reliable guide through life's changes, a means of sanctifying earthly existence and fulfilling its challenges with courage, clarity, and joy.[15]

Astrology is not just a set of predictive methods, but also a form of contemplative knowledge that can awaken inner peace and wisdom and aid us in achieving enlightenment. Reflection on the language of the planets teaches us to discern the will and intention of the cosmos, to attune ourselves to the "cosmic guru," the spirit of guidance. It helps us to become centered in the here and now, and to understand the meaning of events—including painful ones. Since a full elucidation of this subject would take us somewhat far afield of our current topic, I refer those interested to my book *Astrology and Spiritual Awakening*.[16] I consider knowledge of one's individual birth chart and current planetary transits an important tool for every spiritual apprentice.

## Experiencing the Power of Sacred Images

The teacher can appear in the subtle form of a spiritual icon or image that moves us deeply. One day I walked quite spontaneously into an art store. There, seated upon an antique wood cabinet, was the radiant form of a meditating Shiva. I was magnetized to it immediately. My immediate response was to bow down on my knees before this perfect, serene yogi. Something inside me said, "Oh, this is my guru." I looked up into Shiva's eyes and saw the bliss of his inner state. As I gazed at the statue I fell into a deep meditation. I sat there for a long time. The statue was much too expensive for me to buy, and I didn't. But over the next few weeks I couldn't get the image out of my mind. I was obsessed with the idea of bringing Lord Shiva home with me and installing him on an altar. I have rarely in my life been drawn to any form of external worship. Later I realized that to meditate upon the absolute, a form that represents the light of Spirit can be a very helpful aid. We worship the form or *murti* of God in order to merge into the object of our devotion. This is also the basis of the practice of guru yoga. We meditate upon the embodied form of Spirit in order to realize its formless essence.

Eventually I went back to the store determined that, if I could bargain the owner down to a particular price (greatly reduced from the asking price), I would purchase the statue. The owner came over to me, and, without my saying a word, he offered the statue to me for the exact price I had decided I was willing to pay. I picked up the statue, and as I held it and looked at it I saw golden light emanate from it; and then I could have sworn that Shiva smiled at me! I was committed. This had to come home with me. He is sitting in my living room right now.

The meditating Shiva has four arms. In one he holds a drum, symbolic of the power of music, rhythm, tone, and dance—primary expressions of Spirit's power of unending expansion, emanation, and creativity. The drum beat sends the shaman into visionary trance states. The drum is also a symbol of the cosmic rhythms and cycles that govern and organize our lives. It represents our consciousness of time, the changing of seasons, the marking of transitions with ceremony and recounting of the tales of ancestors. The drum also represents the time it takes for everything to unfold to completion. In another hand Shiva holds a trident, symbol of his fierceness and fearlessness. Shiva is lord of the wild animals, the tamer of beasts, the tamer of our passions. In another hand his palm is lifted, facing outward in benediction, symbolizing the bestowal of grace. In his fourth hand he holds a begging bowl. Shiva is an ascetic and a renunciate. He has fully surrendered and is merged in the ocean of consciousness. He does not grasp or cling. His hair is long and matted and filled with snakes. He is ever-delighted in the presence of his consort, kundalini, the serpent goddess, who is coiled around his neck. His eyes are filled with bliss, lifting up into the vast inner sky. Energy lifts from his root chakra up to his crown chakra, where he is fully merged in the sea of tranquility and eternal being. For me, contemplating this image is a powerful catalyst of inner awakening.

## Disembodied Teachers

We may also find ourselves drawn to a teacher who is not physically alive, feeling the presence of a being we meet on the astral plane in meditation or a dream state. We might feel a strong connection to a particular lineage of teachers such as the Tamil siddhas of South India, Christian saints, Tibetan Buddhist yogis, or famous "ascended masters" such as St. Germain and El Morya. We may feel connected to a deceased teacher through books, transcripts of lectures, or audio or video recordings. We may also experience a connection with a being on another plane of existence who communicates through the phenomenon known as channeling.[17] We may adopt a disembodied teacher as our own through our willingness to practice their teachings and contemplate their lives. One man had a vision of the Indian saint Swami Sivananda, who left his physical body in 1963:

> I was staying at my mom's condo in Florida. I was sitting by the pool feeling sad because I didn't have anyone to talk to and I had been eating too much and hadn't practiced yoga in a week or so. Suddenly I saw the subtle form of a very large, tall man with an orange robe and a shaved head. I know he wasn't physically present, yet I saw him quite distinctly. He spoke to me, saying, "Rise up and practice! Rouse the serpent energy with vigorous practice!" I went to my room and started doing my yoga routine. After an hour I was in a quiet, blissful state and meditated deeply. And as I sat there I had the sensation of a serpent moving around at the base of my spine, and then I began to feel electricity rising up my back.

As I have continued on my path, I have been strongly influenced by a number of disembodied teachers, for example the great Indian siddha Nityananda, whose silent and oceanic presence I feel whenever I gaze at his pictures or remember him inwardly. I have also been strongly influenced by Sri Yukteswar, guru of Paramahansa Yogananda. He is always an extremely stern presence who reminds me of discipline and ethics, especially when I am on the brink of committing some act of incredible stupidity and poor judgment. I also feel the subtle presence of great mystics such as Nisargadatta and Ramakrishna when I read their written words.

One can feel the spiritual power of great beings long after their physical bodies have died. Those visiting the shrines of deceased masters often report receiving healing and blessings. Many seekers have had powerful experiences doing sadhana at the shrines or *samadhi* places of great saints and siddhas. Regardless of whether or not we have found a living teacher, it is always a good idea to visit the tombs of great teachers of the past. While meditating next to the tomb of Sri Aurobindo at his ashram in Pondicherry, India, I felt immediate connection with the exalted consciousness of this sage. I felt my boundaries gently dissolve; then a quiet descent of peace.

There are both advantages and disadvantages of becoming a disciple of a teacher who is not in a physical body. The advantage of such a relationship is that the external teacher becomes less of a distraction because the student is forced to search for the presence of the teacher within, and to deeply study the teachings that are available in written or other form. We may feel a connection with a teacher through written words, through pictures (which are often seen as possessing great spiritual power), or through visiting sanctified places associated with the teacher's life.

The disadvantage of disembodied teachers is that they are not accessible to guide us directly through the many difficult stages of our spiritual development, and thus we have to rely on our own judgment in situations where a living teacher's guidance might be very helpful. There is more room for error and less access to feedback, which can be detrimental to us in the event of inflation or a loss of balance.

There is a tendency among some circles to say that only a living, physically embodied teacher can liberate us because we need the fire of face-to-face contact and the purification. Some say that adherence to the teachings of disembodied spirit guides is not authentic spirituality because it leaves us subject to our own delusions, desires, and projections, which we can mistakenly believe are the authentic voice of the inner teacher. But for some spiritual aspirants, receiving guidance in this manner is a valid pathway. For example, a woman named Beth has received rich personal instruction through regular channeled conversations with a nonphysical entity over more than a decade:

> One day I saw a vision, an inner picture of a man. Looking into his eyes was like looking straight into the cosmos. I said to myself. "Oh, he's not human." It was an overpowering experience. I began having sessions with a channel, who told me, "He's your teacher." At first I got very into the idea that I had a guru. But the next time I had a session this being came through the channel and told me, "I'm not your guru." The force of that sent me reeling. I felt tremendous shame, dependency, and fear. I felt rejected and complete abandonment. I worked through it and then I understood the teaching, which was a refusal to take that role with me. The next time I talked to my guide he said, "I knew that was going to have a strong effect on you. You've done that in many lives and it has held you back. My task is to make you a teacher, to bring you to my level, not to keep you a disciple." People who follow gurus often don't become gurus. It was a direct severing of that kind of bond I was trying to make with him, and it forced me to confront those parts of me that would like to hide out in that disciple stance. His refusal to do that with me has been a great gift. I've come to see that the guru-disciple setup was a prison for me. I need to keep moving out of that way of relating to the guru, in terms of dependency needs, and inability to separate and individuate. I need to step up next to the guides instead of being a supplicant from way below, which is what I've tended to do.
>
> I understand from my teacher (and I have no reason to doubt it) that I have been under his care for a very long time. We had one life together in physical bodies, and he's been with me ever since. He waited to reveal himself to me until a time in this life when I was ready. And now we are continuing our work together. This doesn't preclude my having other, living teachers, and following practices that they recommend. But it doesn't make any sense to me that things don't continue after you die. A lot of traditions speak of visitations by disembodied teachers and I don't feel like it's anything particularly out of the ordinary. In Tibetan Buddhist tradition it's common to have visitations, dreams, and visions in which long-dead teachers come and give teachings. These beings are considered part of the refuge tree. We are to honor all the Buddhas that have ever been, all the dakinis, and all the teachers. It's not just imagination. It is assumed that these non-physical beings are really there to help you.

## *The Formless Guru, Gnosis, and the Invisible Guide*

The centrality of the personage of the physically embodied, human teacher gradually dissolves, leaving a formless but tangible presence that we experience guiding our lives. Sufis call it the Spirit of Guidance. Yogis call it Shiva, Krishna, the eternal guru, the witness, the Self. Ohers call it the Will of God, and see it as revealed through the events of our personal and collective histories. Relationship to this formless presence, divinity, or infinite consciousness becomes the new reference point around which the aspirant's life is organized.

A spiritual apprentice may now begin to feel that he or she has become attuned to an invisible inner guide. In the Islamic tradition there is a strong emphasis on guidance from the subtle, angelic realms. A legendary figure in Islam known as Khidr, "the guide of the mystics,"[18] an invisible spirit of assistance and grace, is said to come to the aid of seekers of Truth. Khidr, the patron saint of travelers, is also known as the prophet Elijah. Earlier I cited Schimmel's comment that, "Sometimes the mystics would meet him on their journeys; he would inspire them, answer their questions, rescue them from danger."[19]

I believe that once I may have had an encounter with this mysterious figure. One night in 1980 while I was wandering in the woods near Mt. Ashland in southern Oregon I was lonely and scared. I was camped under a tree, and as I sat there under the stars tears came to my eyes. I began to rock gently back and forth, which felt very soothing. It was as if there were an invisible presence reassuring me and looking after me. I closed my eyes and became quiet. Suddenly I began uttering the sounds of the name Elijah. I knew absolutely nothing about the figure of Elijah, but the name resounded like a mantra. I repeated it numerous times and was filled with peace. I have no idea why. I have never done it again. Something was with me there that night, and the name I voiced does match that of the guide and protector of travelers.

Henry Corbin has written at length about Islamic texts that describe the visitations of the invisible Guide. For example:

> In the charming book entitled The Shepherd of Hermas, . . . which was formerly part of the Biblical canon, the epiphany of the personal angel takes place. . . . Hermas is at home, sitting on his bed,

in a state of deep meditation. Suddenly a person of strange appearance enters, sits down beside him, and says: "I have been sent by the most reverend angel to dwell with you the rest of the days of your life." Hermas thinks that the apparition has come to tempt him: "'But who are you? for . . . I know to whom I was handed over.' He said to me, 'Do you not recognize me?' 'No,' I said. 'I,' said he, 'am the shepherd to whom you were handed over.' While he was still speaking, his appearance changed, and I recognized him, that it was he to whom I was handed over." In this dialogue we clearly discern the familiar Gnostic figure of the angelic Helper and Guide, who is the celestial archetype of the human being entrusted to him.[20]

In the Islamic tradition, the guide is not just a human teacher but also an imaginal being, an archetypal figure of the seeker's inner world. According to Corbin, Islamic philosophers, mystics, and poets such as Avicenna and Suhrawardi wrote mystical texts known as visonary recitals, which describe a series of inner initiations that mystics experience.[21] These texts are expressions of a wisdom tradition known as gnosticism, the search for liberation or salvation of the soul through sacred knowledge. Gnosticism appeared in the Hellenistic era in Jewish, Christian, and Islamic forms, as well as in the Hermetic tradition.

There are two themes common to all gnostic texts and teachings: the motif of Estrangement and the motif of Return to one's true origin. The gnostic experiences himself or herself as a consciousness originating in realms of light beyond the physical and astral worlds—a spark of light that has become estranged from its divine nature, trapped in the physical world, hidden and encased in the tomb of the body. The motif of estrangement suggests that the soul must find its way back home to the Pleroma, the original realm of light, the fullness and unity of unformed, unmanifest Spirit, with the help of an invisible, celestial guide. Corbin writes:

> The soul must find the way of Return. That way is Gnosis and on that way it needs a Guide. . . . There is synchronism between the soul's awakening to itself and its visualization of its guide. . . . At the moment when the soul discovers itself to be a stranger and alone in a world formerly familiar, a *personal* figure appears on its horizon, a figure that announces itself to the soul *personally* because it symbolizes *with* the soul's most intimate depths. In other

words, the soul discovers itself to be the earthly counterpart of another being with which it seemingly forms a totality that is dual in structure. The two elements of this *dualitude* may be called the ego and the Self, or the transcendent celestial Self and the earthly Self.... It is from this transcendent Self that the soul originates in the past of metahistory.... The Self is neither a metaphor nor an ideogram. It is ... the heavenly counterpart of a pair, or a syzygy made up of a fallen angel, or an angel appointed to govern a body, and of an angel retaining his abode in heaven. The idea of syzygy ... corresponds to a fundamental gnostic intuition, which ... individualizes the Holy Spirit into an individual Spirit, who is the celestial *paredros* of the human being, its guardian, angel, guide, helper, and savior.... The soul cannot emerge from this cosmos without its Guide, and reciprocally, the Guide needs the soul in order to perform and celebrate his divine service.[22]

Moments of visionary illumination reveal to the spiritual apprentice that he or she is, in essence, a spirit, intelligence, or "angel" appointed to govern a body, yet always connected with that Guide whose center of awareness and functioning is still in the heaven of formless, infinite Spirit. This invisible Guide is the one who has from the beginning accompanied the aspirant, leading the soul on an inner voyage out of Egypt, out of exile, back toward its true home in the realms of light. The Guide is the seeker's spiritual twin, still rooted in its divine nature. The realization dawns that the Guide and the individual soul are eternally wedded; the two now become conscious of one another, and indeed merge into one. The Guide is the "rainbow bridge" linking our human nature and our higher spiritual nature. And in special visionary moments the Guide leads us into realms of light, the vision of which awakens us to our true identity as the boundless Self, the tranquil, formless field of Consciousness. The Guide is the subtle form and messenger of our own Self. It is both the goal and the method that leads to the goal—which is to abide in the Real. The Guide is the one who has always been with us, who has always walked beside us, who never left us.

Sri Aurobindo, the sage of modern India, eloquently described the aspirant's growing awareness of the formless inner Guide:

But in proportion as this contact establishes itself, the Sadhaka must become conscious that a force other than his own, a force transcending his egoistic endeavor and capacity, is at work in him and to this Power he learns progressively to submit himself and delivers up to it the charge of his Yoga. In the end his own will and force become one with the higher Power; he merges them in the divine Will and its transcendent and universal Force. He finds it thenceforward presiding over the necessary transformation of his mental, vital, and physical being with an impartial wisdom and provident effectivity of which the . . . ego is not capable. . . . When the human ego . . . learns to trust itself to that which transcends it, that is its salvation. . . . The inner Guide, the World-Teacher. . . destroys our darkness by the resplendent light of his knowledge; that light becomes within us the increasing glory of his own self-revelation. . . . This inner Guide is often veiled at first by the very intensity of our personal effort and by the ego's preoccupation with itself and its aims. As we gain in clarity and the turmoil of egoistic effort gives place to a calmer self-knowledge, we recognize the source of the growing light within us. . . . We feel the presence of a supreme Master, Friend, Lover, Teacher. We recognize it in the essence of our being as that develops into likeness and oneness with a greater and wider existence; for we perceive that this miraculous development is not the result of our own efforts; an eternal Perfection is moulding us into its own image.[23]

## *Sacramental Plants*

Along the way I had an encounter with another teacher that impacted me powerfully, even though this is a teacher I probably won't choose to meet again in this lifetime: the peyote cactus. While the use of entheogens (mind-altering substances, also known as psychedelics), is associated with complex social, moral, and legal issues, many traditions attest to their usefulness as agents of profound teachings for individuals who are properly prepared for the experience.[24] For example, to the Huichols and Tarahumara peoples of Mexico, peyote is the grandfather, the teacher of the people, the healer, the one who reveals a sacred path. The Huichol make an annual sacred pilgrimage to Wirikuta, the land where peyote grows. For centuries these peoples have eaten the cactus as part of collective celebrations, dances, and feasts. Its usage was fully integrated into social customs and relationships. Indeed, it was an essential part of the glue that held the tribal group together. As the use of peyote migrated north to the native american tribes of the United States, it became associated with more introspective, meditative ceremonies such as those practiced in the contemporary Native American Church. Members of this church revere peyote as their teacher, receiving visions from the cactus that they use to guide themselves and their tribal affairs. They eat the cactus only in the context of group meetings and ceremony. Thus, use of the sacred cactus is both a shared ritual that promotes social cohesion and a tool for individual vision questing and inner initiation.[25]

My experience with peyote occurred in 1980 when I visited Healing Waters Hot Springs in Eden, Arizona. Soon after I arrived, a man who lived on the premises offered me some fresh, juicy cactus. I chowed two of them for breakfast and wandered out to soak in the pools. I walked around the desert hills gazing at the beauty of the colorful spring wildflowers, and I experienced a deep feeling of love for a hummingbird that seemed to remain suspended in space for eternity. Then I returned to the water and began to meditate. My legs locked into the lotus posture and I began to do spontaneous *bhastrika pranayama*, the breath of fire, the same breath that had made me pass out one night when I was fifteen years old. I felt myself rising up, ascending through all the colors of the spectrum into white light. I lifted my chin up so that my throat began to open, and as I did so I began to roar and breathe fire like the plumed serpent, Quetzalcoatl. I felt myself become the plumed serpent, the dragon of Spirit, the ascending snake of coiled power. I still feel that flying bird-serpent alive within me to this day. Later, a song came to me: "Peyooooteeee! Father of visions, keeper of the door!" I sang it over and over again as that wondrous day's sun finally set.

As a brief digression, let me recount a dream I had about a year later that relates to the experience of the plumed serpent just recounted. In this dream, a very powerful, ancient golden bird with an *enormous* wingspan descended from the sky and landed on the branch of a tree, and slowly lowered its wings. It just rested there, emanating presence and *power*. It would stay down on the ground for a while. Later it would take flight again. I felt that this dream was a message from my unconscious that right now it was not time for visionary journeys, kundalini awakening, or rising of the phoenix. The dream conveyed to me the awareness that my work now was to become more grounded, and to trust that the ascending current would return in its own good time.

## *Relationship Partner as Guru*

Most of us receive most of our most important teachings in more mundane circumstances, in the company of those we love. Thus, another place we find the teacher is through our personal relationships.[26] Sri Ramakrishna was ecstatically in love with all women as embodiments of the Divine Mother and would go into trance at the sight of women. In contrast, the great Indian poet-saint Tukaram was sexually fixated on his wife, who told him, "If you only loved Ram (God) as much as you love my body you would be enlightened by now." This statement forced Tukaram to look at himself closely and awakened a spirit of renunciation and one-pointed devotion to the divine that led to his eventual enlightenment. My own partner Diana has a special knack for revealing my impurities and imperfections—my egotism, carelessness, stinginess, and defensiveness, my sloppiness in daily living. I no longer need a spiritual teacher to expose my ego because she does it for me every day.

Just the other day Diana taught me a marvelous lesson. We were cleaning spider webs out of the house with a broom and dust rags. While searching through a bag of discarded items, Diana found a worn-out, faded old, long baggy orange swami shirt that I bought in Benares in 1978. When she attempted to use it as a dust rag, I objected vehemently! This shirt had sentimental value, I said. It was an important symbol of my first journey to India and my commitment to the spiritual path. I could not just use this as a rag to clean up spider webs. She asked me, "How long has it been since you actually wore that shirt?" It had only been fifteen or sixteen years. She said, "Well, if you're such a swami you should know the importance of non-clinging and not being attached to material possessions—which is exactly what you need to practice right now." And with that, she tied my swami shirt to the end of the broom.

> Delight in the presence of your own shakti or shiva.
> It is with your human partner
> that the great tantric feast is consummated.
> This is the burning grounds of the ego, its place of cremation.
> Pick up the ashes of yourself that you are handed
> and of them make an offering
> at the feet of the eternal.
> This is your companion
> on the journey to the stars.[27]

Over the years, Diana has tried a number of the spiritual disciplines I am involved with, but most of them have not felt right for her. For a long time, I encouraged her to try various practices because I had the concept (or hang-up) that "spiritual" people practice a discipline of consciousness expansion. When I start talking like this, she always gives me a funny, slightly disgusted look and says, "Greg, *you* want to do that practice. You *need* to do that practice. But I don't need to. I have my own path." Diana likes to perform rituals of attunement to the four directions, to the elements, and to the spirits of trees and animals. After she spends a few hours outside with plants she exudes the same clarity, peacefulness, and expanded awareness as anyone I've ever seen after a meditation retreat. She has her own way of "being peace."

The essence of wisdom is attention and care in our relationships. Recall what Joshu Sazaki Roshi told me: "The highest discipline of Zen is to manifest silence when you meet others." This attitude serves us well as we continue our journey and begin to share with others what we have learned along the way.

# Notes

1. *The Hundred Thousand Songs of Milarepa*, translated by G. C. C. Chang (New York: Harper & Row, 1962), pp. 240, 54.
2. See the section on Astrology and Multi-Level Initiation in my book *Therapeutic Astrology* (Berkeley, CA: Dawn Mountain Press, 1996), pp. 101–87.
3. P. L. Wilson, *Sacred Drift* (San Francisco: City Lights Books, 1993), pp. 103–19. Obviously, Martin Luther made a similar point when he questioned the need for the ecclesiastical hierarchy of the Catholic Church and in his call for a return to a direct relationship between the individual and God.
4. H. Corbin, *Avicenna and the Visionary Recital* (Dallas, TX: Spring Publications, 1980); S. Hoeller, *The Gnostic Jung and the Seven Sermons to the Dead* (Wheaton, IL: Quest Books, 1982).
5. Rumi, *Unseen Rain*, translated by J. Moyne and C. Barks (Putney, VT: Threshold Books, 1986), p. 25.
6. D. Frawley, "All Gurus Great and Small," *Yoga Journal,* March–April, 1997, pp. 28, 31, 32.
7. B.K.S. Iyengar, *Light on Yoga* (New York: Schocken, 1965).
8. G. Bogart, "Profile of Allan Bateman," *Yoga Journal,* September–October, 1988.
9. G. Bogart, "How to Learn From an Injury," *Yoga Journal,* May–June, 1992.

10. Judith Lasater's approach to yoga is conveyed in her excellent book, *Relax and Renew: Restful Yoga for Stressful Times* (Berkeley, CA: Rodmell Press, 1995).

11. The text of this lecture is available as a monograph: G. Bogart, *Creative Response to Cultural Crisis: The Prophetic Vision of Dane Rudhyar* (Berkeley, CA: Dawn Mountain Press, 1993).

12. A transcript of this talk appeared in B. Somerfield, "To Dane Rudhyar, Who Inspired My First Steps on the Path," *Planet Earth*, Spring, 1995.

13. Two of my favorite books about dreams are S. Krippner (Ed.), *Dreamtime and Dreamwork* (Los Angeles: Jeremy Tarcher, 1990); and E. Whitmont & S. Perera, *Dreams: A Portal to the Source* (New York: Routledge, 1989).

14. G. Bogart, *Finding Your Life's Calling: Spiritual Dimensions of Vocational Choice* (Berkeley, CA: Dawn Mountain Press, 1995).

15. G. Bogart, *Astrology and Spiritual Awakening* (Berkeley, CA: Dawn Mountain Press, 1994), p. 5.

16. G. Bogart, *Astrology and Spiritual Awakening* (Berkeley, CA: Dawn Mountain Press, 1994). Also see G. Bogart, *Therapeutic Astrology: Using the Birth Chart in Psychotherapy and Spiritual Counseling* (Berkeley, CA: Dawn Mountain Press, 1996).

17. J. Klimo, *Channeling: Investigations on Receiving Information from Paranormal Sources* (Los Angeles: Jeremy Tarcher, 1987); A. Hastings, *With the Tongues of Men and Angels* (Ft. Worth, TX: Holt, Rinehart and Winston, 1991).

18. A. Schimmel, *Mystical Dimensions of Islam* (Chapel Hill, NC: Univ. of North Carolina Press, 1975), p. 102.

19. Ibid., pp. 105–6.

20. H. Corbin, *Avicenna and the Visionary Recital* (Dallas, TX: Spring Publications, 1980), pp. 22–23.

21. Ibid.

22. Ibid., p. 20–21, 44.

23. S. Aurobindo, *The Essential Aurobindo* (R. McDermott, Ed.) (New York: Schocken, 1973), pp. 139–40, 142–43.

24. *Entheogens and the Future of Religion*, edited by R. Forte (San Francisco: Council on Spiritual Practices, 1997).

25. E. Anderson, *Peyote: The Divine Cactus* (Tucson: Univ. of Arizona Press, 1980).

26. For in-depth discussion of the path of relationship as a spiritual path, see J. Vissell & B. Vissell, *The Shared Heart: Relationship Celebrations and Initiations* (Aptos, CA: Ramira Publishing, 1984); J. Welwood, *Challenge of the Heart* (Boston: Shambhala, 1985).

27. This passage is from one of my unpublished poems.

# *Teaching Others*

I am a tide in the sea of life, bearing toward the shore all
who come within my enfoldment.
*The Complete Sayings of Hazrat Inayat Khan*[1]

In all forms of apprenticeship the student at some point achieves sufficient mastery of a particular skill or body of knowledge that he or she
becomes capable of practicing independently of the teacher. At some
point, too, we may be asked by other aspiring apprentices to provide
guidance, instruction, and mentorship. As a variety of contemplative
practices and lineages take hold in the West and become more prominent features of contemporary cultural life, more and more people are
seeking guidance on the spiritual path. And more and more people, as a
natural stage in their own maturation, are being called upon to serve as
guides and teachers. Even if we are not yet fully enlightened, we can
help others along the way, whether informally or through such roles as
yoga instructors, meditation teachers, or spiritual counselors. Whatever
level we have reached in our own practice, becoming a teacher will challenge us to deepen our spiritual wisdom.

There are a few factors that make it more likely we will be successful in this work and that we will actually be helpful to others. First, it is
important that we are deeply immersed in our own spiritual practice
and that we continue this practice once we have begun teaching, rather
than relying only on past experience. Our integrity as teachers derives
from the intensity of our own spiritual discipline. Personal experience is
always the root of effective teaching. Indeed, teaching others should
inspire us to practice more, not less. Second, it is important to receive
either the encouragement or blessing of a qualified teacher or a strong

inner calling before we begin teaching. It is especially helpful if a teacher who is deeply familiar with our character and our level of experience recommends or requests that we begin to teach. Or the call to teach may come from within. When we are impelled by this inner sense of calling we need to rely on the principle of *self-appointment* discussed earlier. If we examine our own motives and sincerely believe we are undertaking the work of a teacher with the right intention then we may appoint ourselves to the role. Training and preparation to become a teacher may be very helpful, such as courses in spiritual direction, counseling methods, or yoga instruction. Third, it is essential that we have the right attitude about teaching, not making inflated claims about our level of attainment, maintaining our humility, and understanding our limitations and the scope of our competency and knowledge. When the teacher is ready, the students will appear. The way the universe shows us that we are ready to begin teaching is that students start appearing.

Also, it is also important to know when to stop teaching for a while so we can replenish ourselves and develop other aspects of our lives. I taught hatha yoga from 1981 to 1995. At that point I stopped because I needed more time to devote to my own practices of yoga and meditation, and to my work as a counselor.

Recently I spoke with a woman named Suniti, who began studying with a teacher in 1970 and moved to the teacher's community in 1981. She has been there ever since, serving for many years as a yoga teacher. Life changed dramatically in her community when her teacher was accused of sexual impropriety and forced to leave the community. Her comments demonstrate how we can gracefully meet the challenges of separating from a teacher while continuing to evolve spiritually. This interview also illustrates how a maturing spiritual apprentice can very naturally assume the function of teaching and leadership for others.

> When my teacher resigned it was a sad time for me, but I do not feel responsible for his life or his karma. I am grateful for the teachings he gave. I don't believe other people betray us. I believe we get stuck where our karma sticks us. He never said that he was completely evolved; to the contrary, he was in the thick of it. And I took him literally to mean that. My intention in being involved was always my growth in service, not to monitor where the master is or his level of evolution. I listened to the teachings and absorbed them, and I thought he spoke them quite eloquently.

I have matured tremendously through his leaving. I always believed in internalizing the teachings, and I have a great opportunity to do that now. I feel very strong inner guidance come through in my meditation. I've had to empower myself because there isn't the same sense of community anymore. In our group we don't speak about our spiritual values the way we used to. A lot of people were very disillusioned. We've become much more business-oriented. I'm challenged to accept the changes that God is bringing me and to be grateful for these changes. I miss the structure to support inner work that used to be much more visible. But I also see that this is an opportunity for me to grow.

When my mind becomes quite silent I find there is always instruction and inner guidance there for me. I have recently begun to write that down as I hear it. I've also begun to read it to myself as a reminder of how my life is unfolding and what my cutting edge is—to serve and care for the people around me.

*When we lose a teacher or when a relationship with a teacher changes it is often incredibly liberating.*

Yes, it is grace. But it has to be after you have a solid grounding in the teachings, otherwise it is devastating.

*How do you counsel others who may not have had as deep a relationship with the teacher and who may have been interrupted at a different stage of the process?*

I teach them classical *ashtanga yoga*, especially the yamas and niyamas [moral precepts and recommended acts of self-purification] because I consider these the foundation to absorb the practices of asana, pranayama, and meditation.

*Sounds like you're finding inspiration in the age-old traditions and practices of yoga.*

I feel more connected to my lineage now than I did when I had a teacher, because it feels more pure because it is just their energy, rather than taking the teaching through a human being. I am inspired by the teachings my teacher gave, but I don't consider them his. If any other teacher of this lineage spoke it would be the same teachings.

*So you are stepping into a role of spiritual leadership, as part of the natural process of your own spiritual growth.*

The vacuum will be filled by a number of us, who are already stepping in.

*You seem to have maintained a positive feeling about your teacher, despite his trangressions, preserving the memory of the positive experiences, the grace, the guidance, and the transmission you received.*

My teacher's teacher said, "See the strengths in others, and the weaknesses in ourselves." I've chosen to work with that. The bottom line is that my path is inside of myself. Focusing on the weaknesses of others doesn't facilitate my sadhana at all.

A couple of months before my teacher left I was in a darshan with him, and I shared with him how deeply I had taken the teachings in, and I felt that the work had been done. I felt that the guru was inside. I expressed my gratitude for that. So it was as if he came into my life and I did the work, and he left just after I finished it. He is part of that energy that took me through that process, but he is no longer a distinct human being in my life. That is not true for other people, but that is true for me. Other people have been left less complete in the process than I was.

*You seem to have come through this with a sense that you received teachings that have transformed your life, you accept what has happened, and you're moving forward, unimpeded by blame. Some people never get over these situations. They remain stuck in losing their teacher, not seeing that this is just another stage of discipleship.*

The guru is an opportunity for us to look at ourselves. But if we stay stuck in thinking our process is all about the external human being, the outer teacher, then we won't grow. We have to learn to get beyond being reactive and feeling betrayed. Feelings of betrayal come out of fear and I don't choose to live in fear.

Suniti has found the teacher within, maturing in spiritual practice to the point where others in her community entrust her with the responsibility of leadership. Her story illustrates how a student can mature into a teacher with a high degree of integrity in the role.

Not every spiritual apprentice ultimately becomes a teacher, but for those who do, it is helpful to have a few basic guidelines. The suggestions I offer here for those engaged in the spiritual guidance of others are quite similar to principles that are implicitly followed by any successful and effective educator.

## Basic Guidelines for Teachers

A genuine teacher is dedicated to the welfare and progress of students and always has their best interests uppermost in awareness. Otherwise we are no more than egoists or spiritual vampires. This does not mean that we never challenge, surprise, or in some instances outrage students.

But it does mean that we don't deliberately and recklessly injure, exploit, or endanger any student. We remain accountable for our actions and consider how they will impact others. Our actions are unjustifiable if there is no valid reason why they will assist a student on the path.

A wise teacher does not put himself or herself above students. We know something that students wish to know, and as we share knowledge with them, we will also learn something from each of them. An effective spiritual teacher remains open to questions, and tries to find the answer together with students. We don't have to pretend or claim to know everything. We explore questions in an atmosphere of open inquiry. One of the joys of teaching is that it spontaneously draws forth from us insights that we may have never articulated previously.

The ultimate reason for us to teach is to further our own evolution. A great teacher loves the learning process and is always learning through the act of teaching. Being a teacher is the greatest opportunity for growth because a person in this role is constantly challenged to manifest new levels of truth, clarity, and tolerance. A teacher is asked to bring wisdom to bear on the problems of students with widely varying needs, and facing very practical challenges in their lives. It accelerates our own growth to try to assist others in this way.

It is advisable to be mindful of the dynamics of overvaluing or devaluing within the student-teacher relationship. Is the student idealizing us? Does that make us uncomfortable? Do we get trapped in believing that we are more powerful, wise, or liberated than we really are? Alternatively, do we feel the student is devaluing us and causing us to doubt our knowledge and effectiveness as a teacher?

A skillful, compassionate teacher does not treat students with disdain just because they disagree with us or struggle to grasp a teaching. Students want to be challenged and to receive instruction; but at times they will also resist and be afraid. It is important to honor the student's fear, knowing that it is an intrinsic part of the learning process.

## Curb Your Cruelty

Teachers need to remember to curb their own aggression and cruelty. Being in a position of power and authority sometimes activates unconscious tendencies toward condescension, abusiveness, or tyrannical behavior. A teacher is a companion to others, not a queen or king. If we are true to our own ideal, make good on our promises, and treat others well, our students and spiritual friends will love and respect us. If we plant greed and exploitation, we will harvest bitter fruit.

Gentleness is a teacher's greatest ally. Even the thickest student's ego will usually respond better to a gentle teaching than an annihilating or humiliating one. There is no excuse for hurting a student physically or emotionally. There are some so-called spiritual teachers who hit students, hurl objects at them, insult them in front of other people, intentionally embarrass them, and financially exploit them. Remember that there is a difference between fierce teaching and injurious behavior. "It takes years to make an ideal, and it takes but a moment to break it."[2]

Many teachers contend that their abusive conduct is the only way they can cut through their students' fears, illusions, defenses, and ignorance. I consider this lousy pedagogy. Even when a teacher has to tell a student something he or she does not want to hear, there is a way to do so that is respectful of the student as a person who is learning and growing, even if he or she makes mistakes.

## Avoid the Pedagogy of Humiliation

The best spiritual teachers avoid the pedagogy of humiliation. One famous teacher is known for his harsh, humiliating treatment of students, who often feel mocked and criticized for asking sincere questions, or because of their fears. I would avoid such a teacher like the plague. It is rarely helpful to humiliate a student, unless the person is grossly arrogant and conceited. In most cases, it breeds self-doubt in the student and resentment toward the teacher. The habit of humiliating students is a sign that the teacher has unresolved, unconscious psychological issues that need to be examined. Such a teacher has a lot more inner work to do.

It is important that we don't try to bind students to us. If they want to study with us, they will do so, without our needing to coerce them. Some teachers insist on making the student's undying devotion an end in itself, and thus never let the student "graduate." However, sooner or later this is bound to make the student feel angry and frustrated.

# *Tests of Character*

> A good reputation is as fragile as a delicate glass. . . . A good
> reputation is a trust given to a man by other people, so it be-
> comes his sacred duty to maintain it.
>
> *The Complete Sayings of Hazrat Inayat Khan*[3]

All teachers go through many tests of character, to determine if we are
truly worthy of guiding others. We will be forced to examine our true
motivations for teaching: Sex? Power? Money? Fame? It will all be exposed. If we are vain, cruel, or disinterested toward students, it will be
obvious. People are completely transparent. Our character is fully visible to others.

Part of our work is to disarm our defenses and admit our mistakes.
It is common for students to confront teachers about some insensitive,
critical, hurtful, or confusing statement they have made in a class or
other teaching situation. A woman with whom I had not spoken in ten
years called me and said, "In the last yoga class I took from you I felt
that you were impatient with me. And I've been a bit angry at you ever
since." Imagine having someone harbor angry thoughts about you for
ten years! After our conversation she said, "I'm not angry anymore, but
I just needed to tell you." We learn through experience the importance
of remaining mindful of our actions and how they will impact others.

## *Money*

As teachers we need to keep our policies about money fair and clear. I
believe that it is totally acceptable for us to want to fulfill certain personal goals and desires—to want to be well-received by the public or
to want adequate financial reward from our work as teachers. We do
derive various forms of personal satisfaction from our work as teachers, otherwise why would we want to do it? In some cultures, spiritual
teachers are supported financially by the generosity of followers and
by institutions such as monasteries, so often it isn't necessary for them
to charge money for teachings. In America, however, it is difficult to
survive without money. Thus, a teacher who has the intention of serving others can feel justified in charging reasonable fees for their knowledge and guidance. We don't have to be completely selfless saints. The

question is whether we can earn our livelihoods as teachers without being excessively venal, maintaining our commitment to serve others.

Some people may disagree with me on this point, believing that wisdom should be available to everyone free of charge. My own policy is that I charge what I feel my services (classes, counseling, private instruction) are worth, but if someone wants to study with me and can't afford to pay the requested fee I try to accommodate them. Sincerity of interest is more important to me than the ability to pay in full.

## Expect Complications

Our work as teachers brings us into many complex and very human relationships where we sometimes have to resolve conflicts with others. For example, a woman once called me to say that she had been injured in a yoga class because I encouraged her to do a twisting pose that turned out to be too difficult for her. My first impulse was to dismiss her claim. I had not physically touched her, nor had I *forced* her body into the twist. Was she not responsible for her own body? She said that I had encouraged her to do a posture that was too difficult for her and therefore she had exceeded her capacity and that now her back was sore and she had to visit the chiropractor and it was all my fault. She said, "I told you I had a history of back problems, but you had me do that posture anyway."

For a moment I felt irritated with her. There had been many students in the class, and I did not remember the complete medical history of each person. Then she became even more upset with me because in the few minutes we had been speaking on the phone I had not yet offered to refund her money for the series of classes for which she had registered. The situation was escalating slightly, but fortunately I kept my cool and backed off from my initial defensive reaction. I tried to listen and empathize with her. I sent her back her money and told her I was sorry she had gotten hurt in class. The situation was resolved harmoniously.

This interaction reminded me the importance of allowing the student to express complaints and negative feelings, while reacting nonpunitively. I truly didn't feel that I did anything to hurt her, but her experience was that I had. I had to accept some responsibility by virtue of my position as the teacher. It is entirely possible that she had explained her physical limitations and that I hadn't listened or didn't take her seriously. She later told me that it meant a lot to her that I responded without becoming angry, that I had taken her feelings into account, and that I refunded her money. This experience taught me to not be too quick to dismiss claims of injuries. It taught me to look at myself and my actions carefully, to admit my mistakes, and to make amends if appropriate to do so.

We cannot hide behind our role as a way to avoid conflict or confrontation with the effects on others of our words or actions. Even masters of a spiritual or contemplative discipline usually have personalities with shadows and flaws that need to be understood and gradually transformed. The work of teaching others demands continuous exposure and purification of a teacher's imperfections. Those not willing to keep working on themselves should not become teachers.

Of course, there are also students who are chronic complainers, who look for any excuse to find someone whom they can blame for their unhappiness. Such students teach the teacher the lesson of patience. On the other hand, sometimes we may need to ask such a student to find another teacher.

We do not have to be perfect. We do, however, need to be open to feedback from others, and to admit our flaws and weaknesses. The best teachers demonstrate a willingness to examine themselves and to change as needed, so that they might better carry out the sacred role with which they have been entrusted. They face their shadow and even acknowledge it in public when necessary. True humility, not false humility, is all that will cut it. It's okay that a teacher is human.

## Avoid Sexual Misconduct

In our role as teachers, we guide students who place their trust in us. It is incumbent upon us not to violate this trust. Most fundamentally, teachers must not exploit students sexually. Life is much simpler for teachers who avoid sexual intimacy with students, and such teachers are less likely to cause pain to themselves or to others.

In reality, attractions do occur between students and teachers. Some people adamantly insist that a wise teacher will never become intimate with any student. But what about when the student wants to make love with you, and you want to do it, too? Teachers frequently face temptations to get involved with students. And trying to forcibly suppress people's desires very often does not work. This is America, where sexual liberation is an established trend. Priests certainly have a difficult time resisting the forbidden pleasures of the flesh with their congregants, even young children. Yet in some professions, such as law, medicine, and psychology, there are legal constraints on sexual involvement with clients. In these fields, sexual contact between client and practitioner is considered unacceptable behavior on the part of the professional, and is often punishable by serious civil or criminal penalties.

For spiritual teachers there are no such explicit and formal laws, except relating to the age of consent. Yet the careers of numerous prominent and highly respected teachers have been compromised or destroyed as a result of allegations of sexual misconduct. It is not just the fact of engaging in sexual intimacies with students that has led to the downfall of such teachers, but also a general pattern of deceit and mistreatment of students, who end up feeling used and betrayed, and whose trust in the teacher is often seriously compromised. If a teacher does choose to get involved with a student, then he or she has to prove himself or herself responsible to the other, just as anyone else involved in a caring relationship needs to do. It is exploiting rather than cherishing the other person that often becomes the central issue. Think back to what June Campbell told us earlier. For her, the most damaging part of her intimate involvement with her teacher was the forced secrecy and hypocrisy that surrounded the relationship.

Even when a teacher feels genuine affection toward a student, it is wise to think of the student's well-being first. Teachers need to examine their motives honestly, and consider peer consultation to resolve any conflicts. The teacher is rarely aware of the power he or she has in the eyes of a student. It is certainly simpler to avoid such situations. But when they do occur, it is preferable to avoid excessive secrecy and false pretensions of holiness. Be authentically who you are. People had less trouble with the sexual behavior of a teacher such as Chogyam Trungpa because he was open about it, he never hid it, and he never said that he was celibate. It's the inconsistency between a teacher's words and deeds that often becomes the greatest source of mistrust.

Stories of teachers who cannot find consenting adults with whom to enjoy intimacies but who, instead, choose twelve-year-olds are especially distressing. While in Asian countries, girls of eleven or twelve years are considered to be of marriageable age, in the cultures of the West it is not morally or legally acceptable for adults to have sexual contact with children or adolescents.

Avoid sexual manipulation and coercion. One supposedly great yogi actually used to fondle students during classes—sometimes while they were lying prone with their eyes closed relaxing at the end of a class—an inexcusable violation of personal boundaries. Another groped all of his secretaries and awkwardly pounced them in his quarters. One teacher was sued in court by several female ex-devotees who claimed he had forced them to go to bed with him, saying, "You'll never achieve enlightenment unless you do this with me."

## *The Art of Spiritual Direction*

An important insight emerges through reflection on the nature of spiritual direction within the Christian tradition. In Catholicism, the teacher-student relationship takes the form of the act of confession. Here a clergyman serves as an impartial listener providing an experience of purification by allowing the individual's expression of conscience, and also providing specific moral, behavioral, and spiritual guidance. However, monks and nuns have traditionally received more in-depth guidance in contemplative prayer from a spiritual director who oversees the novice's inner spiritual life.[4] William Barry and William Connolly write:

> Spiritual direction is concerned with helping a person directly with his or her relationship with God.... The ministering person helps the other to address God directly and to listen to what God has to communicate.... The focus of this kind of spiritual direction is the relationship itself between God and the person. The person is helped not so much to understand the relationship better, but to engage in it, to enter into dialogue with God. Spiritual direction of this kind focuses on what happens when a person listens to and responds to a self-communicating God.[5]

Barry and Connolly suggest that spiritual direction should not focus on the personality of the teacher or director, who is there only as a reminder, to point the student inward, toward direct communion with the true source of blessing and guidance. This understanding of spiritual guidance contrasts with the tendency to focus excessively upon the teacher's personality. The teacher should not become the primary focus of the student's attention; instead, the teacher's job is to help the aspirant become receptive to the inner revelation of the great Mystery. Moreover, spiritual direction need not involve enslavement of the student to the will of the teacher. Barry and Connolly note:

> The person who receives direction must always retain personal responsibility, and the mode and content of sound direction will help him to retain and develop personal responsibility, not make it more difficult for him to do so.[6]

I find this approach quite healthy, both in emphasizing the student's responsiblity, but also in providing a practical guideline for teachers who are not fully realized. As we have seen, there are some teachers who, as a result of their high level of spiritual attainment, are able to serve as agencies for transmission for those who attune to them. Others, who know that they can best serve others as "helpful guides," learn to direct the attention of their students toward the truth within themselves.

The greatest test of teaching others is to maintain transparency to the light of Being, which is always the ultimate source of guidance. The teacher strives for realization of the most expanded state of consciousness, and by example and vibrational influence draws students forward toward that same state. The teacher is an instrument and visible embodiment of the eternal archetype of the Teacher—a messenger of the truth that is greater than any human guide.

## Notes

1. H. I. Khan, *The Complete Sayings of Hazrat Inayat Khan* (New Lebanon, NY: Sufi Order Publications, 1991).
2. Ibid.
3. Ibid.
5. W. Barry & W. Connolly, *The Practice of Spiritual Direction* (San Francisco: Harper & Row, 1982), pp. 5–8.
6. Ibid., pp. 10, 43.

# *The Cycle of Apprenticeship Complete*

This book has explored the full cycle of spiritual apprenticeship and mentorship. One approaches a teacher, receives instruction and transmission, and learns that the Guide is none other than one's own luminous awareness. The student grows into a person of knowledge, an illumined one. The initiate emerges from the ordeals of transformation with an open heart that honors each and every being.

As we walk this path, we feel our guides within and above, their subtle presence revealed through a thousand sacred moments—in which we perceive a living force evolving through us toward its own expanding freedom. We learn methods of self-liberation, and we pass through many tests of character and faith. Nisargadatta Maharaj said:

> Life itself is the Supreme Guru; be attentive to its lessons and obedient to its commands. When you personalize their source, you have an outer Guru; when you take them from life directly, the Guru is within. Your own self is your ultimate teacher. . . . It is only you inner teacher that will walk with you to the goal.[1]

Finding the teacher in many forms, grow toward the wholeness that is your true nature. Follow your own path toward your own vision, and tend the fields of wisdom until the harvest yields enough so that others too may share. Listen to the voice of truth within, and it will teach you all you need to know.

# *Note*

1. N. Maharaj, *I Am That* (Durham, NC: Acorn Press, 1973), pp. 131, 51.

# About the Author

Greg Bogart is a licensed Marriage, Family, and Child Counselor (MFCC) in private practice in Berkeley, California, specializing in depth psychotherapy for adults. Greg received his B.A. in Comparative Religions from Wesleyan University, his M.A. in Counseling Psychology from the California Institute of Integral Studies, and his doctorate in Psychology from Saybrook Institute. He teaches at Dominican College, the Institute of Transpersonal Psychology, and the Rosebridge Graduate Institute of Integrative Psychology. His writings have appeared in *The American Journal of Psychotherapy*, *The Journal of Humanistic Psychology*, *The Journal of Transpersonal Psychology*, *The California Therapist*, *The Journal of the Society for the Study of Dreams*, and *Yoga Journal*. Greg was trained and certified as a yoga instructor by the Iyengar Yoga Institute of San Francisco, and is also an astrological counselor who has taught and practiced professionally since 1981.

Greg is a musician and songwriter, and a member of the Berkeley Jazz Workshop, an experimental performance ensemble. Greg is also an avid runner, finding much peace jogging in the hills of Wildcat Canyon, in Richmond, California, where he currently resides. You can write to him c/o Dawn Mountain Press, P.O. Box 9563, Berkeley, CA 94709.

*See order form on next page*

# Order Form

Please send me the following books. I understand that if I am not completely satisfied, I may return them for a full refund—for any reason, no questions asked.

_____

_____

_____

**Name:** _____

**Address:** _____

**City:** _____ **State:** _____ **Zip Code:** _____

Send check or money order to:
Dawn Mountain Press
P. O. Box 9563
Berkeley, CA 94709

Shipping: Add $2.00 for first book, $1.00 for each additional book. Allow three to four weeks for delivery. For first class shipping, add $4.00 for first book, $1.00 for each additional book. Overseas shipping: Add $10.00, $5.00 each additional book.

Sales Tax: California residents please add 8.25% sales tax.